CW01272495

THE PRESENT PROFESSOR

TEACHING, ENGAGING, AND THRIVING IN HIGHER ED

James M. Lang and Michelle D. Miller, SERIES EDITORS

THE PRESENT PROFESSOR

Authenticity and
Transformational Teaching

ELIZABETH A. NORELL

University of Oklahoma Press : Norman

Library of Congress Cataloging-in-Publication Data

Names: Norell, Elizabeth A., 1977– author.
Title: The present professor : authenticity and transformational teaching / Elizabeth A. Norell.
Description: Norman : University of Oklahoma Press, [2024] | Series: Teaching, engaging, and thriving in higher ed ; volume 3 | Includes bibliographical references and index. | Summary: "A guide to help educators navigate the often-stressful landscape of contemporary higher education through the pursuit of mindfulness and presence"—Provided by publisher.
Identifiers: LCCN 2024013580 | ISBN 978-0-8061-9468-4 (hardcover ; acid-free paper) | ISBN 978-0-8061-9469-1 (paperback ; acid-free paper)
Subjects: LCSH: College teachers—Psychology. | College teachers—Job stress. | Transformative learning. | Presence (Philosophy) | Authenticity (Philosophy) | Mindfulness (Psychology) | BISAC: EDUCATION / Teaching / Methods & Strategies | EDUCATION / Schools / Levels / Higher
Classification: LCC LB2333.2 .N67 2024 | DDC 378.1/25019—dc23/eng/20240723
LC record available at https://lccn.loc.gov/2024013580

The Present Professor: Authenticity and Transformational Teaching is Volume 3 in the Teaching, Engaging, and Thriving in Higher Ed series.

The paper in this book meets the guidelines for permanence and durability of the Committee on Production Guidelines for Book Longevity of the Council on Library Resources, Inc. ∞

Copyright © 2024 by the University of Oklahoma Press, Norman, Publishing Division of the University. Manufactured in the U.S.A.

All rights reserved. No part of this publication may be reproduced, stored in a retrieval system, or transmitted, in any form or by any means, electronic, mechanical, photocopying, recording, or otherwise—except as permitted under Section 107 or 108 of the United States Copyright Act—without the prior written permission of the University of Oklahoma Press. To request permission to reproduce selections from this book, write to Permissions, University of Oklahoma Press, 2800 Venture Drive, Norman OK 73069, or email rights.oupress@ou.edu.

CONTENTS

Acknowledgments — vii

Introduction: Why a Book About Presence? — 1

Part I. Defining Presence and Its Importance — 7

Chapter 1. Presence Defined — 9

Chapter 2. Relational Teaching and Presence — 31

Chapter 3. Academic Culture: Minefields and Shelters — 54

Chapter 4. A Dozen Present Professors — 92

Part II. Tools for Cultivating Self-knowledge — 113

Chapter 5. Mindfulness, or Getting Quiet With Yourself — 117

Chapter 6. Movement—Clarity Through Embodiment — 127

Chapter 7. Playing Big — 143

Chapter 8. Who Am I? As Seen Through the Enneagram — 157

Chapter 9. Confronting our Biases — 172

Conclusion: A Roadmap Forward — 188

Notes 195

Bibliography 203

Index 221

ACKNOWLEDGMENTS

I owe enormous debts of gratitude to a host of people, including many I'm sure I will forget here (please excuse my feeble memory if so):

To my fantastic yoga community, including my teachers, Anna Guest-Jelley, Liz Eskridge, Michael Johnson, Libby Hensley, and Sara McIntyre. You've taught me how to hold space for human bodies to move in human ways. My CYTT crew remains the most sacred circle of women I've ever joined, and I miss you all constantly: Katie, Lorriana, Mary, Kelly, Jen, Elizabeth (the other Liz), Deja, and Sarah.

To my Enneagram teachers and friends: Nan Henson, Jillian Gillian, Shari Fox, and especially Shelley Prevost, who I hope to be more like when I grow up. You helped me recognize my own self-defeating patterns and choose a different way. Viktor Frankl would approve.

To my CWLI friends, who show me how to be brave and empowered every day: Kim Shumpert, Sharayah Scott-Caouette, Stacey Nolan, Sheba Chacko, Karen Estes, Autumn Witt Boyd, and Julie Cook Elsea.

To a motley assortment of dear friends scattered from sea to shining sea, including those I met in high school, college, multiple rounds of graduate school, and jobs in Texas, Washington, DC, Arkansas, and Tennessee. And now Mississippi! You challenge me, inspire me, and support me, even when we don't talk for very long periods.

To a veritable trove of Kaplanites who, among other things, have kept the memory of Dworkin, homing pigeons, the dead cat bounce, and Mrs. Hignett alive much longer than they might have otherwise. Nerding out with you gave me a treasured community for more than a decade.

To all the people who stood by me, defended me, and quietly reached out when things went sideways at The Bad Place, your encouragement helped me through the hardest months of my life. A special thanks to Emily (and Heather and Pay!), Kathy, Tania, Michelle, Sondra, Kristi, Crystal, and Paige, who kept me afloat.

To the #AcademicTwitter community, which helped me find my place in an academic culture that has often felt hostile. I mourn the loss of that community, even as I remain forever indebted to the friends, callings, and brain trust that I gained from it.

To the people who fought me, tested me, disagreed with me, judged me, and found ways both overt and insidious to push me out of spaces where my love of teaching was not wanted, I am grateful that those experiences forged this book. The setbacks and heartaches have only convinced me further how vital my life's work is. I deserved better than you gave.

To the hundreds of people in the POD Network, both known and not-yet-known, the heavens truly shone upon me when I got to join your ranks. I simply love learning from your brilliance and care.

To my definitely-not-a-family team at UM, I will forever be grateful that you truly saw me and invited me to join you. Working with you has healed so much trauma for me. Witnessing your humor, grace, and passion for great teaching is a daily inspiration.

To the canines whose presence in my life has added infinitely more joy than the sorrow of losing them, including His Royal Highness Sir Rags o'Muffin, Bailey, Huxley, Naffy, Brandy, Jack, Lexie, Ginger, and Stein: I have never felt such unconditional love as I've experienced with each of these sassy creatures.

To the Drinens and Grigsbys in Oklahoma and Minnesota, who are still going strong with biweekly family Zoom meetings, which remind me to celebrate incremental progress, no matter how small: I'm immensely grateful to have you as my found family. Especially Uncle John, who's definitely the reason any of this could ever happen, I swear.

To my brother: I love you deeply and miss you tremendously. Maybe someday. Maybe someday.

To the squad, the carb coven, of Julie, Mollee, Andrea, and Amanda: You are the girl squad I always wanted and still can't believe I've found. We Maine in March; we sing to Celine Dion and Disney show tunes. We take an hour-long detour to take pictures of silly water towers. We visit Bahb in Bahr Harbha for lobstah. We always eat the bread. And, above all, we cry: yi yi yi!

To Jen Louden for believing in me, helping me get my bother on, and hosting the best writing retreats in the world: the work you do is so, so valuable, and I'm grateful you've been a big part of my writer's story.

To Edward, to whom I promise one day I actually will write a novel. To Scott, for whom I have just a few questions about what the hell is happening on his side of the aisle. To Erbey, with whom I disagree on (almost) all current events, but whom I love to the very depths of my soul. You will always be my first greatest champion. To Tim, who celebrates great words with a panache unmatched by anyone. To Nancy, whom I miss desperately. To Guy, who has the best forearms and the biggest heart. To Derik and Moon, who were there for me during a challenging time and embody joie de vivre, except darkly. To Adam ATT Taylor, I just freaking love you. I beg you to NEVER go on a *Bachelor* franchise show, no matter what your siblings tell you. To Lauren, who is a terrific mother and compassionate woman, and whom I now inexplicably think of as a friend, even though that was never the expected outcome. To Jen and Barb, who buoyed my writing heart as I was finishing this book. Fortune smiled upon me when our paths crossed, and just FYI I plan to keep you forever.

To Matt, who will never stop being the nerd who dragged CPUs through the lobby of a hotel in 1995 with me, because locally accessible internet was a treasure not to take for granted. Your courage in letting your true self shine into the world makes my heart happy.

To Fred and Dalis, who are smart and sassy and slightly foulmouthed in ways that have been a constant source of love and joy in my life. You are my favorites, but don't tell the others.

My parents remain the most generous and hardworking people I know. Visiting them always means feeling at home . . . and also often doing a lot of work. Marshella and Paul Norell are the heroes of my story. I pledge to buy my parents a new cutting board with the proceeds from this book, one that has pictures of ALL of our faces on it, so they, too, can know the joy of having potatoes cut on their noses.

To Derek, Jim, and especially Michelle, your trust, guidance, and belief in this book truly have meant the world to me. Your mentorship means even more. Susan Hrach and Rebecca Campbell substantially strengthened this manuscript with their generous feedback. Stephanie Marshall Ward sharpened my prose with good cheer and kindness . . . even as I quibbled over a couple of tiny details as though they were mountains. What I'm trying to say is that OU Press has only the best people. This book could not have happened without each of you.

To Blake and EJ, the very best bonus kids any woman could ever ask for. You are both genuinely delightful humans who have introduced more than just a little je ne sais quoi into my life. Watching you become the brilliant, kind, dynamic, passionate humans that you have become has been the honor of my life.

To Doug, even though you never finished reading this draft before it went off to the publisher, I never doubted that you supported this project and whatever it would become. Nothing in these pages should be construed as a judgment of your talents as an educator. You are the very best math professor, MY math professor, and I feel endlessly grateful that I get to do life alongside you. Your generosity, unwavering support, and love of people who are both calm and thoughtful are precious to me. You bear my tendencies toward workaholism and my at-times-insufferable love of dogs with grace and good cheer. I love you.

To all of the people working in higher ed who know that this sector can do so much more, and so much better, I champion your engagement in the good fight. I implore you to take care of yourself. And I dream of a day where we can lay down the fight and embrace this beautiful, messy, inherently human exercise of learning and growing together.

To every teacher I've ever known: You gave me either a shining example of great teaching or a foil to my subsequent pedagogical commitments. I hope you see the impact of your work in this book. A special note of appreciation for Charles Puffenbarger, who died before he could see me graduate from GW, but who saw a glint of talent in me that I couldn't see myself. You were a once-in-a-lifetime mentor, Puff. The world is dimmer without you.

Finally, to the thousands of students who have trusted me with their hearts and minds, often vulnerably: You will never know how much you have changed my life. Your tenacity, curiosity, and willingness to give me the benefit of the doubt are the reasons that teaching has been such a source of consistent joy in my life. I can never repay the debt that I owe you for inspiring me so much. You are the reason that teaching has never felt like a job. Thank you. Thank you. Thank you.

INTRODUCTION

Why a Book About Presence?

When you cannot be present, you cannot teach effectively.

What's good for our students is good for us, too.

These two deceptively pithy sentences form the core arguments of this book. Put another way, our presence is necessary for truly transformative teaching and learning. Our working conditions (and cultures) are also our students' learning conditions (and cultures). While no individual can change the cultures and conditions of higher education writ large, each of us exercises influence and agency within our teaching spaces. This book centers on the opportunity each instructor has to approach their students with a grounded, authentic, and truly present version of self.

Drawing from an unusually diverse body of research, this book will equip you, the reader, with a compelling case for engaging in some inner exploration in service of your craft of teaching. Along the way, you'll read about the experiences of other instructors and be invited to reflect on your own teaching past. To do so is to recognize that learning and teaching are inherently *human*—and inherently *social*—enterprises. As such, this book will engage you in exploration of your own thoughts, emotions, experiences, and values. We'll start with a well-timed a-ha! moment of my own.

Emotional Co-regulation

Fortuitously, as I was finishing this manuscript, MassBay Community College hosted a virtual conference from the Institute for Trauma, Adversity, and Resilience in Higher Education. The opening keynote address was given by Dr. Bessel van der Kolk, author of the runaway *New York Times* bestselling book *The Body Keeps the Score*. In his forty-five-minute talk, van der Kolk synthesized the themes of his book in urgent terms, rooted in our biology, centered on humanizing education, and in service of learning.

As in his book, van der Kolk touched on the ways our body unconsciously reacts to stress. We often think of this as the fight-or-flight response, though there's ample research to suggest there are two other F's to consider (freeze or fawn). The flood of cortisol and adrenaline that comes when we perceive stress is automatic and unavoidable. You cannot white knuckle your way out of how these hormones impact your body. Decades of research have revealed that a brain flooded with these hormones becomes less focused, poorer at recall, and significantly worse at learning new things.

Research on the long shadow of trauma in the body has always fascinated me, but until I listened to van der Kolk's keynote, I hadn't quite put together how that research aligns with the purpose of this book. It all snapped into focus when he said, "We, as teachers, need to be living examples of people who it is worthwhile to become like. . . . [It is] very important, when you work with troubled [students], that you are a living *example of someone who actually has their stuff together*. That, of course, puts a big *burden on teachers to actually do their own work and to take care of their own issues*" (van der Kolk 2023, emphasis added).

Because humans are an imitative species—we mimic the body language and verbal communication patterns of those around us—this makes a lot of intuitive sense. As educators, we occupy a place of power in any classroom; our students will look to us for cues about acceptable behavior, ways of being, and communication. If we are entering classroom spaces with our trauma unresolved, it will complicate that process and make it harder for students to co-regulate their emotional states with us as safe role models. By doing our own inner work, we can create environments that are healthier both for us individually and for the students we aim to teach.

A Different Lens for Trauma

The day before van der Kolk's keynote, I had attended a workshop facilitated by my friend Sheaba Chacko, a therapist and coach who works with high-achieving women experiencing burnout (Chako, 2023). Sheaba's session focused largely on the four F's (fight, flight, fear, and fawn) and how they relate to unprocessed traumas or emotions from our past. If we don't address those root causes, we'll continue to experience one or more of the four F's in stressful moments. Sheaba shared a definition of trauma, greatly simplified, that has helped her in her work with clients: *trauma = overwhelm + isolation* (Kelly and Marriott 2018). Traumas, both large and small, spring from situations that invoke emotions we do not have the capacity to regulate *and* when we lack trusted others to help us co-regulate.

As higher educators, the impact of stress is all around us—because, well, stress is all around *everyone*. No matter what institution you currently labor within, the people around you are experiencing stress daily; many of those stressors are small and managed relatively well, but a significant number of our colleagues and students (and us) have lives significantly disrupted by stressors. We rarely acknowledge or address those stressors, thinking that admission of stress is weakness, somehow. We lament how exhausted we are at the constant need to hustle. But the underlying stressors? The pain points in our past? Those are too often bottled up.

The same is true for our students. They walk into our learning spaces day after day often flooded with stress hormones, making our work nigh on impossible. We cannot teach brains hijacked by stress. Let me say that again: *we cannot teach brains hijacked by stress.*

There are really two ways to deal with this reality—one more productive, one less so. I'll let you guess which is which.

Option one is to proceed as normal. Whip up a class plan, write some learning objectives, give students assignments, try to get some active learning going when your students are gathered, read student work, give meaningful feedback, and hope for the best.

Maybe you incorporate some alternative assessments or some engaging classroom activities. But basically, in this option, you're proceeding as "normal," whatever that means to you.

Option two is to address the underlying stress head on. There are ways to interrupt or complete the stress response; Emily and Amelia Nagoski's book, *Burnout: The Secret to Unlocking the Stress Cycle* (2020), is my favorite resource for this. While it's not feasible to commit your class time entirely to this work, if learners are entering your class flooded with stress hormones, you can incorporate activities that will help discharge some of those and, as a result, promote greater learning. In other words, you become the trusted other who can help humans experiencing stress regulate the emotions arising within them.

OK, I sort of gave away the answer, didn't I? Obviously, option two is the more effective strategy. Sadly, this is not the kind of teaching you've likely seen modeled, much less been taught to do. The reality of our stressful lives, particularly since COVID-related disruptions generated so much stress, overwhelm, and trauma, has made trauma-informed teaching a sought-after topic of learning and growth for student-centered educators. This is a wonderful trend and one this book fits nicely within.

However—and this was the key takeaway from van der Kolk's talk—you cannot help co-regulate your students' emotions and stress if you're experiencing them, too. When you're facing your own burnout or overwhelm or trauma, you don't have the bandwidth to help your students de-escalate theirs.

When you cannot be present, you cannot teach effectively.

Who This Book Is For

I wrote this book with midcareer educators in mind—those with some teaching experience under their belts and who are committed to growing their skillsets as teachers. Those earlier in their careers will find tools here that are useful, but I stress throughout the book (especially in chapter 3, about academic culture) that some of the ways we model presence in the classroom are riskier for some than others. Women, instructors of color, those with disabilities, and people with other minoritized identities will likely find the work of classroom presence more risky than do their white or male colleagues. Awareness of how those dimensions of identity impact our classroom presence is woven throughout this book. Indeed, this book highlights the importance of understanding your own identities and positionality so you can choose a safe and appropriate way of being with your students and colleagues.

The book is organized into two sections. In part 1, I lay out the research and theory that frame the core arguments of this book, including consideration of the academic context in which we do our work. Chapter 1 defines "presence" and looks at several disciplinary literatures on presence and authenticity, including the complicated concept of imposter syndrome. Chapter 2 turns to teaching and focuses on how positive relationships, grounded in authentic presence, can turbocharge learning. Chapter 3 explores the minefields and shelters of academic culture to guide you to the relatively safe places for authentic presence. Chapter 4 provides a dozen examples of present professors who've followed their own idiosyncratic paths to self-awareness and presence.

In part 2, I provide multiple tools for doing the work of examining your identities and fostering greater presence. Largely, these tools are ways of examining your core values, beliefs, and commitments, surfacing them so you can reflect on how your work self is (or is not) congruent with your desired way of being. Some may be familiar; others may not. Chapter 5 focuses on mindfulness; chapter 6 on mindful movement and embodiment. Chapter 7 pulls from Tara Mohr's resources on how to play bigger in our work. Chapter 8 looks at personality frameworks, specifically the Enneagram, with a bunch of caveats about the utility versus the scientific validity of personality frameworks. Chapter 9 concludes this section by considering the implicit biases we all carry.

In the book's conclusion, you'll find guided reflection questions to help you continue your own inner work journey.

Ultimately, the aim of this book is to persuade you of the importance of becoming more self-aware—of doing the inner work that these tools facilitate—so that you can bring greater authenticity and presence into your teaching and working spaces. While the book can make the case for why this work is important and can give you lots of ideas on how to do it, no book can actually *do the work* for you. That process unfolds differently for each person and depends largely on your own experiences, preconceptions of personal development, and willingness to sit with discomfort. Some of us need accountability to engage in this work, and that's where finding communities of practice (such as through your center for teaching) can be incredibly helpful to navigate these sometimes-fraught waters. Others will find working with a therapist or coach helpful. Unfortunately, for many of our colleagues—about half of college faculty are contingent and without institutional or affordable health insurance—seeking a therapist or coach is simply not feasible. This is where, as a community, we can support one another in creating spaces to speak vulnerably and honestly about the tender spots inner work can reveal. However, we must do so in ways that are psychologically and emotionally safe, and, unfortunately, that's not always something higher education does especially well.

Despite some of the harder parts of academia's culture and challenges, I remain optimistic that our very smart and purpose-driven colleagues can create an environment that's safer for all—us, our colleagues, and our students—to engage in meaningful learning and growth. You made it this far in your career by working hard and learning a lot. If we are willing to make use of the tools in this book (or your own curated set of tools), I am convinced that we can make the enterprise of higher education more accepting, fulfilling, and transformational for ever more diverse groups of learners—and for us as educators, too.

PART I

DEFINING PRESENCE AND ITS IMPORTANCE

> Most professors must practice being vulnerable in the classroom, being wholly present in mind, body, and spirit.
>
> bell hooks

In part 1, we'll establish the *why* of this book—why focusing on presence unlocks instructor authenticity and transformational teaching and learning. Let's be honest, though: The word "presence" is a bit of an enigma. It could mean being physically present (your body is in a seat in a classroom, regardless of where your mind or attention is directed), it might mean intellectual engagement with academic puzzles and challenging texts, or presence can even be a *suggestion* of some force within a space without any physical evidence of that thing actually being there (such as the chilling sense that a house might be haunted by some sort of supernatural presence).

One effort to define the term came in Amy Cuddy's popular book *Presence: Bringing Your Boldest Self to Your Biggest Challenges* (2018). That book followed her immensely popular TED Talk, "Your Body Language May Shape Who You Are," which at this writing had been viewed some seventy million times (Cuddy 2012). In both the TED Talk and her book, Cuddy explores the interplay of nonverbal communication, particularly body postures, and the way we are seen by both others and ourselves. While some of the concepts she discusses will turn up in this section, my focus here is on how presence applies to the particular work of teaching. When we take on the work of teaching, we assume a position of power that can be fraught, particularly for those with historically minoritized identities or who experience any imposter-like feelings. What does "presence" mean when we're not even sure it's safe to be authentically ourselves, or when our experiences and the culture make us feel like we should be someone other than who we are?

In the pages ahead, we'll think through the relationship between *presence* and *authenticity*, particularly as it relates to our teaching. We'll do so in a way that recognizes that authenticity is a nuanced goal when teaching. There will always be differences in our ways of being in our everyday life and our ways of being in teaching spaces—as there should be, just as there are between the version of ourselves we present at work versus with our trusted friends versus with our elementary-school-aged children. We must distinguish between needing to moderate our personas depending on context and inhabiting fictional versions of ourselves in service to some idealized notion of How a Very Serious Academic Acts.

To the extent that we can root our teaching personas in more authentic-to-us ways of being, we can engage our students more meaningfully and more fully in the transformational learning we aspire to achieve—at least, that's what part 1 will argue. Let's start with taking a focused look at what "presence" means, at least in the way this book discusses it.

Chapter 1

PRESENCE DEFINED

> The most precious gift we can offer others is our presence.
>
> Thich Nhat Hanh

It was a Monday morning in early August, and I was making my way to my first faculty meeting as an assistant professor. I tentatively entered a classroom with a wall entirely made of glass, blinds up, overlooking a sunken seating area in a building originally designed to hold "advanced technology" programs. It now housed social scientists, teacher educators, and a high school operating on a community college's campus. Our meeting was starting at 10:00 a.m., and I'm chronically early even when not worried about making a good impression—so I walked into a nearly empty room, trying to fold in on myself to evade notice. I knew nobody. It was my first semester as a full-time instructor working on a single campus.

Honestly, I'm still astonished that I managed to right-place, right-time my way into this gig. For nearly a decade, I had been toiling away in the trenches of adjuncting, teaching as many as ten classes—on no fewer than three campuses—in a single semester. The previous year, I had braved the academic job market, and for my trouble I had received only a single nibble: an interview for a non-tenure-track teaching job eight hours away from my partner, stepkids, and dogs—only to watch that gig go to one of *their* adjuncts. Then, out of nowhere, I got a call one April afternoon after I'd just finished teaching a class. On the line was the department head of a local community college, one of the many institutions where I'd taught a class or two.

"Our full-time political scientist is leaving. Are you interested in the job?" he asked.

I was gobsmacked. This does not happen.

I sputtered, seriously wondered if I was being punked, and took a few deep breaths before exclaiming, with somewhat unprofessional enthusiasm, "YES!" People two doors down from my office heard me. Suffice it to say, I did not play it cool.

The next day, I visited the campus to fill out paperwork and talk about the position. I'd be hired on a one-year contract to start August 1; in the spring semester, they'd do a formal search for a tenure-track faculty member. The future colleague I met that day, Dan, would be my mentor for that all-important year in limbo. He encouraged me to do all the things my tenure-track peers would do, including putting together a digital portfolio that faculty completed annually to progress toward tenure or promotion. He confided they had a strong record of hiring adjuncts into full-time positions. I left in something of a daze, feeling like I'd just won the academic job-market lottery. Probably because I had.

Months later, two weeks before classes began, two or three dozen people trickled into the glass-walled classroom, where I sat anxiously. I both wanted to be noticed and hoped to fade into the background. I watched as they threw high fives and hugs around like confetti at a junior-high New Year's Eve party. Just like confetti, that energy went everywhere in the most wonderful way. As their collegiality settled all around me, I felt at once envious of their easy rapport and eager to join in.

It didn't take long for my mind (the voice sometimes called the inner critic) to start fixating on how much of an outsider I was. My new colleagues had inside jokes and easy laughter; I had awkward uncertainty and a fear that I was the convenient—not the ideal—hire. I had no idea how to go about becoming a part of this tight-knit team of rambunctious rabblerousers. I just knew that I wanted to.

Slowly, cautiously, day by day, I began to befriend them. The people whose offices were nearest mine were the easiest targets. As I found my footing with them and started learning about the relationship dynamics of the department, my confidence grew. I felt comfortable with almost everyone in my department... except for one woman, Kathy, one of the longest-serving faculty, who seemed to avoid eye contact and keep to herself. My anxious, inner-critic-dominated mind was certain she disliked me, even though I had no idea why. A cascade of possible explanations flooded: Maybe she loved my predecessor? Maybe one of her friends had wanted my job? Maybe she preferred people who had more confidence, wore glasses, or supported the Green Bay Packers? I wasn't sure what was happening, but I wasn't about to risk face-to-face rejection by asking.

Instead, my inner critic went on a galloping romp in the land of worst-case scenarios. That prompted my raising my defensive shields, fighting back against those imagined critiques. An all-out war was unfolding in my ready-to-assume-the-worst imagination. The battle threatened my tenuous efforts to find my place in this new department, all because of an imagined rebuff.

I can look back now and see that I was so caught up in my own story, my own insecurities, that I was unable to be present with my new colleagues. Consumed by my uncertainty about fitting in, I got distracted from the more pressing business of finding my way. I think about that each time a new semester begins, each time I greet a class of new students wandering tentatively into a classroom, trying to fold themselves into smaller versions, and hoping they fit in. Hoping that nobody will realize they actually don't belong in college at all. Wanting to be seen but fearing the rejection that might follow.

I see my experiences in those early days as an example of what happens when we are robbed of the ability to see a situation clearly, how confirmation bias can seize upon every facial expression or casual remark as evidence that, indeed, we are outsiders and unwelcome. The opposite state is what is sometimes called presence, and it is the key to creating transformational learning spaces. Presence in learning spaces must begin with the central authority figure in every classroom environment—the teacher. *You.* Students cannot be present if you are not, and you cannot be present without knowing how to spot, quiet, and soothe your own insecurities.

Presentation of Self

To wrap our minds around the amorphous concept of presence, let's think about the way we inhabit different spaces and different roles. Sociologist Erving Goffman develops what he calls the dramaturgical model of social life in his 1959 book, *The Presentation of Self in Everyday Life*. Using the theatrical stage as a metaphor, Goffman suggests we have different versions of ourselves that we present, depending on the audience.

When an actor takes the stage for a performance, they are inhabiting a character who may bear little resemblance to the actor's authentic self.[1] When TED speakers stand up to give the talk of their lives, they likely don't bring many dimensions of their authentic selves to that task, either. These "front-stage" selves are not necessarily lies, but they are delivered to an audience with certain expectations. The person on stage moderates what aspects of their personality, insecurities, and inner dialogue seep into their performance to meet those audience expectations.

Away from the spotlight of the front stage, the "back-stage" self appears when we aren't engaged in that demanding process of moderating our behaviors and speech. The back stage is a place where the stage makeup can come off, where lines aren't delivered after extensive rehearsal, where the actors can relax and be themselves.

The performances we give around others are motivated by what Goffman calls impression management. Intended to prevent embarrassing ourselves or others, this effort is demanding and exhausting. It's also core to the human condition, one predicated on our evolution as social creatures dependent on others to survive. If we are ostracized, our physical safety is threatened. Presenting ourselves as in alignment with the expectations of others is, evolutionarily speaking, smart thinking.

If this all seems rather vague, try this thought experiment. Think back to the last time you attended a national disciplinary conference, then call to mind your most recent gathering with your closest friend(s). Chances are the way you dress (costume), words you say (dialogue), and actions you take (choreography) are different in those two contexts. It is possible that, apart from the basics of your physical appearance, you appear to be two entirely different people in those situations. The person you appear to be around your closest friends would be, in Goffman's model, your "back-stage" self, whereas your buttoned-up, professional self is your "front-stage" self.

The drain on cognitive resources to keep up these different versions of yourself is substantial, though. As Bentley University professor Bill Schiano highlights, there are two kinds of cognitive load (sometimes referred to as cognitive bandwidth) worth educators' consideration (Schiano 2021). Intrinsic cognitive load has to do with the content we're teaching; extraneous cognitive load is all the other things we attend to while teaching—such as how we present ourselves and monitoring our students. "To avoid feeling overwhelmed," Schiano writes, "the key is to reduce extraneous load as much as possible and free up working memory to focus on what's intrinsically valuable." In other words, work we do to reduce how much attention we must pay to our presentation of self increases the cognitive bandwidth available to attend to more important matters—namely, to what we're teaching and the students to whom we are teaching it.

Slow Your Thinking

Another useful model for understanding the ways presence manifests in our teaching draws from the Nobel Prize–winning work of Daniel Kahneman (and his collaborator, Amos Tversky, who sadly passed before he could be jointly awarded the Nobel). In his book *Thinking, Fast and Slow* (2011), Kahneman adopts language originally proposed by psychologists Keith Stanovich and Richard West (2000) to distinguish two ways of thinking: System 1 and System 2. Kahneman explains: "System 1 operates automatically and quickly, with little or no effort and no sense of voluntary control. System 2 allocates attention to the effortful mental activities that demand it, including complex computations. The operations of System 2 are often associated with the subjective experience of agency, choice, and concentration" (21–22).

When we are teaching by rote, perhaps leaning on our previous experiences teaching a familiar course or students, we engage in System 1 teaching. It doesn't require a lot of effort or attentiveness, such as when a seasoned educator pulls out a yellowed sheaf of lecture notes and tells the same anecdotes they've been sharing with students for decades (not that I recommend this as a teaching strategy, by the way!). Lecturers who lean on the same material they've always taught are engaging in cognitively efficient teaching—but they also devote so few cognitive resources to the task that they may not notice nonverbal student communications that indicate a lack of engagement or comprehension.

System 2 teaching is present teaching. It is cognitively and emotionally demanding because it requires concentration and in-the-moment reactions to what is unfolding with students as they struggle to understand our topics and answer our questions. To be present is to be attentive; doing so requires more than falling back on our habitual practices.

The notion of applying Kahneman and Tversky's work to teaching is not new to me. I first encountered this idea in John Tagg's book, *The Instruction Myth* (2019). Tagg cleverly applies these two systems for thinking to the process of *learning*, which is of use to us here as educators and as learners ourselves. When we (or our students) encounter new challenges, we have no System 1 expertise to lean on, so we must engage in System 2 cognition. It's hard. It feels uncomfortable. It's exhausting. When we're already operating at reduced cognitive capacity—say, because we're not getting enough quality sleep, we're working two jobs, or we're dealing with life challenges—then System 2 thinking is going to feel nearly impossible. Admonishments to simply *try harder* or *believe in yourself* aren't going to bring online the resources necessary to meet the challenges of System 2 work.

In this way, I hope you see that any resistance you feel to engaging in the cognitively challenging work of teaching with presence is entirely rational and defensible. We only have so much attention, energy, and resources to bring to our work. Existing in burnout or feeling under resourced can contribute to teaching in System 1. And, indeed, this is precisely why this book exists: if we cannot identify our own cognitive and emotional roadblocks, we cannot gather the resources needed to help our students do the same.

Maslow, Reconsidered

For many, the notion of bringing a more authentic self into the classroom feels threatening on multiple levels. We'll get into those, but let's first consider the framework we so often turn to: Maslow's "hierarchy of needs." Scott Barry Kaufman is quite possibly the world's greatest living Abraham Maslow fan. In writing his book reconsidering Maslow's theories, Kaufman read every bit of Maslow's writing that he could find. By doing so, Kaufman was able to get to the heart of Maslow's beliefs about self-actualization. Kaufman's recent book *Transcend: The New Science of Self-Actualization* (2020) revisits this model. Here's Kaufman's big A-HA: Maslow did not literally mean a hierarchy. As Kaufman writes, "Maslow emphasized that we are always in a state of becoming and that one's 'inner core' consists merely of 'potentialities, not final actualizations' that are 'weak, subtle, and delicate, very easily drowned out by learning, by cultural expectations, by fear, by disapproval, etc.,' and which can all too easily become forgotten, neglected, unused, overlooked, unverbalized, or suppressed. Maslow made it clear that human maturation is an ongoing process and that growth is 'not a sudden, saltatory phenomenon' but is often two steps forward and one step back" (Kaufman 2020, xxvii)

In other words, our journeys toward self-actualization will likely never end. But in the struggle to reach that destination, we grow, mature, and overcome challenges. If we are diverting precious mental resources to perform for an audience, we aren't just taxing our very limited cognitive resources; we're also limiting our ability to engage in the self-actualization journey that Maslow describes.

Kaufman's book proposes a different metaphor for understanding Maslow's theory—not the familiar pyramid, but a sailboat (Kaufman 2024). In the hull of the boat are the elements that are fundamental to security: safety, connection, and self-esteem. If there are holes in the hull of a sailboat, all available energy and attention will go toward plugging them so the boat doesn't succumb to the sea. But when the hull is seaworthy, when these three aspects are working together reasonably well, we have the stability we need and can turn our attention and energy to moving forward, which Kaufman represents visually with the sail. Those elements all have to do with growth: exploration, love, and purpose.

To let loose the sails of our lives, we must make ourselves vulnerable. Exploring the unknown, allowing ourselves to love others, and pointing our efforts in the direction of something we value deeply come at the risk of criticism and even failure. That's why, Kaufman says, unfurling the sails of our boats requires that we are sufficiently grounded in physical, emotional, and psychological safety; that we have social connections to support us when we inevitably fall short; and that we believe in our ability to persevere.

Connecting Goffman's theory of the presentation of self with Kaufman's work on self-actualization provides the conceptual framework that underlies this book. I define "presence" as the state of being that occurs when the differences in our front-stage and back-stage presentations of self narrow. When this happens, we're able to bring our more effortless, more authentic selves into the spaces in which we might otherwise feel nudged to engage in impression management. We can grow when we're present. But to do this, we must invest effort in reinforcing the hulls of our sailboats, metaphorically speaking, so that we can withstand the winds that will challenge us when we unfurl the sails of our life's work.

Put another way: when stepping into your classroom, you will be better equipped to engage students in authentic, transformative learning experiences if you are secure enough in who you are, if you have a sense of safety, connection, and self-esteem sufficient to allow yourself to be more authentic with your students. Doing so won't get you all the way to what psychologists call self-actualization, but it's a necessary step in that direction.

The ultimate goal of Maslow's work, self-actualization, shows up in some of our most beloved pedagogical literature, such as bell hooks's argument: "Professors who embrace the challenge of self-actualization will be better able to create pedagogical practices that engage students, providing them with ways of knowing that enhance their capacity to live fully and deeply" (hooks 1994, 22). If you can decrease the number of personality and behavioral changes you undertake, consciously or otherwise, when you don the role of a Very Smart College Professor, your students will be more likely to show up fully, embrace your teaching, and learn more meaningfully—because you will have modeled for them the safety, connection, and self-esteem to do so. That will benefit your students *and* yourself, as you embrace the challenge of self-actualization.

Teaching as a Serving Profession

We often hear teaching described as one of the world's helping professions, like health care or social work. Students and their families entrust us with their most precious resource (time), hoping to leave our classrooms as better versions of themselves. But the way I think about our role as educators was fundamentally altered the first time I encountered Rachel Naomi Remen's essay "In the Service of Life" (see sidebar). Remen makes an important distinction between *service* and *helping* or *fixing*. Only service honors the other person's humanity and wholeness. Helping and fixing both imply judgment and inequality, and others can feel their sense of worth weaken if we operate from a posture of helping or fixing. Remen's essay captures the essence of what presence in our profession looks like: It recognizes that when we are self-aware and do not feel pressured to assume a persona of bulletproof expertise, we can serve our students human to human. Not only is this a more authentic relationship, but we also gain as much from those exchanges as our students do, creating a positive emotional cascade that propels us forward together.

IN THE SERVICE OF LIFE

by Rachel Naomi Remen

In recent years the question how can I help? has become meaningful to many people. But perhaps there is a deeper question we might consider. Perhaps the real question is not how can I help? but how can I serve?

Serving is different from helping. Helping is based on inequality; it is not a relationship between equals. When you help you use your own strength to help those of lesser strength. If I'm attentive to what's going on inside of me when I'm helping, I find that I'm always helping someone who's not as strong as I am, who is needier than I am. People feel this inequality. When we help we may inadvertently take away from people more than we could ever give them; we may diminish their self-esteem, their sense of worth, integrity and wholeness. When I help I am very aware of my own strength. But we don't serve with our strength, we serve with ourselves. We draw from all of our experiences. Our limitations serve, our wounds serve, even our darkness can serve. The wholeness in us serves the wholeness in others and the wholeness in life. The wholeness in you is the same as the wholeness in me. Service is a relationship between equals.

Helping incurs debt. When you help someone they owe you one. But serving, like healing, is mutual. There is no debt. I am as served as the person I am serving. When I help I have a feeling of satisfaction. When I serve I have a feeling of gratitude. These are very different things.

Serving is also different from fixing. When I fix a person I perceive them as broken, and their brokenness requires me to act. When I fix I do not see the wholeness in the other person or trust the integrity of the life in them. When I serve I see and trust that wholeness. It is what I am responding to and collaborating with.

There is distance between ourselves and whatever or whomever we are fixing. Fixing is a form of judgment. All judgment creates distance, a disconnection, an experience of difference. In fixing there is an inequality of expertise that can easily become a moral distance. We cannot serve at a distance. We can only serve that to which we are profoundly connected, that which we are willing to touch. This is Mother Teresa's basic message. We serve life not because it is broken but because it is holy. If helping is an experience of strength, fixing is an experience of mastery and expertise.

Service, on the other hand, is an experience of mystery, surrender, and awe. A fixer has the illusion of being causal. A server knows that he or she is being used and has a willingness to be used in the service of something greater, something essentially unknown. Fixing and helping are very personal; they are very particular, concrete, and specific. We fix and help many different things in our lifetimes, but when we serve we are always serving the same thing. Everyone who has ever served through the history of time serves the same thing. We are servers of the wholeness and mystery in life.

The bottom line, of course, is that we can fix without serving. And we can help without serving. And we can serve without fixing or helping. I think I would go so far as to say that fixing and helping may often be the work of the ego, and service the work of the soul. They may look similar if you're watching from the outside, but the inner experience is different. The outcome is often different, too.

Our service serves us as well as others. That which uses us strengthens us. Over time, fixing and helping are draining, depleting. Over time we burn out. Service is renewing. When we serve, our work itself will sustain us. Service rests on the basic premise that the nature of life is sacred, that life is a holy mystery which has an unknown purpose. When we serve, we know that we belong to life and to that purpose. Fundamentally, helping, fixing, and service are ways of seeing life. When you help you see life as weak, when you fix, you see life as broken. When you serve, you see life as whole. From the perspective of service, we are all connected: All suffering is like my suffering and all joy is like my joy. The impulse to serve emerges naturally and inevitably from this way of seeing.

Lastly, fixing and helping are the basis of curing, but not of healing. In 40 years of chronic illness, I have been helped by many people and fixed by a great many others who did not recognize my wholeness. All that fixing and helping left me wounded in some important and fundamental ways. Only service heals.

©1996 Rachel Naomi Remen, *Noetic Sciences Review*, Spring 1996. Reprinted with permission of the author.

The longer I've taught, the more I've understood that serving students requires a very different mindset than helping students. The chapters to follow provide tangible tools for developing these skills and strategies for improving our classroom cultures. Remen's essay provides a vision for what our teaching can be when we bring our authentic selves into our classrooms and remain present to what's unfolding in those spaces.

Experimenting with Presence

When I began teaching at my current institution, I was convinced that my years of teaching out of my car's trunk, as a roving adjunct, would lead my colleagues to see me as less than, as undeserving of a full-time tenure-track job. When my colleague Kathy didn't warmly welcome me into the fold, it was all the evidence I needed to begin erecting protective barriers.

Thankfully, as I began that job, I was also halfway through a 200-hour yoga teacher training (YTT) program. I hadn't been able to articulate why a YTT felt like the right choice for a political scientist, but I knew it was something I wanted to do and signed up without giving it too much thought.

Through that YTT, one of the strategies I was slowly learning, through studying yogic philosophy (see chapter 6), proved instrumental in changing the trajectory of my entry into my new faculty role. It's pretty simple, too: I asked myself what evidence I had that I'd done something to offend, annoy, or disappoint Kathy. The answer, I confessed to myself, was nothing—certainly, nothing intentional. What I did have was a woman who wasn't smiling at me each time we crossed paths.[2] When I realized that I was girding myself against what I imagined to be her disdain for my ineptitude, without any evidence? That's when I knew I needed to change my mindset and my tactics.

I decided on an experiment: What if I just *pretended* that she'd already accepted me? What if I just acted as if we had already laid the foundation for a collegial relationship? You know, kind of like dressing for the job you want rather than the job you have? It felt like a bold assumption to make, but nothing else was working, so I decided to give it a go. I would smile at her and say hello when our paths crossed. I paid closer attention to her body language and started asking her questions about how her classes were going. Rather than projecting my own insecurities onto her, I responded to what she was actually saying, both verbally and nonverbally. Over time, we became friends. When I was up for tenure six years later, she was one of my most forceful advocates in our department. The shift in my assumptions yielded a change in my behavior, which led to a different outcome. Getting out of my head and being present with a colleague led to a far richer relationship.

Years later, I was chatting with Kathy, and I decided to share with her my experience when I first arrived. She laughed and said, "Noah thought I hated him at first, too!" referring to a colleague who had since joined our department.[3] It turned out that she had been going through a lot of stressful life events at the time, and I had mistakenly read her stress as judgment of me. The whole thing was entirely in my head, but it had the power to completely change my experience of this new department—and, indeed, my entire future.

Everything changed for me when I made a conscious decision to push back against the anxious voices in my head and look for evidence of what was real. I realized that I had been moving around my work environment waiting for someone to call me out as a fraud, and I was doing so in a place where a whole slew of other people were likely doing the same. They didn't know me; for all they knew, I was some hotshot political scientist hoping to take over the joint. The shift to being present with my colleagues required me to get out of my own head and pay attention to each moment, as it was happening, with whoever happened to be in front of me. It meant listening closely to what the people around me were saying, with both their words and their body language.

This shift allowed me to be genuinely happy to see others and genuinely concerned when it was clear they were having a hard day. None of this attentiveness was possible when I was too busy looking for evidence that I fit in (or was failing to do so). As Dr. Brené Brown writes:

> Stop walking through the world looking for confirmation that you don't belong. You will always find it because you've made that your mission. Stop scouring people's faces for evidence that you're not enough. You'll always find it because you've made that your goal. True belonging and self-worth are not goods; we don't negotiate their value with the world. The truth about who we are lives in our hearts. Our call to courage is to protect our wild heart against constant evaluation, especially our own. No one belongs here more than you. (Brown 2017a, 158)

I simply couldn't hold genuine care alongside that fear-inspired intelligence gathering; it was too cognitively demanding. Assuming I fit in and focusing on how I could relate to others was a conscious decision that quite literally changed how I experienced my life.

Classroom Presence

The same dynamics appear in our classrooms. As Schwartz (2020) tells us, "Intellectual and emotional availability between teachers and students is *central in productive teaching, learning, and other intellectual endeavors*" (15, emphasis added). Unfortunately, many academics—myself included—experienced the opposite of this in our school experiences, particularly in graduate school (more on this in chapter 3). As a result, many academics suffer from imposter syndrome.[4] As York University philosopher Diane Zorn says, "Scholarly isolation, aggressive competitiveness, disciplinary nationalism, a lack of mentoring, and the valuation of product over process are rooted in the university culture. Students and faculty alike are particularly susceptible to [imposter syndrome] feelings" (quoted in McDevitt 2006). Although many who work in higher education may experience imposter feelings, faculty and students are especially susceptible. For example, someone who works in institutional research may rarely encounter those with similar levels of expertise in their areas of specialization. Most faculty members and students, however, will come into regular and persistent contact with others who are studying the discipline in which they specialize. This kind of close contact with others invites comparison, and any sense of insecurity or uncertainty can quickly morph into confirmation bias when presented with the slightest hint of judgment or critique, real or imagined.

The experience of imposter syndrome leaves us feeling anxious, like we don't belong and might be called out at any time. The greater the sense of being an imposter, the less present one can be. Feeling like an imposter floods our extraneous cognitive load, reducing the intrinsic load available for our students and our teaching. Imposter feelings are shameful, and we naturally try to hide things that feel shameful. As Brené Brown describes in an SXSW talk, shame in the classroom merits our attention because shame inhibits learning. "Learning is inherently vulnerable," she says. When we feel shameful feelings arising, we grab one of the coping mechanisms Brown calls "shame shields," each of which creates a block to learning (2017b). What's more, as Brown writes elsewhere, "Because true belonging only happens when we present our authentic, imperfect selves to the world, our sense of belonging can never be greater than our level of self-acceptance" (Brown 2010, 26).[5]

If you yearn for a more authentic and engaging dynamic in your classrooms, you simply must find ways to let go of any shameful feelings you possess, no matter how well you're hiding them from others (or yourself). The best pedagogical tools or lesson plans will fall short if you are not present with your students. Chris

Emdin (2021) writes, "The two subjects that the teacher needs to have the most expertise in is themselves and their students. Your subject is not your content area" (28–29).

Moving away from imposter feelings and toward a more authentic presence comes as we work toward self-actualization. As the saying goes, self-actualization is a process, not a destination; we never quite get there, but the journey is rich and rewarding. This book is designed to equip you with the tools to move along in your own journey.

SYNDROME OR CULTURE?

A 2021 *Harvard Business Review* article cautioned us to stop telling women they have imposter syndrome (Tulshyan and Burey 2021b). The authors argue that defining feelings of inadequacy as "imposter syndrome" inherently lays the responsibility on the individual, rather than on a culture steeped in systemic misogyny, racism, xenophobia, classism, and other biases. Instead of fixing the workplace culture, thinking of someone—including ourselves—as experiencing imposter syndrome demands the individual fix her—or him—self. In her Substack newsletter, *Academia Made Easier,* Loleen Berdahl makes this point as well: "Imposter syndrome is *structural* (rather than personal). Evidence suggests that imposter feelings are both ubiquitous and patterned. Individuals who do not fit the norm for 'professors' a century ago (read: white, male, able-bodied, heterosexual, cisgender, neurotypical, non-immigrant, privileged background) are more likely to report imposter feelings" (Berdahl 2023).

These are compelling arguments. Higher education is not immune to the cultural stagnation found in corporate America; if anything, much of higher education is slower to change than other sectors of society. Still, as the authors note in a follow-up piece, a better strategy is to take a "both/and" posture (Tulshyan and Burey 2021a). We recognize the individual experiences of imposter-like feelings, *and* we must call out a culture that makes those experiences common.

Perhaps you're reading this book and not identifying with the sense of imposter syndrome. If so, fantastic! But for those who have felt the "fairly universal feeling of discomfort, second-guessing, and mild anxiety in the workplace," know that there are ways to reduce those feelings *and* fight for a workplace culture that is more inclusive and supportive (Tulshyan and Burey 2021b). In fact, the premise of this book is that we cannot create that better workplace culture if we haven't done some inner work to reduce our own feelings of less-than.

Moving toward Self-Actualization

What I know for sure is that people who are doing this work—who are more able to be present and authentic around others, even those they do not know well—are just easier to be around, especially when building relationships (including student-teacher relationships). To spend time with someone who is more present and authentic just takes less effort; their way of being is disarming and more vulnerable, which gives you permission to engage in less impression management. You leave their company feeling psychologically safer, able to be more vulnerable and authentic, too. When you are near someone who embodies this kind of presence, you might notice that you feel more accepted, comfortable, or drawn toward them by forces you can't quite describe.[6]

Presence means that you're able to see your own thoughts and reactions in close to real time. Presence does not require that you're perfectly capable of controlling your thoughts or reactions, though, only that you can step back from your ego and see what is happening with less reactivity.

Possibilities

"How did you know I belonged here?"

This question, posed by a student after class ended, caught me off guard. After seventy-five minutes of focusing on the students in my classroom, attending to the nuances of their nonverbal communication while trying to keep a lively verbal volley going, my attention was utterly scattered. Most immediately, I was trying to gather up the miscellany I seem to carry with me everywhere I go: articles, books, Post-its, legal pads, class rosters, a jump drive or two, cell phone, ID card lanyard, sunglasses, face mask, pencil case stuffed to the gills with every style of pen imaginable. I tend to bring every possible reference or resource to class, you know—*just in case*. The students had filed out of the room, and I was frittering away, collecting the detritus, physical and mental, that I'd strewn about haphazardly near the front of the room.

Sandy had lingered, which was not unusual.[7] She had a languid way of being, a slow and quiet presence that meant people often overlooked her. During the first seven weeks of the semester, I had become accustomed to coexisting quietly with Sandy before or after class, both of us seeming to appreciate the chance to be in a space without the oppressive need to fill it up with words. Her clothing reflected her observant and thoughtful identity, mostly thrift finds she'd upcycled with patches, long links of safety pins, and her own knitted embellishments. Everything about her read as considered and conscientious—and introverted. So, so introverted.

Her unexpected question came after we had wrapped up our last session before fall break, and Sandy was reflecting on how unexpectedly comfortable she felt in the course. She had been recruited (after I recommended her) into a by-invitation-only student leadership course. Thirteen students were nominated by a professor or club advisor as having strong leadership potential. The goal of the course was to help those students understand their own leadership talents, make connections to campus and community leaders, and design a service project.

Sandy was one of two students I'd nominated, after she had taken my introductory American government course. While she was typically quiet during class, her writing demonstrated strong critical thinking skills. She'd also expressed a desire to get involved in some of the campus events I occasionally mentioned in class. Others in the class deferred to her thoughts when discussions unfolded, paying attention to the points she made or listening carefully if she shared a story from her past. From my vantage point as her (present) professor, Sandy had tremendous potential to take on more official leadership roles; from her perspective, as an introverted and uncertain first-semester college student, she was just trying to succeed while flying under her peers' radar.

Thanks to the rapport we'd established over the course of the prior semester, though, Sandy decided to trust my faith in her and sign up for the leadership course. She flourished. After a half-term of twice-weekly meetings, she had connected with every student in the course. They were meeting outside of class times, carpooling to community events, and working on a project together. If you compiled a list of behaviors that predict student persistence and success, you would have an excellent case study of Sandy that semester. She was finding her people and clarifying her purpose.

But that question—how had I known? It was a vulnerable question.

I turned my attention back to her, away from my distracting mess of the moment. I saw a young woman with a curious face and a guarded stance, someone looking for validation but afraid it might not come. I knew that what I said would matter to her, maybe a lot. I worried that I might not be able to capture something sufficiently tangible to satisfy her need for validation.

A thousand tiny moments had coalesced into my general sense that she had the potential to step into a more visible leadership role. How could I boil them down into a succinct answer?

"You are an incredibly thoughtful person, Sandy. Your classmates look to you because they know you won't judge them. They trust you to focus on what really matters. You aren't interested in fitting in with someone else's idea of what you *should* be. You are more interested in changing the world to fit what you think it *ought* to be."

She maintained eye contact, absorbing my words.

"Almost since I met you, I knew you were intelligent and capable. But what I've seen in this class is how others gravitate to you. You make others feel comfortable being themselves because you appear to be comfortable with yourself. That is gold."

I do not think I could have found those words had I been caught up in my own insecurities. I had developed a nuanced sense of her because I was mentally, emotionally, and intentionally present with her and her class for an entire semester. It wasn't just Sandy that I'd come to know; most of the students who attended regularly were on my radar in similar ways. Connecting them to opportunities and resources that align with their goals is a big part of what I think of as my work.

I think every student has the potential I saw in Sandy. What made her different, what attracted my attention, was that she became increasingly willing to engage with her classmates as she grew more comfortable in the classroom. She spoke up more often and began sharing more of her experiences. I've learned to look for those subtle shifts and respond in kind.

Another student in the leadership course—the other I'd nominated—was struggling. Jesse's attendance was spotty; his attention was flagging. The students had set up a group text message thread, and he rarely engaged in the volleys of messages around class days and campus events. When he did come to class, he said very little, even sitting a bit apart from others.

Jesse was a student whose career trajectory I had already invested significant effort in directing. A political science major and my advisee, Jesse had secured a prestigious internship as a freshman. Like Sandy, he was a quiet but thoughtful contributor to discussions. In a previous semester, he'd taken my honors course on world politics; in that class, students participate in several National Security Council simulations on thorny foreign policy problems. (See Model Diplomacy in the bibliography for those tools).Jesse was the first student to volunteer to play the role of US president, a role that required taking in a huge volume of information from the other students and deciding what the US policy directive would be. His curiosity and ability to listen to competing perspectives made him an ideal pretend president, one that his peers would seek to emulate in subsequent simulations.

Then, Jesse's life got tricky. I had known that Jesse was in the process of getting a divorce and negotiating custody over his two kids. I later learned that, as our leadership class got underway, those proceedings turned acrimonious. He was consumed with worries about losing custody of his kids, his finances were a mess due to the unanticipated legal costs, and school was rightly the last thing on his mind. When we spoke over fall break, I saw all the signs of deep stress: exhaustion, distraction, rumination, anxiety spirals, and so on. To be clear, attending to Jesse's obvious life struggles is not in my job description. I'm no therapist, and my first responsibility is to ensure my students can be academically successful. However, attending to my students as whole human beings sometimes necessitates listening to what's on their mind. Just doing that is a powerful gift of affirmation. As Jesse spoke, I listened carefully and expressed a willingness to help him identify resources where I could—if he wanted me to.

Eventually, our conversation turned to the leadership class. Jesse confessed, "I know I'm not very talkative in class. I just feel like everyone else is next-level, and I'm learning from them. They're all so amazing."

Most of the thirteen students in the class struggled to see themselves as leaders, particularly early in the course. But in that moment, I realized something bigger was happening with Jesse. He saw talent and ambition in them that he perceived himself as lacking. Realizing this broke my heart. I felt empathy for his life's trials, but I now also felt compassion for how those trials were affecting his ability to see himself positively. With his relationship with his children threatened, *of course* school was going to become a lower priority. He hadn't accepted the tradeoffs, though, and he was trying to continue playing the part of Student with His Life Totally Together. Jesse felt like he had to keep going without help because he'd never needed help before.

Jesse was doubling down on his front-stage performance; he didn't feel comfortable being his authentic self with his classmates or me, fearing we'd realize he wasn't accomplished or promising or talented. In Jesse, I saw what I frequently observe in students, colleagues, and friends: a fear of being found out, a hesitance to speak up, a preference to stay quiet and hope nobody noticed he was drifting away. I recognized it because it was the same impulse I had felt on my first day at that school.

As Sandy was demonstrating in the same class, though, having someone else see you fully has the power to transform uncertainty into courage. Jesse would get there, too, with time. But none of it could have happened without Sandy's and Jesse's instructors and peers escaping their own uncertainty spirals and staying present.

When you are present with yourself, when you can bring that presence into the classroom, magical things can happen. Genuine connection happens, which leads to genuine learning. And that is where the next several chapters will take us.

Chapter 2

RELATIONAL TEACHING AND PRESENCE

Start by trusting students.
> Jesse Stommel's four-word pedagogy

Relationships are engines of education. A litany of scholarly research underscores the importance of relationships in driving learning at all levels, as well as many studies that demonstrate how relationships propel learning in higher education, particularly regular interactions with faculty and quality engagement with peers (e.g., Cozolino and Sprokay 2006; Lundberg 2003; Lundberg 2014). Other books—particularly Sarah Rose Cavanagh's *The Spark of Learning* (2016) and Kevin Gannon's *Radical Hope* (2020)—highlight the ways in which relationships have an impact on student learning and motivation.

Two recent books that center relationships in teaching and learning in higher education have received wide critical acclaim. Peter Felten and Leo M. Lambert's *Relationship-Rich Education: How Human Connections Drive Success in College* (2020) and Harriet L. Schwartz's *Connected Teaching: Relationship, Power, and Mattering in Higher Education* (2019) dive into the centrality of relationships in our teaching work. As Felten and Lambert write, "The classroom remains the most important place on campus for meaningful relationships to take root" (Felten and Lambert 2020, 152). They quote Randy Bass of Georgetown University as saying, "Relationships are essential because there is no learning without relationships" (Felten and Lambert 2020, 1).

This context allows us to embrace what Schwartz advocates: "A relational approach is intended to create a learning environment in which students trust themselves and us as educators. This increase in trust promotes students' intellectual risk-taking, motivation, and belief in their own potential, which then facilitates deeper engagement and learning" (Schwartz 2019, 63; see also Brookfield 2017). Closely related is what James Lang calls "cognitive belonging," or "affirming to students that they are intellectually capable of success in our courses" (Lang 2021, 167). Relationships make it possible for students to trust our encouragement and to rise to the challenges we set before them.

But here's the thing that matters for us: if we're going to create meaningful relationships with our students, the kinds of relationships that lead to the greater engagement, motivation, and learning we aspire to foster, we cannot do this while hiding integral parts of our identities. It simply requires too much cognitive and emotional bandwidth to inhabit a role *and* meaningfully connect with another human being. The effort required cannot be sustained over the time-consuming process of building a relationship grounded in trust. In this chapter, we'll review the research, from a variety of perspectives, on how to build more meaningful relationships. Throughout this discussion, we'll focus on specific strategies and techniques we can use in the classroom, along with the rationale behind how and why they work.

Eating Cookies in Law Class

When I was an undergraduate at George Washington University, I was required to take one honors course per semester to maintain my standing in our honors program (and keep my scholarship). My sophomore year, I signed up for a First Amendment Law honors course taught by a law school professor and the university's marshal, Jill Kasle. Among the many ways that Professor Kasle tried to create a welcoming class environment was her insistence on ensuring we had a volunteer "Cookie Guy" for each class meeting. Cookie Guy would bring some sort of sweet treat to class each day. She didn't have to work hard to persuade us that an afternoon class just worked better with cookies.[1] The fact that this was a nonnegotiable part of our class persuaded me (and I assume others, too) that she cared about our experience of the class and ensuring that our brains had the fuel they needed to perform well with the class's tough material and unfamiliar law-school-esque Socratic discussion format.

Her focus on comfort went beyond just our classroom space, though. Professor Kasle's office was a cozy space with a rocking chair for student visitors to occupy while chatting. She was attentive, invested, and demanding. In my undergraduate program, she was a rare exemplar of holding high expectations and compassion simultaneously.

Having always been a strong writer and student, I assumed the course would be challenging but manageable. When I got back my first essay for the course, though, I was crestfallen; it was returned with a sea of red ink and a note to come visit her during her office hours and no grade. Sitting in that rocking chair, I was near tears as she told me that she wanted me to rewrite the paper entirely. I couldn't fathom having completely failed this assignment—it was so bad, I had to *start over?!* But Professor Kasle sat across from me, in a chair that looked less comfortable than mine, and said, "I know you're going to be an amazing lawyer someday. You can do better. I know you can."

A coach and friend of mine, Shelley Prevost, says that "you know you've healed when you can celebrate your failures." Today, I celebrate that challenge. Because it turns out, legal analysis is just qualitatively different from any other kind of writing students are asked to do. I think nearly the entire class had that same conversation with her in her office about our first essays. She was certain we'd all succeed, and she wasn't going to let us stop trying until we did. Her class was, incidentally, my first exposure to growth-mindset-centered pedagogy. In the end, I grew so much as a writer and thinker in that class that I signed up for another class with her the following semester, on constitutional law. The challenge of the course was a selling point, but only because Professor Kastle made it so abundantly clear that she trusted I could meet the challenge. The cookies were just one more way she demonstrated care alongside her high expectations.

Very few of my professors in my undergraduate career were nearly as invested in my success and in mentoring me as a student. At many points in my teaching career, I've told my own students about Cookie Guy and suggested we adopt the practice, with varying degrees of success. Years ago, I bought an IKEA POÄNG rocking chair from a neighbor and installed it in my office for students to use when visiting. (That lasted only as long as I had an office big enough to accommodate it . . . which wasn't for a very long time, sadly.) Nevertheless, I *have* had success with finding my own authentic ways of creating welcome, things like affixing stickers to exit slips for in-person classes, creating an online space where students can share (explicitly PG or safer) memes and funnies with the class, and bringing snacks anytime I gather with students. Efforts at hospitality aren't just frivolous means of buying students' appreciation; they're meaningful mechanisms for showing genuine care and welcome. (More on this in chapter 3's sidebar about Priya Parker).

Relational Teaching

In chapter 1, you learned a little about the critical importance of belonging, the feeling of social acceptance, to creating a safe environment for learning. This is true of any learning space, and it's true for both teachers *and* learners. The secret, of course, is that everyone in a learning space should, ideally, be learning—regardless of their title or the role they occupy. As the professor, your job is to design conditions that facilitate learning; to do so effectively, you must simultaneously engage in a process of learning—about your students, your subject, and, most importantly, yourself.

The reason may not be self-evident, at least not until you dig a bit more deeply. As Parker Palmer (2007) tells us, though, "We teach who we are. . . . When I do not know myself, I cannot know who my students are" (2–3). The academy has traditionally prioritized what we conceive of as rational thought over emotional awareness and, as such, we've often been directed away from this inner exploration. However, trying to forget ourselves and let our subjects absorb us only leads to a divided life, one in which Parker says "community cannot take root.... Only as we are in communion with ourselves can we find community with others" (92).

Let's try a thought experiment. Think back to an experience from your past where you felt truly in community with others. This might have been in a traditional classroom setting, such as a high school or college class where you felt the grip of excitement while exploring a topic you found highly engaging. It might have been a moment with friends where you were playing a round of Cards Against Humanity or enjoying a band you particularly love. Or maybe you were playing softball in an adult league, going kayaking on a summer afternoon, or spending time with family members whom you especially enjoy being around. What was it about that moment that felt so deeply communal? What were the physical sensations that let you know you were in community with others? How did it feel in your body?

Got that memory in mind? Good. Now I want to ask you a few more questions that might surprise you, maybe even confuse you: How did you feel about yourself at that moment? Did you accept yourself? Embrace yourself? Perhaps even celebrate the fact that you have an interest that others share with you? Or did you entirely forget yourself, finding yourself fully immersed in the moment?

If you were feeling *truly* in community with others, it's highly unlikely that you spent that time thinking negative thoughts about your inner worth, performance, or belongingness. You were probably feeling like one of the very best versions of yourself—able to exist with people whose company fosters feelings of acceptance, love, and even celebration.

In those moments, we are most receptive to learning. It might be that we're learning about academic subjects, but it's more likely that we're learning about ourselves and how we fit into the world. For example, if you felt fully enmeshed in community while playing a concert with your high school band, as I so often did, at that moment you were learning about the power of music to unite diverse groups. You were internalizing the importance of practice to create something beautiful. You understood that mistakes are inevitable, but you didn't stop just because someone made one—you kept going, turning the momentary blip of mistake into barely a passing thought as you focused on the notes ahead. You experienced a state of flow, that unmistakably enjoyable feeling of total absorption into something challenging enough to require concentration but feasible enough to accomplish (e.g., Csikszentmihályi 2008; Csikszentmihályi, Abuhamdeh, and Nakamura 2005). You were learning a lot, but you didn't experience it as *learning* so much as *doing*.

Now compare that communal experience to what happens in most of our classrooms. How do we generate those moments in an institutional box with rows of chairs oriented at a whiteboard or overhead projector screen? Most of our academic learning spaces aren't designed to foster community; they're designed with the banking model of learning (Friere [1970] 2018) in mind, that tired old "sage on the stage" metaphor. But despite our ever-growing knowledge of what makes for an engaged, active-learning classroom, our facilities designers haven't quite caught up, have they? We are left trying to discern how to make transformational learning happen for our students in an English composition or world history or chemistry classroom.

The answers won't come by ordering new furniture, wreaking chaos on the meticulously arranged rows of chairs, or leading your students through a think-pair-share activity.[2] Those things might help, but they can only help if you're also creating space for true belonging and genuine connection. Until your students—and you—can let down their guards a little and be real. Until the inhabitants of your learning space are doing something that taps into their deeper emotional, intellectual, and social needs. In other words, your best efforts at pedagogical innovation will only succeed to the extent that you've created a space for the people there to be human *beings*, not just human *doings*.[3]

The authors of *Make It Stick: The Science of Successful Learning* teach us that most learning happens *outside* of formal learning spaces (Brown, Roediger, and McDaniel 2014).[4] The work we do in our classrooms matters, but it probably isn't where the deepest levels of learning happen. Instead, we lay the groundwork in our shared spaces before sending learners out into their lives to make meaning and apply what we've introduced and explored together. The relationships we develop with students can either smooth or impede the way for them to deepen their work outside of class.

But how? The rest of this chapter provides some clues from a variety of literatures—from pedagogy, the social sciences, and business. Some of these may feel resonant; others may not. That's okay. Like most of this book, consider this to be a menu of options, each with an invitation to explore further. The goal is to start thinking about how to generate the conditions that allow for genuine connection and belonging to take root in your learning spaces. None of these efforts will succeed if they aren't grounded in your authentic way of being—which, don't worry, we'll talk more about exploring in the next set of chapters. For now, though, focus your attention on what this work can unlock in your relationships with and between students. Let's see what might work for you.

RELATIONSHIPS MATTER

The consensus of decades of psychological research is clear: Relationships matter. A lot. Having at least one close relationship is vital to health and happiness (e.g., Frederickson 2013). They matter to our health; those with stronger relationships enjoy protective benefits, including living longer, better recovery from stress, and fewer and less severe illnesses (Kreitzer 2022). As Sbarra and Coan (2018) write, "The evidence is unequivocal: High-quality, low-conflict relationships are associated with better health, and this conclusion holds in both healthy and medically-involved samples." Our primal desire to form strong bonds with others comes from our tribal ancestry, where belonging to a tight-knit clan served as protection against invaders. Maslow's framework to understand our needs underscores this. As we saw in chapter 1 with Kaufman's sailboat metaphor, strong relationships reinforce the hull of our life's ship and allow our sails to unfurl. In more direct terms: We are safer, more connected, and have higher self-esteem when we have strong relationships; we can explore, love, and fulfill our life's purpose when those relationships bolster us further. Security and growth require strong relationships.

As we'll explore more deeply in chapter 3, though, the process of earning an advanced degree and pursuing a career in higher education often teaches us to ignore our natural social impulses. Horror stories about graduate school or academic hazing abound. Academic career coach Karen Kelsey started a Facebook group called The Professor Is Out that, at last check, boasted nearly 30,000 members, where person after person has shared traumatic experiences from graduate school and beyond.

Likely you've felt some of this, too, in your own educational and teaching career. When we turn to the literature on psychological thriving—including happiness, life satisfaction, and self-actualization, we see how important strong relationships are to combating the potentially isolating side effects of living a life of the mind. If we imagine the continuum of quality, meaningful relationships with others as running from left to right, from completely isolated to completely satisfied, we can look to the far left to see the consequences of lacking strong relationships. As surgeon general Dr. Vivek Murthy writes in his book, *Together: The Healing Power of Human Connection in a Sometimes Lonely World* (2020), there are three dimensions of loneliness—and three dimensions of connection to combat them:

Intimate, Relational, and Collective. We all need close friends and intimate confidants with whom we share deep bonds of mutual affection and trust. We need casual friendships and social relationships that offer shared support and connection. And we need to belong to communities of people—neighbors, colleagues, classmates, and acquaintances—with whom we experience a sense of collective purpose and identity. (Murthy, 218–19)

What is good for our students is also good for us; we need these three levels of connection in our personal and work lives. If you start to feel resistance to the lessons of this book, pause for a moment and think about the relationships you have on your campus or within your organization. Do you have people whom you consider close friends? Do you have casual friendships that support you? Do you feel you belong to a community with a shared purpose and identity? If the answer to each question is yes, congratulations! Spend some time thinking about how those different kinds of relationships influence your job and life satisfaction, how they sustain you when you're feeling stressed or frustrated. If you answered any of these questions with a no, reflect on how the lack of that type of relationship impacts your work life. What might be different about your work or life satisfaction if you had some of these relationships? How might that change your experience of your work community?

After you've reflected on these questions, you can apply the lessons you've learned to the students in your classrooms. They need the same kinds of relationships—if not with people on your campus, then with others in their lives. The classroom is a natural space for collective relationships to form, but to do so, they must come to represent a shared purpose for the students gathered. And to create that shared purpose in service of something productive to learning, your thoughtful, purposeful intervention is necessary.

Building Relationships: What Pedagogy Tells Us

So much terrific work has emerged on higher education pedagogy in recent years—in no small part thanks to the work of James M. Lang, Michelle D. Miller, and Derek Krisoff to bring books like this one to life at the West Virginia University and University of Oklahoma Presses. One of the best resources I've read in recent years was Kevin Gannon's book, *Radical Hope: A Teaching Manifesto*. Gannon advances a view of students as collaborators—co-conspirators, even—in learning. One of the most powerful moments of his book comes in his discussion of the role of grades in the college classroom. As a faculty developer, Gannon hears the common refrains about students who engage in grade-grubbing behaviors, but he responds by asking us all to think about how the K–12 education system has prepared those students. "When instructors lament their students only seem to care about what's on the exam, they fail to see that their emphasis on weeding people out has rendered grades existentially important for their students," he writes (Gannon 2020, 34). His book includes several terrific prompts for reflection on your own practices and pedagogy, and I find these two especially helpful:

Make a word cloud from your syllabus, using one of the several free online word cloud generators (like wordclouds.com, for example). Using this visual representation of your syllabus text (and disregarding results like "the" and "of"), what words appear most frequently? Does this pattern align with the type of tone and approach you want your syllabus to have (108)?

In your immediate teaching environment, what are the connotations and practices associated with concepts like *rigor* and *compassion*? Is there a culture of one or the other? What implications might that have for your practice? Consider journaling about your sense of the environment and its effects on the teaching and learning around you (38).

I'm also fond of the practical tools in Zaretta Hammond's excellent book *Culturally Responsive Teaching and the Brain: Promoting Authentic Engagement and Rigor Among Culturally and Linguistically Diverse Students* (2015). Hammond provides a set of "trust generators," or a set of actions that will facilitate more meaningful connections with others and thus open the door for building trust (Hammond 2015, 79). Below I list these five actions, along with an illustrative example from my own experiences:

1. **Selective vulnerability:** Sharing a personal experience that demonstrates you are human, not perfect.

    On my liquid syllabus website, I tell students about my experience failing on a graduate qualifying exam and being pressured to leave a doctoral program—one of the most personally challenging experiences of my life. I explain how it made me feel, how hard it was to move past that failure, and how I now think about the experience. Namely, facing down that "failure" helped clarify what was most important to me—and it was not earning a pedigree PhD and becoming an R1 researcher. Ultimately, I earned my PhD from a program more aligned with my career goals and was able to pursue a teaching-centric job with the full support of my mentors. Releasing anxiety by no longer swimming upstream, I now see, was an incalculable relief.

2. **Familiarity:** Becoming a more familiar fixture in another person's life through everyday interactions.

    The most straightforward way I've found to create trust through familiarity is to simply be available to students—in the physical and virtual spaces where they are already spending time. That may look like attending student organization meetings or events, supporting the sports teams (especially at smaller schools), or just scheduling some of my office hours in the library or another central campus location. It also means I run a Discord server for students (and former students) in my classes where they can chat with one another and me informally. These impromptu meetings become even more powerful if you find ways to demonstrate you know your students, such as by using a student's name, when you encounter them outside of the classroom.

    Creating an office environment that is inviting also goes a long way toward breeding familiarity with your students—because having an inviting office space will reduce barriers to students seeking you out. One of my favorite ways to encourage students to make that important first visit to my office is to build a student photo roster with selfies taken at my office door. On the first day of class, I tell students that I want them to find my office before the second week of the semester. Many of them follow me to my office after that first class meeting. I have each of them take a selfie—and I'll make a silly facial expression in the background if I happen to be in my office when they come by. Then I have them email or text it to me with their name. Not only does this make our first one-on-one encounter far more enjoyable, but it emphasizes to them that learning their name is important to me. They'll get a peek inside my office without needing to stay for a long time, and they'll see the softer lighting (I abhor overhead fluorescent lights, so I use a scattered array of lamps), the plentiful snacks I keep on hand, and the collection of travel tchotchkes I have decorating my space. All of these careful choices about how I designed my office space are meant to create a nonintimidating and welcoming space for students to visit.

I also share with students (and post outside my office door) that I keep emergency supplies on hand for students to take as needed—no questions asked. These include snacks, pens and pencils, Post-its, paper, bandages, and feminine hygiene products. I want students to know that my space is a place they can land without fear of judgment. When they show up to chat, I know that I'm making inroads in this direction.

3. **Similarity of interests:** Sharing likes, dislikes, hobbies, and other personal details with others.

    Over the years, I've experimented with alternative ways of engaging with students outside of class time and outside the official course learning management system. Among the technologies I've used are Remind, a texting app that obscures phone numbers; GroupMe, a group texting app once popular with students—and maybe still? I'm not cool enough to know . . .; Slack, a popular collaboration and communication tool most often used in business; and Discord, another collaboration and communication tool, most often used by gamers, and hence one that gains a lot of street cred with that population of students. In these spaces, particularly in Slack and Discord, I've made a habit of providing spaces (channels, they're called) for nonacademic chatter. In Discord, which I'm currently using with students, I have a "just-for-fun" channel where I regularly post (rated-G) memes I find on the internet.

Students can react with basic emojis or post their own reactions. These no-cost and low-maintenance channels are great ways to engage students in off-topic but pro-social connections.

4. **Concern:** Demonstrating genuine concern for issues or events important to another person.

    You've been teaching a little while, so it's a bit trite to remind you of this at this point, but perhaps the most important way you can demonstrate concern for students is to learn their preferred names and how they're properly pronounced—and then use those names. I remind myself often of Dale Carnegie's observation that our favorite word is our own name (Russell 2014). Using students' preferred pronouns is also an easy way to build trust through showing concern. I have a former student, now a dog- and house-sitter and friend, who uses they/them pronouns; I don't always manage to use the correct pronouns, but I *always* correct myself (or welcome their correction) and offer a sincere apology. The student once said to me, "That's all I ask." It's such a low-cost and high-reward gesture.

    But genuine concern goes deeper. Like many professors, I often get emails from students describing meaningful—often challenging—life events. These range from transportation challenges (a broken-down car or a missed bus) to childcare issues (sick parent, closed childcare facility, or unaffordable options) to illness and death. Very early in my career, I would sometimes ask for some sort of documentation—but I quickly stopped after a student in a graduate seminar sent me photos of his split-open forehead after an accident in an afternoon basketball game. I wish I'd never seen those photos, and I immediately started telling students *not* to send me photographic evidence. *Please.*

    In statistics, we talk about Type I and Type II errors. My (mathematician) partner and I have joked nearly since the day we met that we'll never remember which one is which, but one is a false positive and one is a false negative. (If you want to know which is which, I recommend Banerjee et al. [2009]; it's my go-to reference when I really need to know which is which with accuracy—which I rarely do.) In the case of students and the challenges they face, I can assume everyone is lying and sometimes be overly harsh with students legitimately experiencing challenges, or I can assume everyone is telling the truth and sometimes be taken advantage of. When I think about the complex lives of my students, the choice is quite simple when framed this way. I'd always rather get taken advantage of occasionally than doubt someone genuinely in crisis. Put another way: I'd much rather be occasionally naive than inflict even more trauma on students who have often already experienced so much trauma. In fact, I know that giving students the benefit of the doubt, oftentimes giving them *many* more opportunities to right the ship than others might, is the only way my conscience can find peace. You may be comfortable with a less forgiving posture regarding students, as is your right as an educator, but taking the time to investigate and reflect on that choice is critical. In other words, intentionality and reflection are more important than where your process ultimately lands you. Don't implement a policy because it seems like what everyone else is doing; really take the time to think about what your values are and how your student-facing policies embrace (or fail to embrace) those principles.

5. **Competence:** Exuding skill, knowledge, and the will to help and support others.

    For years, I'd wanted to create a one-page snapshot of the work I expected students to do. I've always liked to bake a fair amount of student choice into my course design, but as the number of choices rises, students need significantly more structure to understand how to make those choices (hat tip to Karen Costa for helping me more fully understand this). In recent years, I've required very few specific assignments or activities of all students, instead giving students access to a large choice set of potential learning activities. While many appreciate the opportunity to pursue learning that doesn't feel redundant or irrelevant to their existing knowledge, the initial reaction to this degree of freedom is almost always overwhelm and confusion. As a result, about a year ago I created the "course planning worksheet" (available on my website, liznorell.com/book), which is indeed a single-page snapshot of the requirements of the course. This worksheet undoubtedly helped students, but designing it also made my own expectations crystal clear *to me*, which was an unanticipated positive impact. My colleague Emily Pitts Donahoe did something similar with her Progress Tracker, which she describes at length in a series of Substack posts (Donahoe 2023).

#HipHop educator Chris Emdin writes brilliant and provocative works on multicultural education. His book *For White Folks Who Teach in the Hood . . . and the Rest of Y'all Too* was my introduction to what he calls reality pedagogy. It focuses on meeting our diverse students where they are and with deep respect for the wisdom found in their cultures. In forging relationships with our students, Emdin cautions: "When differences between the teacher and students are present and go unaddressed, they multiply quickly" (Emdin 2016, 83). He continues, "The key to becoming an effective educator is acknowledging the differences between students and teacher and adjusting one's teaching accordingly, which often requires nontraditional approaches to teaching and learning" (83).

What I love most about Emdin's work is its relentless focus on student-centered learning spaces. One of the tools he develops in his book is the cogenerative dialogue, or cogen. Working with a small group of students, the faculty and students engage in "co-creating/generating plans of action for improving the classroom" (65). Emdin recommends recruiting four students who will meet weekly with the teacher in "secret"—outside of class time and without sharing it with the rest of the class. These students should broadly represent the different identities and backgrounds (social, ethnic, academic, etc.) present in the course. For a set period, the participants (including the teacher) will sit in a circle, partake in some food, and discuss how to create a more inclusive, supportive, and productive classroom environment. Each member of the cogen has equal responsibility for implementing the actions decided upon by the group. In addition to helping the instructor develop closer relationships with the student cogen members, this can help build a stronger community within the classroom by ensuring the instructor is alert to the dynamics often occurring outside their awareness. What's more, it builds confidence and agency among the student members of the cogen, which can help move what Hammond describes as dependent learners into more independent identities. For a full discussion of cogens, I recommend chapter 4 of his book to explore the benefits, processes, and potential speed bumps.

Building Relationships: What Business Tells Us

More often than not, academics instinctively grimace at the notion of finding anything in business literature of relevance to their own academic work—and I count myself as one. Still, a growing body of writers has much to teach us about the importance of and techniques for building relationships. While I encourage you to explore the work of those mentioned below more fully on your own, here are a few key insights I've gleaned from reading this literature:

Know your why. Simon Sinek has done some of the best work on the power of why; you can check out his TED Talk and his books on the topic. In short, though, Sinek's formula for writing your why looks like this: "To _____ (contribution) so that _____ (impact)." For example, Sinek's why is: "to inspire people to do what inspires them so that, together, each of us can change our world for the better" (Sinek 2024). Sinek's workbook,

Find Your Why, is an excellent resource if you want to spend some time exploring and crafting your own why statement (Sinek 2017).

There is no substitute for psychological safety. In a piece for the *New York Times,* Charles Duhigg shared the results of an extensive study conducted by Google to unearth why some of the company's project teams were successful and others were not. It was called Project Aristotle, and the researchers eventually stumbled upon a set of team dynamics—group norms, really—that led to more harmonious and productive collaboration. These dynamics are captured by a framework known as "psychological safety" (e.g., Edmondson and Lei 2014), which encompasses "a sense of confidence that the team will not embarrass, reject, or punish someone for speaking up" (Duhigg 2016). In their book *No Hard Feelings: The Secret Power of Embracing Emotions at Work,* Liz Fosslien and Molly Duffy developed a five-question flash test to measure the psychological safety you experience in your work environment. The items are measured on a 1–7 Likert scale, ranging from strongly disagree to strongly agree. They are:

- If I make a mistake on my team, it is often held against me.
- Members of my team are able to bring up problems and tough issues.
- It is safe to take a risk on this team.
- It is difficult to ask other members of this team for help.
- Working with members of this team, my unique skills and talents are valued and utilized. (Fosslien and Duffy 2019, 249).

You might imagine an adapted set of five statements to ask your students to gauge their level of psychological safety in your classrooms:

- If I make a mistake in class, I will be criticized or penalized for it.
- Students can bring up problems and tough issues with how the class is going.
- It is safe to take risks in this class—on assignments or in discussions.

- It is difficult to ask my teacher (or my peers) for help.
- When I participate in learning in this class, my unique skills and talents are valued and utilized.

If your students were to take this assessment, how do you think they would answer? Have you created a classroom environment where the learners have psychological safety? And if not, how might you adjust to create more psychological safety for everyone?

Belonging matters. Educators know that a sense of belonging makes an impact on learners' ability to engage (e.g., Osterman 2000; for a review, see Nunn 2021). The business world is coming to understand this as well. Fosslien and Duffy (2019) provide a few salient points on how to create a culture of belonging in a workplace environment—points that relate to our classrooms just as much as a corporation (191):

Assume good intentions. When someone makes a misstep, give that person room to learn from the mistake. As the professor, you have the opportunity to show students that mistakes are not only acceptable, they're welcomed as evidence that learning is taking place. How can you assume good intentions of your students, particularly early on? Are there ways to celebrate the courage students embody when they're willing to make mistakes, especially in front of their peers?

Belonging starts with onboarding. This means creating a welcoming environment from initial contact—sometimes, even before someone shows up for the first day. At eyeglass maker Warby Parker, for example, someone reaches out *before* a new hire's first day to ask if they have any questions and to let them know what to expect at employee orientation. How might you initiate contact with students before they arrive on your first day of class? What might help them feel less anxiety about the semester ahead? For more on this, look at Supiano and Fischer's 2023 advice guide, particularly Rebecca Glazier's ideas around welcoming students before the first day of classes.

Assign "culture buddies." Pairing a community member with someone who has experience with the culture can help ease the transition. After the first week, the buddies get together to answer questions about the newbie's experience, give feedback, and foster belongingness. An excellent higher ed analog is hosting a panel of former students toward the end of the first week of a new semester, as Brookfield (2015) suggests. Inviting two or three students who have taken your class in a previous semester to chat with new students—importantly, without you present in the room—can go far toward reducing or even eliminating student resistance. This is particularly true if you have a large number of historically minoritized or overlooked students, who are likely to enter the class suspicious of your efforts to invite more authenticity and presence into the classroom. Hearing from another student that you are sincere in your caring and not trying to trick the newbies can be a powerful way to boost belongingness and get your new students on your side quickly.

Avoid command-and-control dynamics. As Kim Scott writes in *Radical Candor: Be a Kick-ass Boss Without Losing Your Humanity:* "Command and control can hinder innovation and harm a team's ability to improve the efficiency of routine work. Bosses and companies get better results when they voluntarily lay down unilateral power and encourage their teams and peers to hold them accountable, when they quit trying to control employees and focus instead on encouraging agency" (2019, xi).

The same is true in learning environments. For true, long-lasting learning to happen, students must be engaged as partners in their learning. Command-and-control tactics will only hijack students' amygdalas, flooding their systems with stress hormones like cortisol and adrenaline, which will severely paralyze their abilities to learn (Hammond 2015, chapter 3). Instead, creating an atmosphere of shared accountability and individual agency will yield an entirely different classroom dynamic—and, importantly, greater learning. As Scott writes, "There are few things more damaging to human relationships than a sense of superiority" (12). Your advanced degree and years of teaching experience mean you almost certainly know more about the *subjects* you are teaching, but they do not mean you know more about the *students* you are teaching. And, as Palmer tells us, "If a space is to support learning, it must invite students to find their authentic voices, whether or not they speak in ways approved by others" (Palmer 2007, 78).

VULNERABILITY, SHAME, AND OTHER EXCITEMENTS

If you spend any time in the inner work spaces of the internet, you've probably heard of Dr. Brené Brown. She's got something of a cultish following—to be honest, I'm just waiting for the podcast *Sounds Like a Cult* to do an episode on her fan base. (I'd happily be a guest to gush about my enthusiastic membership in the cult of Brown.) Brené Brown centers her research on all the things that really get us grabbing for a blanket to hide under: shame, vulnerability, authenticity, brave leadership, and imperfections. She's written multiple books, run two blockbuster podcasts simultaneously, and delivered two highly popular TED talks ("The Power of Vulnerability" has, at this writing, nearly sixty million views). And she had a cameo role in Amy Poehler's 2019 Netflix film *Wine Country*, which is how we know she's well and truly part of the popular consciousness.

Now that I have established her pop culture bona fides, here's why you should pay attention to Brown's work: It's got everything to do with the work this book equips you to do. Do you struggle with feeling imposter-y? Go read *The Gifts of Imperfection* (2010), which will help you embrace your confidence wobbles and move into a more wholehearted way of being. Struggle with having challenging conversations across differences? You'll find a litany of useful tools in *Braving the Wilderness* (2017a), a book that embodies her mantra: "Strong back, soft front, wild heart." So much of academic culture pressures us to hide our uncertainties and failures in the dark corners of our lives; this shame can be paralyzing and prevent us from truly connecting with others. It's tender to do so, but when you're ready to let go of some of that shame, *Daring Greatly* (2012) and *Rising Strong* (2015) are terrific resources to understand the feelings underneath that shame.

Dr. Brown is a social work professor at the University of Houston who focuses on public scholarship. As her career has progressed, she's come to do increasingly more work consulting with businesses who want to improve their workplace cultures. A native Texan, Brown pulls no punches. Her work is an excellent place to begin if you're new to the idea of inner work. And if you've been in this space for a while, take it from someone else marinating in both academic culture and inner work culture: it's *always* worth revisiting her ideas, frameworks, research, tools, and wisdom. If nothing else, watch her RSA animated video on empathy vs. sympathy and then banish the phrase "at least" from your vocabulary (Brown 2013).

Building Relationships: What Social Science Tells Us

One of the worst myths about human relationships is that cutthroat competition belongs in relationships. You'll sometimes hear people apply evolutionary biology to everyday behavior, à la "survival of the fittest"—but research suggests this is simply not true, at least not when it comes to human relationships. I'm fascinated by the work of Duke researchers Brian Hare and Vanessa Woods, who study, among other things, evolutionary anthropology and canine behavior. In their book *Survival of the Friendliest: Understanding Our Origins and Rediscovering Our Common Humanity,* Hare and Woods write: "To Darwin and modern biologists, 'survival of the fittest' refers to something very specific—the ability to survive and leave behind viable offspring. It is not meant to go beyond that. . . . [Darwin] and many of the biologists who followed him have documented that *the ideal way to win* at the evolutionary game is to *maximize friendliness so that cooperation flourishes.*" (2020, xvi–xvii, emphasis added)

Cutthroat competition may yield a larger number of offspring, many of whom may survive, but that doesn't mean they will thrive or find any modicum of life satisfaction. If we want to thrive in this life, cooperation is the wiser route.

However, competition can be valuable. Simon Sinek tells a charming story about a person in the world whom he hates, a person who does the same work he does and writes books that are in competition with his own. Sinek describes checking his book rankings, then immediately checking his rival's, to see whether he's currently beating that rival. At an event where they spoke together and were asked to introduce each other, Sinek went first: "You make me really insecure. All of your strengths are all of my weaknesses. When your name comes up, it makes me really uncomfortable." His rival said, "Funny, I feel the same way about you" (Sinek 2019; Bilyeu 2019). That rival is Adam Grant, whom Sinek describes as a "worthy rival," someone who motivates him to do better work. Once they recognized that they shared the same goal, they were able to work together to move the world toward their hopeful future. Adam Grant's work is similarly useful, inspiring, and worth your time. Their relationship is founded on respect, the kind that comes from recognizing a worthy competitor who makes you want to aim higher.

I love this story, because it really highlights the shift that can happen—in our work, in our minds, in our hearts—when we stop seeing another person (or group of people) as adversaries and start seeing them as allies. Sinek would be the first to agree that his work has gotten better since he made this shift from hating Adam Grant to collaborating regularly. What might happen if you could make a similar shift? What if your resistance to challenging students or obstinate colleagues was trying to tell you something about your own insecurities and not about the shortfalls of others? And what if finding a common purpose and pursuing that together meant everyone was better?

This is precisely what Hare and Woods argue in their work, since buttressed by Melanie Challenger's book *How to Be Animal* (2021). Challenger's book pushes back on the impulse to conceive of humans as having somehow evolved away from their innate animal instincts. She acknowledges the social and hierarchical ways that our species naturally interacts with others. If we are to engage in truly collaborative learning and growth, we cannot fully do so without acknowledging the ways in which our primal instincts lead us to notice and care about how others perceive us moment to moment. In other words, it takes a lot of mindful reflection and inner work to see our animal instincts operating and to understand the unconscious impact they have on our relationships with others.

Chapter 3

ACADEMIC CULTURE

Minefields and Shelters

> Your student experience cannot exceed your employee experience.
>
> Matt Whiat, Chapman & Company

Of all that I considered while writing this book, the content of this chapter gave me the most anxiety. It would be too easy and too facile to extrapolate from my own experiences a cluster of observations about all of academic culture. Even within a single department, at a single institution, the "culture" is going to vary depending on your positionality. Women experience a different culture than do men, to say nothing of the culture for nonbinary faculty. White faculty experience academia quite differently than faculty of color. Other distinctions that will shape our experience of academic culture include status (full-time vs. part-time, tenure-track vs. non-tenure-track vs. tenured), institution type, geography, department, educational background, and more.

Still, there are shared components of academic culture, and I organize my thinking of these shared aspects of our ecosystem into two imperfect clusters: minefields and shelters. In this chapter, we'll survey the landscape to see where the potential minefields are and where we might be able to seek shelter from any potential fallout. Your experiences will vary depending on the particulars of your identity, your history, and the culture you're steeped in. As in earlier chapters, I share here stories from my own experiences, but I wanted to avoid the myopia that writing solely from my own experiences might bring. To add other voices, then, I pursued three avenues of collecting others' experiences.

First, I reached out to about two dozen faculty and staff to request one-on-one conversations about their experiences in higher education; those interviews provided the raw material for the dozen profiles in the next chapter.[1] Second, I created a Google form to allow a wider range of voices to share a little (or a lot) of their experiences with academic culture in entirely voluntary ways, with the promise of anonymity or confidentiality or neither, as they preferred. Another dozen or so folks with experience in higher education—graduate students, former or current faculty members, and staff members—chose to share their experiences in this way. Most didn't want to be named, but many were willing to be quoted anonymously. Finally, I took advantage of the very large amount of crowd-sourced survey data available from Karen Kelsky, who started a Facebook group called The Professor Is Out (TPIO) as an offshoot of her academic career coaching business, The Professor Is In. The survey was announced on Twitter in May 2022, and the anonymous responses are available for anyone to read and download (Kelsky 2023). By reading through these responses, in conjunction with the information I gathered from my peers and colleagues, I was able to integrate many perspectives alongside mine, in this chapter, to highlight aspects of our shared culture. To engage in the inner work in part 2, we must be mindful of the cultural context in which we work—just as, incidentally, we must be mindful of our *students'* cultures in our teaching (Hammond 2015).

Before we forge ahead, though, it's critical to step back and think about the landscape of academia vis-à-vis our reasons for choosing a career in this sector. The central thesis of, and arguments within, this book align well with the descriptions of academic culture in Berg and Seeber's book, *The Slow Professor* (2017). The authors challenge the corporatization of academia, a trend we've seen for decades. Berg and Seeber detail how corporatization trends impact the cultures in which we work. For example, they note that we now embrace the metric of "time to completion" as a measure of academic quality and efficiency (8). For many US states, persistence, retention, and graduation rates are baked into the states' funding. Mired in the quotidian rhythms of academia as we are, these metrics seem commonplace, even sensical. However, when we step back and look at what got many of us into academia—the "very idealism that drives intellectual and pedagogic endeavours" (Berg and Seeber 2017, 17), our goals in pursuing this work stand in stark contrast to the realities of how we run our academic institutions today. In an EdSurge interview, Kevin McClure noted that so-called "academic capitalism tends to shift authority and power within universities toward individuals that are directly connected to revenue generation, and often more in the direction of people that are in managerial and administrative roles" (Koenig 2019). This feels akin to the laments we hear about administrative bloat. By increasing the reliance on adjunct faculty to teach our classes and increasing the number of administrators to oversee the work of the institution, leaders can reduce the strength of faculty in shared governance, weaken faculty opposition, and create a more nimble institution. And by "nimble," I, of course, mean financially lucrative. Or, as Winter (2009) put it, "universities shed their collegiate skins and take on more corporate customer-focused suits" (123).[2]

As Philipson (2002) writes, the sense of idealism that attracted many of us to this sector—in which vast economic returns are by no means promised and rarely achieved—makes it much easier for our institutions to manipulate its workers, as do corporations, with the rhetoric of family and community, "to solidify company cultures and inspire loyalty and commitment in an attempt to boost productivity" (123). Or, as Ruha Benjamin (2022) writes in her searing book, *Viral Justice:* "If passion is believed to be your fuel, the bosses will likely take you for a ride" (180).

Take a moment and ponder that. Do your administrators talk about your campus using the metaphor of family? Do you invest more than you would in a corporate job because of your sense of obligation to the community of your campus? And does it even make sense to think about a workplace as a family—particularly when, as so many of us have experienced at times during our careers, "we will love this career long after it breaks our hearts" (Bowler 2021, 108)?

Throughout this book, I provide caveats to assuage the concerns you might have when looking at advice from the business sector. Ironic, then, that our loathing of that sector is not sent into high alert given how much of our academic culture stresses productivity, efficiency, and overwork. By describing these aims in language rooted in concern for students, including study after study on what predicts student success, graduation, and economic gain after college, we have allowed a fundamentally human activity—learning—to become yet another transaction in a life filled with them (Basile and Azevedo 2022). We pay lip service to buzzwords like "student-centered teaching" and "belonging," but in many ways, we have taken humanity out of our learning spaces and institutions. Consider this chapter an invitation to step back and look at where our humanity is challenged (minefields) and welcomed (shelters).

Minefields

The metaphor of minefields strikes me as appropriate for academic culture mostly because these are *potential* dangers, not necessarily realized by everyone. The distinguishing feature of a landmine is that it makes terrain uncertain and potentially threatening, creating hazards without having to strafe an entire landscape. The minefields of academia are those pockets of our sector that are the danger zones, where a wrong step can wreak havoc. In the post-2020 years, my antennae have picked up far more discussion of the lack of psychological safety in our sector. For example, writer Tom Williams quotes Petra Boynton in a *Times Higher Education (THE)* piece, "Academia is full of exit stories now—either by choice or by being pushed out or having to leave due to being simply broken by a toxic environment" (Williams 2022). "'Staff with expertise in areas such as social care, school teaching, and healthcare know they can get jobs for similar or better pay outside academia'—as Boynton notes, 'without the toxicity,'" writes Williams for *THE*.

Each of us will find our own unique set of minefields, but there are a few that seem to come up again and again in the literature.

In this section, I'll discuss four: graduate school, elitism, what Kevin Gannon (2021) calls performative hardassery, and privilege.

A quick note about language: The astute reader will note that the language of this chapter leans heavily on military metaphors. Somewhere between discussion of landmines and describing my graduate school tours of duty, suffice it to say I've realized just how much my mental models for higher education are rooted in adversarial relationships, which almost certainly tells you something about my career experiences. Because of this, I feel I must emphasize that, at my core, I am a conflict-averse person with borderline pacifist instincts.

Landmine #1: Graduate School

Before I decided I wanted to pursue a PhD and enter the world of college teaching, I engaged in what I have always described as a couple of tours through graduate programs. Neither of those experiences prepared me for the rather different expectations of students in the political science doctoral program in which I later enrolled. I entered that program already feeling imposter-y (see chapter 1), given that I'd only taken a handful of political science courses as an undergraduate and none of them had been particularly research intensive. For the first year or so of my studies, I spoke infrequently and worried everyone else knew a lot more than I did. Our first year, my cohort took almost all the same classes. In our first semester, the director of our graduate program was the instructor of the foundational course introducing the theories of the discipline's different fields. She was a brilliant woman with seemingly sky-high expectations and little use for heartfelt conversations to boost the confidence of her students. I was so intimidated by her, terrified I'd be found out as unqualified for this program.

Thus began what I experienced as many years of academic hazing. To be fair, a lot of that was due to my own insecurities and uncertainties about whether I belonged. (To be even more fair, those feelings mirror closely what many of my students—and yours, too—feel when they enter our classes.) As I started to find my sea legs in the program, particularly when the department hosted job talks or guest lectures, I began to realize that the currency of graduate school was mounting a devastating critique of someone else's research. In seminar after seminar, talk after talk, I watched usually young academics face relentless questions from senior faculty in our department. What I *wanted* to believe was deep scholarly curiosity and interest *felt* a lot more like a squadron filled with locked-and-loaded individuals, each trying to score the kill shot in a decidedly lopsided battle. Nick Rule describes the unease this can create in relatable terms: "Academic culture is built on a scientific enterprise whose foundation is skepticism, doubt, and stringent criteria for survival. Am I, too, just a Type I error in terms of my professional success?" (Jaremka et al. 2020, 10).

At the same time, since we were a fully funded doctoral program, each of us had an assignment within the department. I was assigned to work with a professor whose research interests dovetailed with my own, and I was fortunate that he was an excellent mentor and advocate on my behalf. I learned a lot from Tom Brunell at the University of Texas Dallas, particularly about teaching the American government introductory course that is the workhorse of any US-based political science department. I was fortunate to avoid the landmine of the graduate school advisor who bullies, shames, or works to death their graduate students. Others are not so lucky—and if you're reading this book, chances are good you have either experienced challenging mentorship or have a close friend or colleague who has.

On top of this, given the impossibly grueling academic job market, the pressure to publish begins early in graduate school. A Twitter thread by University of Mull film professor Dr. Laura Mayne includes these observations about academic culture:

> PhDs are training in . . . hooking your self-worth so closely to your career that you become entirely defined by it. It doesn't happen all at once—it happens bit by bit. Do a bit of writing for free here, take on one . . . project because it looks good in the long run on your CV, and then another. Everyone does it. Soon all you begin to talk about is work,

and all you begin to think about, even at 2:00 a.m. (especially at 2:00 a.m.) are the publications you're not writing. Everything is an existential crisis, and that's because your chosen profession is not just a job anymore: it's you. A criticism of an article is not just a criticism of your work, it's a criticism of your very existence. You ask yourself, but what could I do, if not this? You are degraded not all at once, but by inches. You say "yes" to overwork, and with each personal boundary you erode you tell yourself that you have a higher purpose, either to the research, to the students, or to both. You become disillusioned, and you even dream about leaving, but unfortunately the hold the job has over you is emotional manipulation of the most powerful kind: that without it you won't exist, and that no other profession could ever love you in the same way. We wean PhD students on dysfunctional ideals that we accept without question, a process that begins by having them accept that for three-plus years their entire professional development will be contingent on 1 person: their supervisor, & so they better hope they have a good one. (Mayne 2022)

Perhaps the most insidious way that graduate school presents potential for career implosion is in its wholesale rejection of pursuing anything outside of scholarship. Hobbies, outside work, adjunct teaching, having or caring for children or elderly parents—disclosing any of these during grad school runs the risk of becoming known as someone not serious about scholarship. These so-called distractions are most likely to be weaponized against those who are already at risk of marginalization in the academy, namely, those who are not White, male, and economically comfortable. If you find yourself in graduate school as a woman or nonbinary person, a member of a historically minoritized identity, or a person without an economic safety net or financial benefactor, the chances you'll avoid these minefields are quite low. Almost any mistake or perceived slight can be traced back to your lack of devotion to academia.

I especially appreciated a *Chronicle of Higher Education* piece by Liz Mayo that highlighted the need for graduate programs to prepare non-White and non-male graduate students for the expectations of a career in academe. Mayo recommends that we "take women and minorities aside and whisper difficult truths to them: No one is going to stop them from doing too much academic service" (Mayo 2023). The piece, "Women Do Higher Ed's Chores. That Must Change.," highlights something underscoring several trends in this chapter—that different people experience academia differently, depending on their positionality and background. Unfortunately, though, for those who do not present as male or White, the ability to meet expectations and achieve promotion and tenure is much harder than it is for our White male colleagues.

I don't talk about it often, but for a short time during my PhD studies, I transferred to a different doctoral program. My advisors saw potential in my research and writing, and they advised I try to move to a program with more prestige. I ended up at a doctoral program in political science with ambitious goals of becoming one of the best in the discipline. My foray into an allegedly more prestigious program was short-lived, though, and that's largely because of how my life circumstances changed during my time there. Not three months into my time at this institution, my marriage imploded and I moved out of a home where most of my monthly expenses were covered by my ex-husband's salary. To be able to afford expenses like food, transportation, and the marital debt we divided during the divorce, I took on a series of part-time jobs. I primarily worked as an adjunct at a local community college, teaching one or two classes a semester. Even so, I was barely getting by. I largely subsisted on 99-cent frozen Totino's pizzas and off-brand mac and cheese.

One day, I was meeting with a high school student I was tutoring at a local Starbucks, and the graduate program advisor happened to walk by. That chance encounter led to the unraveling of my funded position in that department. I was summoned to a meeting about what he'd seen me doing and, when I explained, he told me this was going to be a problem for me. I sat for comprehensive exams soon thereafter, and the committee that graded my major field comp had several critiques of my responses, though I never fully understood what those issues were and how I'd misstepped. Ultimately, I was nudged out. Years later, a friend who had worked in the department told me that I could've fought it and probably been allowed to stay, but that my time in the department would've been an exhausting fight that I wasn't likely to survive . . . not because I was unfit for graduation from the program, but because the leadership of the department was determined to wage a war of attrition against me (my words, not the friend's).

Landmine #2: Elitism

There's no question that my experience at an allegedly more respected graduate program shaped how I think about what it means to acquire prestige in academia. In many (perhaps most?) corners of academia, we have a kind of caste system that rivals in its durability the racial caste system Isabel Wilkerson so eloquently describes in her book (2020). The human impulse to rank and compare shows up in full force in everything from rating graduate programs in each discipline to peer-reviewed journal rankings to what sorts of jobs we want, apply for, or are willing to accept. In graduate school I heard someone describe a faculty member as having "published her way out of a community college," suggesting that a community college teaching position was something to escape, a kind of punitive sentence one hoped to shorten through good behavior. As one person shared with me confidentially, "When I said I wanted to teach at the community college level, many of my classmates thought that was a silly idea."

The way academics engage in a race for ever-greater prestige sends clear messages to the apprentices they mentor. From my earliest days in a PhD program, I picked up on the language we use to rank and judge, words and phrases like "R1," "impact factor," and "top twenty-five program." Living in a bubble where these phrases are part of our everyday language has an impact on our perception of what passes for acceptable scholarly output. As Rebecca Shuman writes in an "Are You Working?" column in the

Chronicle of Higher Education, "In academe, beating yourself up about your scholarly disappointments is almost embedded in the culture and may even feel instinctive to you at this point" (Shuman 2022). We see this modeled in graduate school, and most of us pick up the mantle of self-flagellation without even realizing we're doing it. But why? As Brian Rosenberg writes in the *Chronicle of Higher Education,* "In the world of colleges and universities, reputation, brand strength, prestige—call it what you will—is now and has long been more important than anything else, including the nature and quality of the actual education provided" (Rosenberg 2022). This impacts those of us working in academia at every turn, but especially when we enter the job market: "It's difficult for even a supremely gifted graduate of a less prestigious university to get past an initial screening of candidates, let alone to get hired" (Rosenberg 2022).

This isn't just a perception. Daniel Larremore's research on the ways doctoral program prestige dominates the academic job market is so profoundly important that the National Science Foundation awarded his work the Alan T. Waterman Award, which "recognizes an outstanding young researcher in any field of science or engineering" and confers a medal and $1 million in funding over five years to support the researcher's work (National Science Foundation 2024). In his Waterman Lecture, Larremore uses the tools of computational epidemiology to trace the networks of academic institutions (Larremore 2022). This lecture makes abundantly clear, through elegant visualizations of where PhD graduates land upon graduation, that perceptions of prestige are nearly exclusively what hiring committees reward.

No surprise, then, that our educational pedigree can open or close doors with little to no additional information needed. When I first wanted to pursue a master's degree, in June 2000, I emailed the graduate chair of the closest university offering that degree to ask what I needed to do to apply the following year. I mentioned that I'd graduated from George Washington University with an undergraduate degree in journalism. On the basis of that piece of information alone, I was offered a spot in the incoming class—*in two months*—and a graduate assistantship with a stipend. I didn't have to apply, I didn't need a transcript, and no letters of recommendation were required for that offer to be extended. Sure, I had to get those things to make it official—but on the basis of the prestige of my undergraduate degree alone, I was moved ahead in line for one of only two funded graduate assistantships. *Without even asking.*

As with so many human instincts, this drive comes with a flip side, a dark reality of marginalization and anguish. Speaking from experience, I can say that those who take community college teaching jobs often feel shunned by their graduate mentors or schools. At a disciplinary conference, we might shrug as we admit we work at a two-year school, and then in the next breath we'll talk about the scholarly work we're doing to become more attractive on the job market next cycle. The well-worn "publish or perish" mantra seeps into our consciousness from the earliest days of our graduate training and pushes us to ignore other parts of our lives in pursuit of the holy grail in academia—an article published in our discipline's top journal. We worship at the altar of the impact factor.[3]

Part of this elitism requires a superhuman dedication to the work of research and writing, often on top of demanding teaching expectations. The flurry of expectations that accompany academic life creates a yearning for time, for spaces in which there are no expectations, where we can pursue our curiosities at our own pace. This is anathema to the culture of higher education. There simply is not enough time in our academic lives for rest, quiet, and reflection. Instead, we are assaulted with publications like the popular (and oft-recommended) 2019 book, *Writing Your Journal Article in Twelve Weeks*, by Wendy Laura Belcher. A friend who was trying to build up her CV so she could apply for a tenure-track position (instead of the NTT lecturer position she'd held for four years) asked me once if I had journal article ideas that wouldn't require an Institutional Review Board application, as she needed to churn out some quick publications before the next hiring cycle started.

All of this leaves us feeling exhausted and inadequate. Parker Palmer describes the dilemma facing academics poignantly: "The very situation that creates our need for safe space seems to prevent us from getting what we need" (Palmer 2007, 72). He continues, "But hidden in that little phrase 'seems to' is the way out of catch-22. The notion that we cannot have what we genuinely need is a culturally induced illusion that keeps us mired in the madness of business as usual." In what ways are you mired in the madness of business as usual? Where and how and when can you escape that madness and really listen to what work your heart, your soul, your vocation call you to do?

Another voice echoing this need to examine our hustle culture comes from Berg and Seeber: "Academic culture celebrates overwork, but it is imperative that we question the value of busyness. We need to interrogate what we are modeling for each other and for our students" (2017, 21). In this vein, I try to remind myself regularly of Chris Emdin's clarion call: "Students must see you struggle with the tension between what is expected of you and what is the right thing to do" (2021, 2). Or as one person in the TPIO survey wrote, "I felt like I couldn't fit in with the culture [of higher education] because my work wasn't the totality of my identity."

At what cost, though? We cannot sustain our health or any sense of self when engaged in a rat race for prestige. Prestige is, in fact, an ephemeral notion we largely make up in our individual and collective minds to assuage doubts that we are valuable, that we are productive, that *we belong*. But as we've seen in earlier chapters, those feelings of value, of productivity, of belongingness? They come from within us, not from the outside. Or, as Rosenberg (2022) writes: "Prestige matters so much in higher education because the industry is the clearest example of what economists and marketers have termed credence goods, that is, 'goods and services that are difficult or impossible to evaluate even after you've experienced them.'" Darn you, economics.

And yet. We exist in this miasma of never-enough-ness, and it is a radical act of defiance to refuse to engage in the chase for prestige. I believe that defiance cannot and will not happen, not in any lasting way, without having done the inner work earlier chapters guided you toward. It won't stop there, though—because, ultimately, we're dealing with a *cultural* problem, not a *personal* deficiency. As Hannah Leffingwell (2023) writes, "The central paradox of academe [is that it is a] capitalist institution that claims it is above capitalism while exploiting students, faculty, and staff for financial gains." Having diagnosed our sector in this stark way, it comes as no surprise that Leffingwell surmises, "In my opinion, we are past the point where [small] steps can offer true relief. We need a revolution, not a revision." To get there, though, the inner work suggested in this book is meant to help you lay a stronger foundation, one built on your values and experiences, to engage in the revolutionary work to make higher education what it aims to be—indeed, what it claims to be.

Landmine #3: Performative Hardassery

Early-career faculty often enter their first teaching role being only a few years older than their average student, which leads to all sorts of compensatory behaviors typical in young faculty members. Years ago, while I was in an NTT lecturer role, a brand-new assistant professor joined the department of my mid-sized regional university. She was fresh out of graduate school and close in age to many of her students. Like most college faculty, she had not really been given much preparation for the teaching part of her job, so that first semester was going to be a challenge for her. As someone who'd navigated those choppy waters, I offered to help her with a second set of eyes on her syllabus, a sounding board for class planning and management strategies, and so forth. She demurred, assuring me she was confident. Maybe she was, or maybe she was faking it. One day, about two weeks into the semester, she hurried into my office after her class with this report: "I did some good professoring today! I called on students and asked them questions about the reading, and when they couldn't answer my questions, I called them out on not being prepared!" She beamed at me. I felt queasy in response. I'm sure my terrible poker face gave me away.

A lot of early-career faculty—especially non-White or non-male-identifying faculty—feel like performing hardassery is what defines their authority in the classroom. The phrase makes intuitive sense to me, but to be sure that we're all operating with the same understanding, I asked Gannon to provide his own definition of the instantly iconic phrase: "To me, it's being a hardass for the sake of demonstrating how much of a hardass you are to others (who are, by definition, not hardass enough). It's a very public and visible form of being inflexible and even adversarial, toward students and curating an image of oneself as the last defender of 'rigor' and 'standards'" (Kevin Gannon, email message to the author, November 27, 2023).

To be fair, this instinct is hardly unique to academia; early-career professionals in all sorts of fields feel like they must command authority by exercising power over others. It's a natural instinct, and it's certainly more evolutionarily sensible than its opposing one—leading with insecurity and fear. But if our goal is to create spaces where students can enter and feel welcomed and supported in their learning? Performative hardassery works against those goals because it erects a giant wall between us (the teachers) and them (the students). It defines the field of learning as a combative one from which shall emerge winners (few) and losers (many).[4]

This performative hardassery is even more understandable when we think about what we saw modeled as scholarship in graduate school. Those job talks we attended as graduate students? They messaged to us that engaging in scholarship is a hostile, take-no-prisoners scene. We've convinced ourselves that being harsh will command respect and obedience—and that those are valuable qualities in the classroom. Particularly in an era when we hear story after story of disruptive classroom behavior and disengaged students, it's only natural that we'd enter our learning spaces determined to ensure students are meeting high expectations and performing to their abilities.[5] The evidence on what will motivate students to do so, though, does not point toward this performative hardassery. In fact, it's the opposite that seems to bring out the best in our students. As Jiddu Krishnamurti (1974) wrote in *On Education*, "Fear is what prevents the flowering of the mind."

Parker Palmer writes about something I'd call adjacent to performative hardassery, and it seems to be a particular affliction among newer teachers. As an example, he points to Jane Tompkins's pitch-perfect essay, "Pedagogy of the Distressed," in which she confesses that her early teaching was consumed with matters other than helping students learn what they needed or wanted to know. Instead, she was concerned with: "(a) showing the students how smart I was; (b) showing them how knowledgeable I was; and (c) showing them how well prepared I was for class. I had been putting on a performance whose true goal was not to help the students learn but to act in such a way that they would have a good opinion of me." (Palmer 2007, 29–30; Tompkins 1990). Some of us build our confidence and, by midcareer, can shed the performative hardassery cloak; others seem committed to the persona for the entirety of a career.

And I get it, y'all. There is some evidence that, as we've returned to campus after COVID interrupted in-person learning, our academic communities lack some of the rich engagement we remember having pre-COVID. Whether that's a reality or a romancing of the past or somewhere in between, living in greater isolation for some period of time has a lasting impact. *Chronicle of Higher Education* reporter Beth McMurtrie quoted Seán McCarthy, an associate professor at James Madison University, whose colleague described the challenges in engaging students as a phenomenon of "militant apathy"—that "students seemed almost defiant in their indifference to school work" (McMurtrie 2023). In that same piece, a student described it differently, though—in terms that I think many of us can relate to, post-2020: "There seems to be this overwhelming fear of failure that is so paralyzing, that instead of turning in subpar work, or work they don't feel good about, [students] just don't turn anything in." That student, Elian Sorenson, is enrolled at Hamilton College, where Professor Frank Anechiarico has found that immersive classes that tackle wicked problems in the community—such as homelessness, as Sorenson's class did—can break through the "anxious malaise" that students feel.

In another *Chronicle* piece, Sarah Rose Cavanagh addressed the issue of student malaise from a different perspective—mental illness, specifically the wisdom of providing so-called mental health breaks (Cavanagh 2023). When the head of Simmons University's teaching center, Jennifer Herman, asked STEM professors what pedagogical challenge they were facing in their classrooms, "Their answer, almost to a person: the number and frequency of students requesting mental health breaks to exempt them from attending class." Rather than reinforcing this impulse, Cavanagh suggests, "We need to create classrooms that draw students in, that are deeply motivating—so that it feels like the best thing for their mental health would be to attend class, rather than stay home." Doing so looks like "encouraging faculty members to build some freedom, flexibility, and choice into their syllabus and course structure." This is, you'll note, the antithesis to hardassery—performative or otherwise.

Other *Chronicle* articles suggest this perceived student apathy is actually many complex things, among them: mental health challenges, a lack of social connection, poor focus/executive function, unresolved trauma, lost confidence, greater life demands, and a perceived lack of relevance of their coursework to their lives (Holstead 2022; McMurtrie 2022).

I'll conclude my discussion of performative hardassery with a quote from bell hooks's *Teaching Community*, where she discusses the political ecosystem of the classroom in the starkest of terms:

> To many professors of all races, the classroom is viewed as a mini-country governed by their autocratic rule. As a microcosm of the dominator culture, the classroom becomes a place where the professor acts out while sharing knowledge in whatever manner he or she chooses.... Incompetence in teaching can be tolerated because the consumer is a young person who is perceived as having no rights. Subordinated by a hierarchal system that indoctrinates students early on, letting them know that their success depends on their capacity to obey, most students fear questioning anything about the way their classrooms are structured. In our so-called best colleges and universities, teaching is rarely valued (hooks 2003, 85–86)

Landmine #4: Privilege

If and when you do some of the inner work I suggest around implicit bias, particularly as it relates to racial bias and systemic oppression (see chapter 9), you'll become quite acquainted with the concept of privilege. It's become something of a caricature by which those on the right side of our current political spectrum characterize others, particularly the straw man "woke liberal" who thinks all White folks have had it easy and owe those with less privilege the opportunity to skip ahead in line. This is too facile to capture the nuance of what we mean when we talk about privilege. Beverly Daniel Tatum mentions a White student who couldn't find the words to describe her ethnic identity, resorting to saying, "I'm just normal!" (Daniel Tatum 2017, 185). Like that student, those who are in relatively privileged positions in our social caste system can find it difficult, nigh on impossible, to recognize the privileges we have.

This is all foundational if we're to understand how privilege in higher education—just as in our broader society—creates minefields everywhere for those who are not in the dominant groups. If you are not male, if you are not White, if you are not heterosexual, if you are not cisgender, if you are not neurotypical, if you are not able-bodied, or if you are not reasonably well off economically, academia is rife with potential for toxic cultural realities. If you studied under someone who was a lightning rod in the discipline, or if you graduated from a "lesser" graduate program, you have an uphill climb ahead of you. In each of these ways, our work is not judged on its merits alone. The reality of who we are, where we come from, and how we show up in academia largely determines the opportunities open to us. What's more, once in an academic role, we are often pressured to negate these nonmajoritarian identities to mollify the privileged among us. "What good is an education," Bettina Love asks, "if you must shed who you are?" (Love 2019, 44).

I've repeated multiple times, at this point in the book, the mantra that emerged from my research: what's good for students is also good for us. As I was reading Kelly Hogan and Viji Sathy's book, *Inclusive Teaching*, I was struck by how their description of students who "might not feel comfortable in higher education" read like a list of *faculty members* who might feel likewise—just replace the word "students" with "faculty" as you read their words: "Students who are underrepresented either at the institution or in a discipline, students who are first in their families to go to college, students who are introverts, minoritized students, those who experience imposter phenomenon, students holding a minority view on an issue, students with learning differences, those with physical disabilities, individuals who identify as LGBTQIA+, international students, and many others" (Hogan and Sathy 2022, 111–12).

Sagacious bell hooks provides us with an excellent overview of the problems of inclusion and exclusion in higher education:

> As students we were socialized to believe that when we entered a classroom and were not regarded with respect by the professor, it was due to some inner lack and not the consequence of unjust hierarchy and dominator culture. The politics of domination as they are played out in the classroom often ensure that students from marginalized groups will not do well. Imagine how crazy-making it must be for students coming from an exploited and oppressed group, who make their way through the educational system to attend college by force of a will that resists exclusion, and who then enter a system that privileges exclusion, that valorizes subordination and obedience as a mark of one's capacity to succeed. It makes sense that students faced with this turnabout often do poorly or simply lose interest in education. . . . Contempt, disdain, shaming, like all forms of psychological abuse, are hard to document especially when they are coming from a person in authority, especially one who is skilled in the art of dissimulation. Usually, the only recourse a student has is turning to the peers of their harasser. Fear, especially fear of betrayal, usually silences the student victims of professorial psychological terrorism. (hooks 2003, 86–87)

Gender. The academy is dominated by the male voices who were once exclusively in charge of our institutions. While many of our colleges and universities now employ more women than men—and, for years now, have enrolled more women than men—the policies and norms that shape our culture are still very entrenched in a patriarchal mindset. We see this in everything from the hierarchies that dominate higher education to the privileging of scholarship over advising and teaching; one boosts perceived prestige, while the other looks a lot like emotional labor—both of which are quite gendered.

A big source of my own anxiety in writing a chapter in this book about academic culture—truth be told, in writing the book at all—came from the potential critiques about the work being gendered. When I conducted extended interviews with scholars across the United States, I recognized my ease with asking women about what "inner work" and "academic culture" mean to them—and my discomfort, even insecurity, in asking those same questions of men. These norms pervade our culture, and that reality shapes how fully non-male professors can be present with their students without risking critique or persecution from their colleagues.

Brenna Clarke Gray's essay drives home the extent to which gendered labor intersected with COVID to create ever-higher barriers to success for academics who do not identify as male. Part of that comes from the reality that "those on the margins of the academy" tend to do what's been called "the housework of the university: mentorship, pastoral care, undergraduate teaching," and other work engaging with students. Clarke Gray calls out the tendency of our institutions to respond to our needs—"adequate staffing for faculty support, smaller classes for instructional faculty"—with ineffective measures: "yet another offer to take a yoga class or a mindfulness workshop via Teams." I felt like I was in church as I read her words: "I have come to see these wellness webinars as positioning my exhaustion, my stress, my overwork as something I can solve on my own, with deep breathing or lunchtime yoga; they invite me to see my struggle as a personal failing. I am not failing. *I am being failed.*" (2022, emphasis added)

One respondent in the TPIO survey wrote that she was leaving academia after "years of playing the academic chess game to survive as a woman."

Race. I am a White woman. For that reason, I cannot write authoritatively about the lived experience of non-White academics. All I can share is what I've read and what others have told me—and it's not good. bell hooks writes about this: "I was continually shocked when individual professors, usually white males, would act hatefully toward me. In those naive years I did not understand the extent to which racist and sexist iconography of the black female body and person had imprinted on the consciousness of many professors the notion that black people in general, and black females in particular, were simply not suited for higher learning" (hooks 2003, 87).

My own work around understanding race and evolving toward a more anti-racist mindset has demonstrated the entrenched White supremacy in every facet of my life, including (and especially) in the academy. My service on a college equity team gave me the chance to craft questions for and analyze the results of a campus climate survey. The quantitative data were presented to the campus in a series of presentations, but the qualitative responses in that survey and in other research efforts on our campus stunned me. The quotidian experiences with racism and inequity on our campus had, until I looked at the results of that survey, flown under my radar, but they were rampant and largely went—I'm sorry to say—unaddressed. As Carolyn Davis wrote for *The Professor Is In* blog in 2020, "White supremacy is the lifeblood of academia."

Historically minoritized faculty and students exist in a world hostile to their very existence, both on and off our campuses. That reality occupies a significant amount of cognitive bandwidth. If you are White and in higher education, you must be aware that your minoritized students and colleagues simply have less available bandwidth for the work you're doing together (Verschelden 2024).[6] This is not because of any deficit on their part, and it is not inherent or genetic or determined by any other naturally occurring phenomenon. It is entirely because they live in a system that privileges Whiteness above all other racial identities, and they must always be on guard for signs of danger. Or, as one respondent in the TPIO survey wrote, "It is difficult to be in an industry which so ostensibly critiques inequality and status-based hierarchy while viewing the contribution and status of fellow scholars and colleagues with so much condescension."

If you are not convinced this is true for you or in your context, I encourage you to engage in some deeper reading, starting with Ruha Benjamin's searing 2022 book, *Viral Justice*. I read it in community with faculty, staff, and graduate students, an experience I found enormously valuable and enlightening.

Economic status/class. My experiences pursuing a doctorate taught me how precarious graduate school can be when you do not have the privilege of economic wealth to buttress the paltry resources made available to graduate students. My parents live a reasonably comfortable life, but by the time I was pursuing a PhD, I was in my early thirties and had been fully financially independent for more than a decade. I was not poor; however, I did not have substantial savings or passive streams of income during graduate school. Living on less than $20,000 annually, in an urban setting and in the early aughts, was simply not easy. For the first few years of graduate school, I was married and had the support of spousal income; however, I divorced in 2008 and was significantly delayed in completing my PhD because of the devastating financial impact that wrought.

It's hard to know how many brilliant minds with the potential to be exemplary educators and researchers are dissuaded from pursuing advanced education because of the economic realities of graduate study. Our system is hostile to those who need to earn a living wage, particularly during our training years. For as judged as I felt for pursuing part-time work outside of grad school, nearly every person I interviewed for chapter 4 mentioned doing at least some outside work during graduate school. This may be an artifact of the non-random sampling of my interviews, but it suggests that the idealized vision we have of what graduate education *should* be does not conform with the experience of those who manage to survive the experience and make it into academia.

Neurodivergence. The academy has the potential to be both a landmine-strewn field *and* a shelter for those who are neurodivergent, which the Cleveland Clinic describes as "a nonmedical term that describes people whose brains develop or work differently for some reason" (2024). The term is most often used to describe those with symptoms or a diagnosis of Attention-Deficit Hyperactivity Disorder (ADHD), Autism Spectrum Disorder (ASD), certain mental health disorders (bipolar disorder, obsessive-compulsive disorder, etc.), intellectual or developmental disabilities, or Down syndrome.

For the neurodivergent who have relatively high levels of intelligence (as measured by, for example, IQ batteries), the academy can be a relatively safe space to pursue a career, at least as compared to for-profit industry, because of the greater flexibility and relative independence of the work. However, when interpersonal dynamics are in play—as they almost always are—the neurodivergent can experience heightened stress in a workplace where systems can be opaque, norms are often implicit, and politics lurk just below the surface of nearly every decision. These unwritten rules (the "hidden curriculum") challenge our students just as they challenge our neurodivergent colleagues.

Imagine how those with undiagnosed neurodivergent traits might feel misunderstood or persecuted by some of the policies, practices, and norms of higher education. These will disproportionately fall to women, who are significantly less likely to receive an autism diagnosis or to even realize they have traits that fall within the autistic constellation of traits (McQuaid et al. 2021). This is also true in non-White individuals of all gender identities (Begeer et al. 2009). As with so many identities associated with disparate treatment or outcomes, neurodivergent individuals likely experience the intersectional challenges of being both neurodivergent *and* female or from a historically minoritized racial group or lower economic class or maybe all of these at once.

In a courageous essay for *The Chronicle of Higher Education* in March 2023, Bradley J. Irish, an associate professor of English at Arizona State University, wrote about his own autism diagnosis seventeen years into his career. His piece is a call to action for academe to make room for neurodivergent faculty and staff members on campus. He recommends including neurodiversity, including autism, in diversity, equity, and inclusion programming and committing to the idea that neurodiversity strengthens organizations—the sort of actions that might have resulted in a very different outcome in my own tenure case (more on this in chapter 7). As Irish writes, "Institutions showing a greater sensitivity to the conditions of neurodiversity would vastly improve the quality of life of people in both categories [of faculty and students]" (Irish 2023).

COMMENTS FROM THE CROWD

The comments below are verbatim responses gathered from a crowd-sourced survey by The Professor Is Out (TPIO) Facebook group. Those who are leaving or have left academia shared reasons why they felt they needed to leave higher education. I include these comments not because I agree that higher education is irrevocably and inherently toxic or abusive. However, as someone who felt very much alone when dealing with a challenging situation, my hope is that if you're feeling at odds with the system in which you work, you'll find something in these comments to let you know you're not alone. And, as someone who successfully extricated herself from a toxic-for-me environment for a vastly more supportive and healing place within higher education, I know it's possible to find shelters and continue doing the work we love—*if we choose.*

- I refuse to inflict and perpetuate this toxic process upon any other human being.
- I could not successfully (or at least not in any healthy way) be both a mother and an academic at the same time. It would have been possible, but untenable.
- Institution rewards mediocrity and meanness.
- Hierarchies that turn smart people into squabbling, territorial bridge trolls.
- I want to use my skills to help people rather than fuel egos.

- I HATE the corporatization and commodification of higher education.
- Toxic or stunningly boring and mediocre working environments. The remarkable narcissism of nearly all academics I have ever met. The mafia-like dynamics of the interactions and hierarchical channels between faculty and administration.
- Constant self-doubt that I was a good teacher or writer.
- Harassment specifically for race and sex and the retaliation goes unchecked in the academic environment.
- The shame of working so hard for almost zero appreciation was really hard.
- I'm finding [it] more and more difficult to justify staying in a profession that seems to only value the amount of work I do.
- I'm tired of hustling and struggling; I'd rather pour my energy into something that feeds me, too.
- The faculty and protective mechanisms failing to do anything but blacklist me for speaking up about what was so clearly not working.
- Even though I put the time [in], I never feel completely accomplished or seen. There is always something else to finish and it is never good enough.

Students and faculty alike are completely run down and demoralized by a constant barrage of demands. The focus on workplace wellness is being used as a way for institutions to show they "care" about their faculty and students while giving no attention to changing the structural and cultural conditions that produce overwork and a toxic academic culture.

Shelters

My sincere hope is that after reading the first half of this chapter, you're thinking, "But Liz! It's really not *that* toxic!" And if you are, good. Education is, as bell hooks writes, "a vocation rooted in hopefulness" (hooks 2003, xiv). Each of us finds our shelters in our academic worlds, out of necessity; otherwise, we'd not be able to persist in our work. Positive psychology, particularly as described by Carl Rogers, identifies the need for "unconditional positive regard," which Rogers said is a universal human craving. The American Psychological Association defines this as "an attitude of caring, acceptance, and prizing that others express toward an individual irrespective of his or her behavior and without regard to the others' personal standards" (APA 2022). If we worked in contexts where all positive regard were conditional, our metaphorical sailboats (see chapter 2) would become unstable, lacking adequate ballast.

Each of us finds our own pockets of emotional and mental safety, but in this section, we'll explore some of the more consistently safe harbors in academia. Specifically, this chapter focuses on four: centers for teaching, faculty learning communities, interdisciplinary or pedagogically focused organizations and conferences, and libraries. This section will intentionally take something of a faculty development lens, as our faculty developers are those tasked with creating environments welcoming of faculty and students in a community of learning. However, the shelters I describe here are open to all of us, perhaps most importantly to teaching faculty.

Shelter #1: Centers for Teaching

By now, most of our campuses have some sort of center for teaching and learning (CTL), be that in academic affairs, the library, technology, or elsewhere (Wright 2023). These centers are generally places where faculty can learn and improve their teaching, and, in my experience, they are some of the safest spaces on college campuses for faculty. A commitment to creating inclusive, equitable, student-success-focused spaces defines the core competency of the teaching center. For this reason, among others, teaching centers are often places where we can let down our guards a bit and be real about the challenges we're facing. The people who tend to staff these centers are often current or former faculty members who found a love for pedagogy and the scholarship of teaching and learning (including me). CTL staff typically relish opportunities to work with others on improving student success and engagement across the institution. CTLs are also quite often bastions of psychological safety, for reasons I explored in a guest column for John Warner's *Inside Higher Ed* blog, "Just Visiting" (Norell 2023).

Too often, centers for teaching are most effective at reaching what many faculty developers call the "frequent fliers," or—more tongue-in-cheek—"repeat offenders." There is usually a devoted cadre of faculty who will show up any time the teaching center doors are open for a program. They become their own kind of faculty learning community (discussed more below). The struggle for teaching centers is so often finding ways to bring the rest of the campus into the fold. To do so, teaching centers will offer a variety of programs, with widely varying degrees of success. Here are some of the most effective strategies I've seen to get a greater diversity of faculty into the center:

Book clubs: A staple offering of many CTLs is the faculty reading group. This works well when the teaching center has the budget to supply the books for faculty—academics are suckers for free books, after all. Even better if food is on offer, too! In my experience, the key to a successful book club is finding the right size and keeping it focused on how the book can be applicable to faculty in the classes they're teaching right now. For example, a group of us read Kevin Gannon's *Radical Hope* in the summer of 2020 and met every two weeks by Zoom to discuss it. We weren't even on contract at the time, so this was done entirely on our own time and voluntarily. Still, because Gannon's book had so many practical, hands-on tips for being more inclusive and empathetic in our teaching, our group of more than twenty faculty and staff did not suffer noticeable attrition over the eight summer weeks we read and discussed together.

Bite-sized professional learning. Give me a microphone or a podium, and I'll talk all day about almost any topic I'm passionate about. That means that no matter how much time I'm given to talk about something, it never feels long enough. But the thing is, our audiences don't always have that same endless well of interest and excitement. What's more, they're busy. Really busy. All of them. All of the time. So while we might want a half day to explore a pedagogical or subject-matter topic we want everyone to embrace, our colleagues will be far more likely to engage with us if it's a bite-sized chunk of time we're asking of them. By this, I mean thirty minutes or less, if at all possible. Rather than trying to address absolutely everything about creating inclusive learning spaces, what if you could just talk about *one* strategy to do this? Borrow from the Universal Design for Learning framework of "add one"—what's *one* thing you could add to your teaching to make it more inclusive (Tobin and Behling 2018)? (Or equitable, or engaging, or relevant, or transparent, or . . .) Make that your professional learning offering, and try to find ways to let your participants practice that one thing before they leave. That means you're not going to be talking much—and we must get comfortable with this because it'll help our colleagues and, by extension, our students. (Incidentally, I hope it doesn't escape your notice that this advice to talk less works well for the classes we're teaching, too.)

Model best practices in teaching. We love to talk to one another about the promises of active learning, micro-lectures, and engagement . . . but when I attend professional learning workshops, I'm astounded by how few of these things we do. Like our students probably do, I confess I groan a bit when a workshop involves some directed discussions or activities . . . but I also retain the information (and the experience) longer and leave feeling like I acquired a new strategy or tool far more often. (Repeat it with me: what's good for the students is good for us!) Some of my favorite programs at our teaching center involved going for a five-minute walk with a colleague I didn't know to get to know them better (with an option to stay in the room for those who would rather not move around), or papering the room with very large sticky notes to write ideas to brainstorm and discuss, or learning classroom engagement techniques from a colleague who once taught kindergarten.[7]

Make it worthwhile. Learning for learning's sake is great, but we are overworked and overwhelmed individuals. We are, hopefully, intrinsically motivated to pick up these new strategies and tools. But a little extrinsic reward helps. Few institutions have the resources to provide stipends for attending professional learning offerings at the center for teaching, but there are plenty of ways to recognize the effort your colleagues are investing, including:

Certificates after completing a program. These don't have to be elaborate—Microsoft Word or Canva will make creating these a breeze. Provide them in print or as PDFs, so faculty can include them in their annual dossiers for review, promotion, or tenure. When I recently organized a writing accountability group, I sent out participation certificates at the end of the semester, and I was astounded at how grateful participants were to have that digital file!

Publicity. Include the names of those who participated in a teaching center offering on a regular basis—this might be monthly or quarterly—in a newsletter or campus communication.

Cohorts. We know learning communities work well in a variety of contexts. Might you be able to create a small cohort of learners based on some shared characteristic—first-year faculty? faculty going up for tenure next year? adjunct faculty?—and create a slate of professional learning offerings for them as a group? (More on learning communities below.)

Investment in sending faculty off campus to learn. Perhaps there are ways to invest professional learning dollars into faculty who are willing and able to share what they learn in your center for teaching. Invite those who go to conferences on the college's dime to share with others when they return.

Highlight your experts. In a time of tightening budgets and challenging enrollment demographics, it's increasingly difficult to find the dollars for bringing in national experts on pedagogy to enrich your faculty's knowledge base. Turn to your faculty. They know so much, and they will feel undervalued if you pay thousands of dollars to bring in a speaker to tell them something they already know. Sometimes it does help to have an outsider speak a difficult truth to a campus community, but not every professional learning offering fits that description. By highlighting the expertise of your faculty, you are communicating that you value their knowledge and want to showcase it. There are few things more motivating in the workplace than that messaging of value (e.g., Schmidt 2023).

Shelter #2: Faculty Learning Communities

Just as first-year experiences help first-time freshmen acclimate to the college culture, faculty learning communities (FLCs) can go far toward creating interdisciplinary relationships and support systems. These groups can be formal or informal, organized spontaneously and sporadically or intentionally and with built-in structure. I've participated in all kinds of FLCs, but the ones that have been most life-giving have been those I've cobbled together on my own. My four closest friends are colleagues—some faculty, some librarians—whom I communicate with primarily via group text. In contrast, I participated in a first-year faculty seminar when I got my first tenure-track job, and while there was some helpful information shared, there was almost no community-building included in that experience. I left that yearlong FLC feeling no more connected to my first-year colleagues than I had on our first day at work. That was a missed opportunity.

FLCs, then, will benefit faculty most when they emphasize the community-building aspects of the group. The knowledge shared is important, but as in our classrooms, that will be far less effective if the participants have no sense of belonging within the group. This is why affinity groups and employee resource groups in the workplace are such powerful practices. Gathering individuals with a shared identity—such as LGBTQIA+ faculty and staff—can provide a safe space to belong and temporarily, at least in part, set aside the emotional armor we carry. FLCs can be extremely powerful when crafted with the same degree of intentionality. (See the sidebar on page 87, intentional gathering, for more on this.)

FLCs are also especially powerful when organized as a community of *practice* (sometimes called a COP). I emphasize "practice" intentionally; "it is *doing* in a historical and social context that gives structure and meaning to what we do," in other words (Glowacki-Dudka and Brown 2013, 30, emphasis added). By exploring the scholarship of teaching with colleagues and committing to applying that scholarship in our different disciplines and contexts, we get all the benefits of learning and of developing the relationships that can sustain us in the more trying seasons of our careers. I can't resist the urge to point out that FLCs—and especially COPs—are part and parcel of what it means to be an institution of learning. For excellent resources on building effective COPs, look at Cox (2004), Martin (2023), and Tinnell et al. (2019).

Shelter #3: Interdisciplinary Organizations and Conferences

Interdisciplinary conferences have been the life-giving force of my career in recent years. Getting faculty (and staff!) out of their silos and talking about higher ed from a more zoomed-out perspective seems to reduce the impulses to peacock and shame. I'm especially fond of conferences focused on pedagogy, as they seem to attract people who are invested in student success and meaningful learning. Examples include the Lily Conferences, offered multiple times a year, the AAC&U and ATD annual meetings, and the Teaching Professor conference, which is now offered in person annually in June and virtually during the fall semester.[8] For those who are now or someday hope to work in faculty development, the Professional and Organizational Development Network conference is also excellent. These meetings have been the most inclusive and invigorating professional learning opportunities of my career.

It feels critical to mention that these conferences and organizations, including the journals they publish, are not universally valued in tenure and promotion packets. For early-career faculty, or those working off the tenure track in the hopes of finding a tenure-track position, the investment of time and personal resources in participating in these spaces may yield few benefits for your long-term career aspirations. Having said that, I have made the choice to engage anyway because great teaching is my aspiration—not a title, not an upward career trajectory into a prestigious institution. I mention this only as a warning for those in earlier career phases.

Early in my career, I went along with the prevailing view of academic work as creating new knowledge within my tiny research niche. I wrote paper after paper for academic conferences during graduate school, and the experience of proposing, writing, and presenting my scholarly research was valuable. I distinctly remember, however, attending the second-largest disciplinary meeting in political science many years ago and realizing I no longer belonged there. I was sitting in the Palmer House hotel in Chicago, drinking a latte and looking over some emails, when I happened to catch tiny bits of the conversation happening at the next table. I listened to these two political scientists (whom I did not know) quibble over the tiniest difference in theoretical perspectives—quibble with *vigor*, as though their very professional reputations depended on winning this debate—and I was struck with a thought that felt more like a scream, "WHAT ARE WE DOING?" It was an inflection point for me. The gap between their perspectives was tiny and, for all but about a few dozen political scientists, completely inconsequential. I don't mean to suggest that all academic research is without consequence. I realized, though, that when we get so focused on impressing the people within our disciplines, we can easily lose track of the real-world implications of our work. It's one of many reasons I was so disappointed when the *Washington Post* ended its partnership with the *Monkey Cage*, a blog by political scientists dedicated to making political science research accessible to the general public (Sides 2022). Thankfully, it has been resurrected, though in a more limited format.

Certainly, attend disciplinary meetings and submit to prestigious journals early in your career or as your research agenda and career goals dictate. But when you want to reinvigorate your teaching, look for interdisciplinary or teaching-specific meetings and journals. They are safe(r) spaces to have real conversations, without the performance of expertise serving as a necessary precondition to entry.

Shelter #4: Libraries

Librarians and library spaces are the gifts we do not deserve but absolutely need.[9] Librarians' entire profession is focused on the free and accessible flow of information and resources to anyone who wants it. Libraries have been the refuges of the outcast and the curious for decades. Millennia. As Louise Capizzo says, "Librarians are committed to lifelong learning in order to create a community of well-informed individuals. Librarians are catalysts to enlightenment for their communities" (Nicolas 2018).

When my department's campus offices were under renovation, we had the opportunity to request a temporary office somewhere else on campus (likely nowhere near any of our departmental colleagues) or to work remotely. I chose the latter option and used the library as my home base for the academic year. It was heavenly. It felt like every time I walked through the doors, my shoulders dropped a little and I could breathe more easily. The welcoming staff at the reference desk, the ambient sound of people milling around, the sight of students tap-tap-tapping away at computers, it all felt so wholesome and encouraging and quintessentially *academic*. Groups of students met in collaborative learning rooms, some with anatomy and physiology manipulables to study for their next A&P exam.

Libraries operate on a principle of open access and equitable service. When every other corner of campus feels overwhelming or oppressive or potentially fraught, the library is the place where you can—or, at least, should—be able to relax and be yourself. To question. To seek. To be curious.

The Association of College and Research Libraries (or ACRL) Standards for Libraries in Higher Education explicitly require, among many other things, the following:

- Libraries are the intellectual commons where users interact with ideas in both physical and virtual environments to expand learning and facilitate the creation of new knowledge.
- Library personnel model best pedagogical practices for classroom teaching, online tutorial design, and other educational practices. (3.3)
- Library personnel collaborate with campus partners to provide opportunities for faculty professional development (3.5)
- The library provides safe and secure physical and virtual environments conducive to study and research. (6.2)
- The library provides clean, inviting, and adequate space, conducive to study and research, with suitable environmental conditions and convenient hours for its services, personnel, resources, and collections. (6.7)

For knowledge workers, the library is like a cocoon of wisdom, a physical embodiment of our highest professional strivings. Engel and Antell (2004) note that many thought the importance of the physical library would diminish in an increasingly digital age. However, the research indicates otherwise. Their interviews with faculty, for example, revealed several themes:

- Faculty space[s are] an oasis of solitude, a place for sustained, uninterrupted thinking or reading, and a quiet place for reflection.
- The faculty space's location within the library enables "serendipitous browsing," which is valuable to faculty members' work.
- Faculty members' "academic upbringing" has habituated them to using the library as the primary place for doing research. Going to the library is a ritual that puts them in the right frame of mind to do serious work. (Engel and Antell 2004, 12)

The symbolic and practical dimensions of the library as a physical space align with the notion of a shelter. Dahlkild (2011) likens libraries to what sociologist Ray Oldenburg calls "third places," or public spaces available for spending time without a particular agenda. They are "important for the vitality of civil society and the foundation of a functioning democracy. They promote social equality by leveling the status of guests, providing informal contacts and discussions, creating habits of public association, and supporting both individuals and communities, and they counteract the isolation of the suburban societies" (Dahlkild 2011, 34–35).

This gets to the very ethos of higher education. Libraries are open to all, and they function as "levelers, where differences seem less important and where place is inclusive rather than exclusive, with a diversity of people and experiences encountered" (Kranich 2020, 135–36; see also Gibson et al. 2017).

In short, the library's mission is, by design, to serve as an intellectual shelter, a space where curiosity unfolds and flourishes. Faculty and students find spaces conducive to studying, collaborating, thinking, learning, and even finding solitude (Lux, Snyder, and Boff 2016). Even when just existing in a library space, users often sense a kind of spiritual or subliminal linkage to "the tradition of scholarship" (Cunningham and Tabur 2012).

INTENTIONAL GATHERING

Pre-pandemic, one of my closest friends and I read Priya Parker's book *The Art of Gathering* together (Parker 2018). Parker is a talented planner of gatherings that often transform the attendees in some meaningful way. Her book shares what she's learned about the importance of being mindful in the design of a gathering, from the invitation to the closing moments, to ensure that it's achieving some purpose—and that that purpose is not driven by logistics (who needs to do what and when) or habit (weekly staff meetings, for example). My friend Julie, whom you'll meet in chapter four, and I put together a short workshop for our colleagues on the lessons from Parker's book. Below, I share some of those key takeaways. I encourage you to read her book—it's magnificent!—or listen to her limited-run podcast, *Together Apart*, about how we gathered during the COVID-19 pandemic, produced by the *New York Times* (Parker 2020).

The ideas in her book are meant to be applied to any context where people gather, including our learning spaces.

Begin with: why are you *really* gathering? If you are going to ask students (or colleagues) to give up time to gather, take the time to identify a clear and meaningful purpose for the gathering, including your class meetings. Parker urges us to remember that a category is not a purpose. Instead, a defined purpose for gathering has meaning, which meets the four criteria below (annotated with how this relates to your synchronous class meetings):

The purpose sticks its neck out a little bit.

How does each class meeting facilitate something challenging, unexpected, or experimental for its attendees? How are you designing experiences that go beyond the expected?

It takes a stand.

Taking a stand doesn't mean preparing for battle, but it does require that you're tapping into something deeper and more meaningful.

It's willing to unsettle some of the guests (or the host).

You don't have to deeply unsettle someone; this isn't about confrontational or conflict-ridden learning spaces.

It refuses to be everything to everyone.

No gathering can satisfy the hopes and expectations of every person who might attend. Similarly, no class—no single meeting, no semester-long study—can be all things to all potential students (and teachers). Being clear about what you will—and will not—tackle is important.

Examples:
- Our discussion of Clint Smith's article "Why the Confederacy Lives On" will challenge us to grapple with the legacy of the Civil War as we build awareness of the unrealized hope of civil rights and civil liberties in America.
- Tuesday's class will explore Bryan Alexander's argument that climate change is a crisis, today, for higher education.
- Today's exploration of the ethics of artificial intelligence (AI) will focus on the resources needed to train AI.
- Tonight, we will use a discussion of the rhetoric in James Baldwin's "A Talk to Teachers" to build greater proficiency in writing persuasively.

Be specific. Make each gathering different from every other gathering. What larger needs in the world does your gathering address?

Transition into the gathering with intention. Before an official beginning, there will always be a time of transition between when students (attendees) arrive and when the event begins. Use this time wisely. You might create a physical or metaphorical passageway into the space, or you might give students (attendees) a task that will prime them for your gathering's purpose. This can include the time between signing up for a course and when a new semester begins; it might also be the time between when students get access to your course learning management system and when you meet them for the first time. How can you use that liminal space to prime them for what's to come?

Do not begin with logistics. The first five minutes of any gathering often get paid the most attention, and we often squander this attention with housekeeping tasks. Or, "syllabus day." We've all heard that our first day with students sets the tone for the semester ahead. Parker urges us to use this precious moment of attentiveness to go directly into the purpose of your gathering. Set the stakes immediately.

Once gathered, create a community. Creating a sense of belonging among those gathered should be your second priority. This means helping each person see the others, which is a critical component of a meaningful gathering. This is not about getting those present to connect with you, the teacher (or host); it's about helping them create a psychologically inter-stitched group.

Diversity is a potentiality that needs to be activated. You may have diverse voices in the room, but if they do not have space to speak, that diversity is an untapped resource. This means both giving time to the perspectives of others and welcoming diverse perspectives, even if they are not ones you personally share. Doing this early on will activate the potential of the entire group to grow and learn together.

Design spaces with intentionality. If you want participants to engage, the design of the space needs to facilitate—indeed, encourage—participation. One of the best ways to do this is to break participants out of their habits; displace them. This might mean disrupting the organization of the room, banishing the rows of orderly desks and chairs. It could also mean moving to a different space for a day or for the semester (if possible), one that facilitates the kind of community you're striving to create.

Protect the people in the room. As the person who is convening a class or group, it is your responsibility to anticipate and intercept instances where students/attendees may not be considering the betterment of the group or the experience. Doing so may mean some of the participants are unhappy, but it's done in service of the purpose of the gathering. This might look like intercepting a student who likes to dominate classroom discussions or redirecting a conversation back on topic when tangents pop up. It may also mean enforcing (yourself or in collaboration with students) a set of community agreements around norms of participation.

Consider pop-up rules. This technique can help create a space that feels separate from the rest of the day or other gatherings. These pop-up rules apply only as long as the gathering lasts and can change with each new meeting. They should be announced at the moment of coming together, so nobody has time to prepare. Some examples: you may not use words that include the letter R; everyone gives themselves a nickname that must be used for the time you're together; you may only ask questions that are not asking for more information. Let your creativity guide you. You could even invite a different student to establish a pop-up rule each time your class gathers.

Vulnerability bonds groups. "In the classrooms where we were supposed to learn what we didn't already know, the culture taught us to avoid sounding stupid in front of one another" (208). Help your group create a space where mistakes are celebrated and questions are valued. Encouraging the telling of stories can be a good method for doing so; the most powerful moments in stories are those moments when vulnerability is shared. As the teacher or convener, you should share even more personal stories than you expect those gathered to share. Bear in mind the need to respect boundaries and to allow those gathered to pass if they do not feel safe or open to sharing.

Come to a close thoughtfully. Too many gatherings (including classes) don't end; they simply stop. Create an intentional closing that helps your attendees face the end. It may be helpful to think of this as an 'outbound ushering.' Pause to reflect on what happened during your gathering. How does what happened connect to our lives outside this gathering? What do I want to take with me? Doing this as a group is more powerful than doing it alone.

As Parker relates, her father-in-law, who teaches at George Washington University, says he teaches because "he likes the idea of investing in citizens of character that [he] is unleashing into the world. The content of his course is incidental to that larger purpose" (277). How can we think about our gatherings—in the classroom, and beyond—as investing in citizens of character unleashed into the world?

Navigating the Choppy Waters

This chapter was meant to identify some of the potential minefields of academia and to give ideas about the places of shelter, of refuge, in our peculiar world. This framework of minefields and shelters is useful, but the specific situations or places that fall under each category are different for each of us. In describing some that I've observed as potentially fraught or potentially safe, I've not intended to suggest that the same will be true for you. My hope is that, in thinking about the physical, intellectual, and emotional places in your own academic communities, this chapter helps you reflect on where you feel safe and where you feel you must don your armor to protect yourself.

Chapter 4

A DOZEN PRESENT PROFESSORS

> There is something of yourself that you leave at every meeting with another person.
>
> Fred Rogers

Writing can be an isolating task—at least, that's what I've read in all the books, articles, and blogs about writing. However, I was fortunate to have excellent examples of present professors around me—physically, intellectually, and technologically—throughout the writing of this book. Because each of us must find our own path through inner work and cultivating instructor presence, this chapter will introduce you to a dozen brilliant professors. In each, I've provided just a slice of their journey toward greater presence in their teaching. I made no effort to create a perfectly representative sample of all higher education faculty; the people chosen here were those I admired, or whom my colleagues mentioned as the best teacher(s) they'd ever had, and who, crucially, fulfilled the necessary conditions of being available and willing to talk to me. Each will give you a different example of what this inner work might look like—and how it might impact the teaching we do.

Note: Throughout these profiles, I consciously refer to the professors I've profiled by their first names. This is a choice I made to try to foster a sense of community and lateral relationships. There are power dynamics involved in choices about how to refer to others in academia, and because many of those profiled have historically minoritized identities, this choice could feel disempowering. I begin each profile with their title and institution, but I believe the power here is in the story, not the resume, in keeping with the overall tone of this book. Each of these professors has my deepest respect and admiration.

Julie Barcroft (she/her)

Professor of English, Chattanooga State Community College, TN

There are two moments in Julie's teaching career that really stand out when you talk to her, and they boil down to two phrases that capture her whimsical nature: the patron saint of vulnerability and Mr. Prison Potato Head.

Starting with the second, Julie feels especially proud of her work teaching at the Bledsoe County Correctional Complex, part of Tennessee's efforts to increase access to education among those serving time. The program launched in 2021, and Julie was recruited to teach the students by her then–department head, who thought she would be empathetic and flexible around the technology challenges of teaching fully online courses to incarcerated students. There were, indeed, significant technological challenges, particularly given the start of the program coincided with ongoing COVID outbreaks in the prison, which limited students' access to the computer lab. Julie and her colleagues had to approach their work with a tenacity few of us require to engage with students.

One student in particular, Greg, was what Julie calls her "lightbulb student." After serving ten years in prison, Greg was pursuing an associate degree in business through Chattanooga State. Julie describes him as "polite, respectful" and someone whom the students regarded as a mediator with the facility staffers and instructors. Students had the option to create a zine. It was not graded: the goal was to give them a chance to create something for themselves. Julie and her embedded course librarian, Amanda Roper, went to the prison one day. Student workers at the library had prepared for this visit by cutting out images from magazines and supplying glue sticks, paper, and the like. The men's class (because the prison classes, like prison itself, are segregated by gender) decided to create a Mr. Prison Potato Head. Among the things they looked for were the "perfect little shank" to give their creation, along with a tattoo and a heart of gold. Julie said, "It was this spontaneous, creative, funny, and completely student-guided effort. They turned it into the mascot of the class, this weird collage creature. It was wonderful to see them being playful." Mr. Prison Potato Head lived on beyond the class, making the rounds of the college president's office and other faculty spaces before taking up residence with Julie and Amanda on campus. Mr. Prison Potato Head lives in a frame and is proudly displayed.

This work was enabled by Julie's commitment to introspection and exploration of her own vulnerability, which she credits to finding Brené Brown, whom she calls her "patron saint of vulnerability." Vulnerability is what allows her to be "comfortable with discomfort"—and she says she can hold that discomfort because of the inner work she's done. For Julie, that has looked like seasons of therapy, of reading books, of talking with friends who are doing that inner work as well. "The ability to have fellow anxious and questioning people to be in community with" has helped her expand her comfort with vulnerability and wrestling with uncomfortable things. She also credits self-exploration through the Enneagram, particularly in wrestling with feelings of shame.

Dr. Susan Blum (she/her)

Professor of Anthropology, University of Notre Dame, IN

When the topic of ungrading comes up in educational spaces, Susan's name is one of the first to arise—and with good reason. Her edited volume, *Ungrading: Why Rating Students Undermines Learning (and What to Do Instead)*, sparked all sorts of important and practical conversations around alternative grading practices in education at all levels. But it might surprise you—as it did me—to learn that, early in her career, Susan was "a very strict grader" and "a stickler for this and a stickler for that." Although, having said that, maybe it's not surprising at all, especially for an anthropologist, someone with well-honed skills in cultural observation and analysis. After all, looking at the prevailing behaviors of educators would lead almost anyone to conclude that assigning grades and embodying the persona of a stickler is just how educating happens.

But somewhere along the way, Susan realized this wasn't working. In her early teaching, fear was a going concern. "I used to be so scared of students—I'm not sure I've ever said this out loud. I felt like I didn't know how to talk to them, except for the few who were like me," she says. Imposter syndrome was part of it, given that she had taken only a few years of anthropology coursework; her background was in linguistics and Chinese. Teaching classes she had never taken felt like something students would easily pick up on. To break down those walls and battle the fear, Susan did what any good anthropologist does—she studied them. Eighteen years of doing ethnographic study of her students gave her purchase on understanding these creatures so often different from her. The softening of her teaching persona happened as a result; "sometimes the heart follows the head," she says.

Recognizing that her class is just "one tiny piece" of her students' "very complicated and multifaceted" lives, Susan says she now thinks of her teaching as being akin to an improv practice. "I want to see what's happening with these actual people in this actual moment. I have plans—I don't just show up. But I'm kind of waiting to see what's happening and what people respond to, along with the content and skills that I hope we're going to get to that day. It's always a question of how we're going to get there." She's present, in other words.

To cultivate this presence, in addition to her ethnographic study of students, Susan has engaged in other kinds of introspection. For her, though, no strategy has been more helpful than writing, which she describes as something she does to think and to understand herself better. It's clear that reflecting on her teaching is something she does often, and often in community with others.

What continues to niggle at her? Susan is concerned by the assumptions made by some of the writers I've drawn from most in this book, like Parker Palmer. She asks, "is [teaching] a vocation that makes us use our entire self? Do we have to? It works well when we do, but what if you don't want to? What if you have an identity where that wouldn't be safe or appropriate or comfortable?" Especially when "the modal professor is contingent, at an under-resourced school with a very heavy teaching load," how can we demand that professors give all of themselves to a job with low compensation? "The affect expected now is, in addition to all the other credentials, a lot. How do you balance the labor along with the emotional labor?"

Susan admits she doesn't have solutions. She's confident that we need to talk more about boundaries in academia, though. Perhaps, she muses, we need to talk about the fact that teaching is one of the few caring professions where we—the professionals—aren't actually doing the most important work. Students, after all, have to invest time and effort to do the learning. We can't control that. As our conversation wrapped up, she asked a question that I continue to ponder: "How do you deal with that lack of power, even though you have power?"

Dr. Holly Bullard (she/her)

Director of Academics, Programs for Talented Youth, Vanderbilt University, TN

A trio of events, any one of which would've rocked anyone's life, led Holly to the inner work that has transformed her relationship with herself and her students. In August 2009, a Ford F-350 truck drove through her family's home; the point of impact was her six-year-old daughter's bedroom. Holly and her then-husband were watching TV, and suddenly there was a big truck sitting where her daughter's bed had been. Miraculously, their daughter had not a scratch on her. Soon thereafter, Holly's grandmother had surgery and passed away unexpectedly afterward, a fluke occurrence no doctor could explain. And then Holly met someone she couldn't stop thinking about, an event that would eventually lead to the unraveling of her marriage. Her sister told her, "You're not special," words Holly embraced as evidence of her own humanity and—in her words, repeated often during our conversation—the fact that "life is fucking hard."

Holly began her inner work with therapy—so, so much therapy, she says. That led her to journaling, which became a regular tool for sorting out the events happening in her life. She gave herself permission to write whatever came to mind, and she knew that when she had resistance to writing about something, that's what she needed most to get out of her mind and heart.

As a result of this work, Holly says she's now much, much more open with her students. "I'm honest, I'm real, I don't try to create a facade," she says. She recalls a dean she worked with once who believed that you check anything and everything negative at the door when you come to work. She embraced that for a season of her life, but not anymore. "I don't check anything at the door. I don't share inappropriately, but you need to create space for people to bring their full selves into the room." Holly believes that this openness and authenticity empowers her students to share things with her they wouldn't with others. "Find out what's meaningful and valuable. Find out how to connect with students," she advises.

One of my favorite moments in my conversation with Holly came when she talked about her time working as a Quality Enhancement Project director at a former institution. They were working with faculty to boost students' critical thinking skills as a part of writing. The focus of their faculty development strategy was something more institutions ought to emulate: "We had [value] *on our campus.*" Her professional learning offerings came from asking colleagues to share their expertise with one another. When faculty asked for institutional support to attend conferences, those grants came with a requirement to share what you learned upon your return. That strategy matters because it communicated the inherent value faculty bring to the institution beyond their work in their siloed classrooms.

Dr. Sarah Rose Cavanagh (she/her)

Professor of Psychology and Senior Associate Director for Teaching and Learning, Simmons University, MA

As a psychological researcher and writer, Sarah says, "Everything I do, all my writing and research, is *me*search. I write about emotions because I find that helpful." I love how she explicitly makes a connection between her research and the questions that she's compelled to answer because she just can't set them aside. This passion, this yearning to understand something that feels personally important, is one of the most important—but so often ineffable—qualities of great teaching.

Although she hasn't written them up yet, Sarah shared some qualitative research findings that speak to this ineffability of teaching. She talked to thirty-five undergraduate students about their college experiences, particularly their best and worst learning experiences. One of the themes that emerged mirrors the themes of this book—presence and attention. Sarah says, "The students used the most interesting language when they were talking about professors who were present. They would say, 'they were just *there*-there.'" When professors seemed less present, students would say, "they're not *there*-there."

Although none of us can explain exactly how or why, we just *know* when someone's brain isn't fully engaged. Sarah says it's "like dogs smelling COVID"—we can detect what's happening in someone else's brain, even if all the obvious outer signals (words, slides, activities) are the same.

I was hoping my conversation with Sarah would shoot off into a decidedly nerdy direction, and I was not disappointed. As she talked about how she cultivates presence—the *there*-there-ness—in her own work, she talked about the ways she engages the default mode network to reach insights in her own intellectual puzzles. Especially important is running to her creative process; she finds that she gets her best ideas about the narrative of a writing project while she's out on a run. "An idea will occur to me, phrases, shapes, emotions, things like that." She also finds creative energy on dog walks and—no surprises here—while taking a shower.

If one wants to be a *there*-there professor, Sarah says, it comes most reliably when one can come into classroom spaces in an "open manner." This is an attitude of expecting you're going to learn something, too, and being willing to explore things that you don't understand well. "It's harder to do when you get more expertise, but it's one of the best ways to be *there*-there and be authentic—learning together."

Dr. Liz Faber (they/them)

*Assistant Professor of English & Communication,
Dean College, MA*

"When I started, I was 100 percent made of imposter syndrome," Liz confesses. They were thinking, "I don't know what I'm doing, I don't know why I'm here ... who trusted me with this?" It's this kind of transparency that has made Liz something of a Twitter phenom, with their daily self-care check-in tweets that encourage their followers to pause and ask: "What did you do to be kind to yourself today?" Liz confesses that they feel like they should be journaling and that stuff, but their brain makes consistency harder, so a daily check-in tweet feels more doable.

This ethos may infuse their teaching work today, but it hasn't always been so transparent.

Liz says that "inner work is really part of being a good teacher—I am able to say to my students, 'you are a whole person, always, but you're not the same person you'll be tomorrow, or five years from now, or twenty years from now.'" This comes straight from their experiences. Gaining confidence in the classroom allowed Liz to shift their pedagogy and approach with students. Early in their career, though, there was that pressure to "put on the air of authority," without necessarily knowing exactly what that meant. As Liz has built experience—and, hence, comfort—in teaching, in working with students, they say, "I've gotten more comfortable with who I am and what I want from my life."

The path of gaining that comfort was informed by the inner work they did, which looked like reading books to work out some of their own experiences and traumas, at times seeking therapy, and finding community on Twitter. While social media often gets a bad rap for its toxicity, Liz (and others I interviewed) notes that "having a community of support" has been enormously helpful. "To be able to hear people going through similar struggles and be able to talk it through with them has been wildly important for me."

A lesson Liz learned earlier in their career is particularly worth highlighting—that there is a "mean girls kind of thing" in academia that permeates many of our institutions. Before getting a tenure-track position, Liz worked off the tenure track. "Woo, buddy, the tenure-track faculty treated us terribly," they say. "We had been teaching longer, but they treated us like we were just out of grad school. It was incredibly toxic." The prevailing attitude, they say, was that adjunct faculty members should be "happy just to have a job." And, unfortunately, the constant sense of being not good enough "shows in the classroom, and students see it."

This is perhaps the clearest call I heard from any of the present professors I interviewed. Finding an authentic way of being that feels rooted in our identity is one of the most powerful ways we have to turbocharge learning.

Liz's willingness to be transparent is incredibly refreshing. They ended our conversation by saying, "I wish I were better versed in the literature of pedagogy, but who has time for that? There is power in intuition. That's sort of my underlying teaching philosophy—I'm going to fly by the seat of my pants, and then I'll think about how that went."

Dr. Eric Fournier (he/him)

Director of Educational Development, Center for Teaching and Learning, Washington University, MO

A friendship with well-known educational psychologist Stephen Chew at Samford University helped Eric reframe what his focus should be in his college teaching—a reframe that has served him well as he's moved into faculty development. "When I first started [teaching]," Eric says, "it was all about me and my learning. Chew pushed me—what about the students and what they're learning? It was a paradigm shift."

It may seem simple, but it's something that comes up often in his work with faculty at Washington University in St. Louis. He's sensitive to the anxiety and insecurity that early-career faculty often bring into teaching spaces. By becoming aware of the challenges that different identities introduce into that equation, he feels he's better able to mentor younger faculty. One example he gives is the challenge early-career female faculty members often have in claiming authority in the classroom. "Younger women end up playing this character that's meaner, stricter, and more strident—because they don't want to be seen as a pushover," he says. But then "they feel this disconnect between what they want to be and what the students need to have."

The incongruence is where the CTL steps in. Eric's first piece of advice for newer faculty is to ensure you have a solid course plan and assessment strategy. "When logistics are well thought out," he says, students will forgive a lot of other behaviors or insecurities. Transparency in assessment will help ensure students don't perceive grades as arbitrary.

Earlier in his career, Eric says he really benefited from a two-hour commute between graduate school at the University of Georgia and an adjunct course he picked up at Kennesaw State University. The commute "allowed me to mentally get into the space on the way there, and then on the way home to reflect on how things went."

He's continued the practice of regular reflection on his practices, particularly when he moved from a tenured teaching position at Samford to the CTL at WashU. He says, "I easily could've continued in [the Samford] job and ridden the downhill slope to retirement." He chose not to—because he knew he wanted a new challenge. In describing how he made that decision, Eric pulls from Eric Erikson's stages of development, particularly the distinction Erikson makes between stagnation and generativity. He saw many of his mid- and late-career colleagues "teaching the same courses, doing the same things, parking in the same spots." The move to a completely new career focus at a different institution appealed because of the opportunities for generativity, to pass on what he knew to others.

Being a reflective teacher is a cornerstone of what he aims to accomplish at the WashU CTL. For example, he's hoping to convene a journaling club for faculty, getting them to commit to journaling about their teaching throughout the semester.

Dr. Yasha Hartberg (he/him)

Lecturer, Veterinary Integrative Biosciences, School of Veterinary Medicine and Biomedical Sciences, Texas A&M University, TX

A lucrative tutoring enterprise for undergraduate and master's-level students at Texas A&M was the best preparation Yasha can imagine for his later work teaching at the college level. It was also where he got his first taste of imposter syndrome. Along with a friend, Yasha offered individual and small-group tutoring and had to think on the fly. "I felt confident in my own ability to do calculus," he says, "but I didn't know if a student would stump me." What he discovered was that helping students develop metacognition was the most helpful—to narrate for his tutees, in other words, how he was thinking through a problem to help them develop the ability to think through how to *think about* the problem, versus the mechanics of any one specific problem type.

Yasha's inner work evolution has taken place over many years and in many phases. He talks reverently about Parker Palmer's ability to put into words something Yasha has felt, the terror of being found out as imperfect. This, Yasha says, "is made worse by the adversarial process of scholarship. We throw stuff out and people are *supposed* to tear it apart. We hope they pick at the tiniest bits but not the major parts." Other avenues for finding greater peace with himself and his work have come from his spiritual explorations, seeking mental health support, and working on productivity.

Like many of the present professors profiled in this chapter, Yasha had an inflection point in his life that redefined how he occupies space with students. As he describes it, "My mental health tanked." It was mid-semester, and he felt he needed to let his students know that he was going through some stuff because he wasn't able to respond to them in the ways they needed him to. "I needed to be authentic, to share what was going on," he says. "Sharing was terrifying. But it was amazing. They were grateful for someone opening up about that, especially a faculty member. They sent me letters of support, emails, and they stopped by my office to check on me."

His emphasis on mental wellness changed everything about his relationships with students and his teaching. It also has clearly infused the way he thinks about the enterprise of higher education writ large. "Academics should be building a better world," he muses. "Kindness can be one of the most subversive things we do in academia." He encourages his colleagues to remember that students won't remember specific facts or even where they learned a concept. They will, however, remember the way they felt about subjects or about the world while taking classes. He says he hopes that his students remember, "There's room for kindness and grace and community and vulnerability."

Dr. Jessamyn Neuhaus (she/her)

Director, SUNY Plattsburgh Center for Teaching Excellence, NY

Magic. The idea of magic and superhuman talents came up a lot when I talked to Jessamyn. You'll see.

Jessamyn credits a vehement opposition to academic gatekeeping and hierarchy as her "inoculation against imposter syndrome" in her early faculty career. Among the ways that gatekeeping plays out, she says, are systemic racism and the air of self-importance built into academia. Instead, Jessamyn's priorities are helping students—and the faculty she works with in her teaching center, as well as the readers of her book *Geeky Pedagogy*—realize that they can get better and that there are all sorts of tools to help us learn, grow, and claim agency over our development.

As a self-described vocal introvert, Jessamyn is passionate about dispelling the myth of the "damned super-teacher stereotype." She says that the perpetuation of this idealized version of a teacher is both entrenched and problematic. It "hampers college teachers (especially) who are disproportionately nerdy or not performative," she says, and it's what she most wishes she could disappear with a wave of a magic wand. Instead, she says, the work of teaching is made up of "daily, incremental, even grinding work to teach and learn."

But her introversion is a gift. When asked about her inner work, Jessamyn exclaimed, "I love inner work! You can do it by yourself! Yay!" The way she conceptualizes pedagogy is just inner work by another name, she says. "You can use your big fat smart brain to figure things out, to think through things." The magic comes when we can shift from questioning whether we're good (or not-so-good) teachers and instead ask questions like, "What's going on here? What could I change? What's working well? What's bothering me? What's a real problem here?" Those questions are vulnerable, but Jessamyn says that inner work, to her, is changing our mindsets around our teaching.

The first time Jessamyn went to a teaching conference, it was such a different environment than what she'd found at disciplinary conferences. "I realized I could sit down next to anyone and say, 'Where do you teach? What are your students like?'" She's also found refuge in the community of scholars with whom she's connected on Twitter, particularly since COVID disrupted our lives in March 2020.

Decidedly approachable, Jessamyn wants all of academia to shed the veil of the ivory tower and focus more on being accessible and relatable. In writing her book, she explicitly focused on making the research interesting. She worries about "how incredibly hard it is to get a college degree" today. She says, "It's more expensive. It's harder to survive adolescence. If I can help someone with non-jargony, non-pompous research help students succeed in college? It doesn't get any better." Magic, in other words.

Dr. Christopher Poulos (he/him)

Professor, Communication Studies, University of North Carolina–Greensboro, NC

"I never followed the straight path," Chris told me when we talked. His teaching career looks like a meandering path and not so much a linear trajectory. For example, he took some time off between his undergraduate and graduate degrees to pay off his undergraduate debt. He got a job working in customer service in the corporate world, then moved into training and development. A chance encounter with a consulting group from the University of Denver during his corporate work helped him realize the work he wanted to do was in communication studies. And so he began his PhD there.

School came easily to Chris, but other parts of life did not. "I was born neurotic and anxious," he says freely. He began therapy while an undergraduate, a practice that he's continued off and on ever since. He also shares that inner work for him has included meditation, yoga, and twelve-step recovery. "I equate inner work with deep digging into the past, to understand why you've come to how you are," he says. The impulse to do that deep inner work and engage in self-care "runs against academic culture," which he describes as based on an efficiency model that's forever seeking to do more with fewer people.

To combat the imposter syndrome he describes having felt well before he began teaching, Chris took acting classes in college. The emphasis on rehearsal and preparation has served him well in his career. "That taught me how to be in a room and not be afraid of what other people were thinking."

The spaces Chris finds most healing in academia now have to do with the relationships he's formed. One of those spaces is the International Congress of Qualitative Inquiry, which he's been attending since 2005. The conference brings scholars from around the world together to engage in interdisciplinary conversation about qualitative research. "It's a community that's like home for me," he says. Another place he seeks refuge is in a reading group with people in Greensboro. The group reads fiction and consists of people from a host of backgrounds—including professors, musicians, and artists—across the community, which is home to five colleges and universities. This commitment has added an "assignment to my life," he says, but it "feeds me because we're not reading for speed, we're doing life in a different way."

As an auto-ethnographer, Chris is an ardent believer that personal narrative can have a transformational impact on a life. He asks his students to write their life story as part of an unfolding semester-long writing project. The last chapter of this project is to project ten years into the future and write what will be happening then, using the conventions of fiction—action, dialogue, and plotting, for example. He's had a number of students reach out ten years later and say, "Wow! This is really close to what my life is!"

Chris points out that in any industry, water-cooler conversation is complaining about the people you serve. But for Chris, this is counterproductive. "What I've taken away is that young people are fascinating and resilient. You have to find them where they are and take them to where they can go. Even if it's just a little bit along the path."

Dr. Christen Rexing (she/her)

Assistant Professor of Public Health, School of Nursing and Health Sciences, LaSalle University, PA

When bad things happened to her earlier in life, Christen was the kind of person to "put my nose down and plow forward." That changed when her brother died suddenly during her first semester in her doctoral program. She instead reflected on her priorities in life and what she wanted to do with her life, and she made a change. "Ever since then, that punctuation in my life, I started to process differently about what I should be doing and where."

Teaching was thrilling for Christen early in her career. As an extrovert, teaching "totally tapped into my personality and my passion." She was surprised to find that teaching was a blast, even if it was way more work than being a research assistant. Working with her students was a joy, and she says that she's learned so much about herself through that work. "I've learned how to be compassionate in ways that I wasn't before, and sometimes being compassionate isn't the right thing to do."

And then, the pandemic arrived. That joy she felt in teaching seems to be gone entirely . . . "and I'm teaching in public health! Here's the moment!" But she's just found that her students have been disconnected and disengaged since 2020 in ways that she's at a loss to mitigate. Christen's tried all the normal hacks for boosting engagement or finding ways to reinvigorate her teaching, but they haven't worked for her.

Some of that has to do with where she's teaching, a small liberal arts college that's very dependent on tuition dollars. "Enrollment numbers are falling every year," she says, which creates perverse incentives to boost enrollment without regard to *how* enrollment is boosted.

Even before the pandemic, though, Christen says she knew she wanted a career reset. She missed the public health work she had done earlier in her career. Unlike the much-discussed phenomenon of "quiet quitting" that everyone was talking about in 2021, Christen says she has been engaged in a process of "LOUD QUITTING"—she started telling people a year in advance, "I am going to quit." Doing so brought her peace, and that's how she knew it was the right choice.

She's disappointed with a lot in higher education, but she maintains that she still loves working with the students who show up to learn. Christen tells a story of a time when students she'd taught seven years earlier texted her from London because they had seen something in the city Christen had taught them about. "We were thinking of you!" they texted her. Those moments are the ones she'll miss.

What she won't miss is the "icky" academic culture that so often feels like "this bizarre land of rules that make no sense, designed by people with a ton of privilege, where nobody says anything. They say they will speak up when they get tenure, but after they get tenure, they've been worn down and do nothing."

Still, she recognizes that her confidence and authenticity have been instrumental in creating meaningful relationships with students. "The people who I've had the biggest impact on are the ones I've been myself with," she says.

Dr. Kate Smith (she/her)

Assistant Professor of Pharmacy, Oklahoma University Health Sciences Center College of Pharmacy, OK

I wanted to talk to Kate specifically because she's such a passionate advocate for the use of the Enneagram in higher education. Like many of us, she grew up "loving personality tests," possibly (probably?) because her dad did, too. It also helps that others in her discipline—Pharmacy Education, known to insiders as PharmEd—have also embraced the Enneagram as a tool for engaging with students.

Learning more about the Enneagram framework helped her better understand how she interacts with students and engages in the classroom. Kate's dominant Enneagram type is a 1, known as "the perfectionist." (See chapter 8.) She says, "Pharmacists like things that we can measure and can control. That's very much me. So much of pharmacy and health doesn't fit into neat black-and-white categories." Seeing the world in yes-no, right-wrong dichotomies is a common trait of Enneagram 1s, who want to do the Right Thing . . . and do it perfectly, always.

This awareness has changed how she relates to students, she says. "As a young faculty member, I was very much about classroom control. I wanted the students' attention the whole time." In other words, orderly and predictable—a 1's panacea. Now, though, Kate has learned to embrace a little more chaos. "There is so much more meaningful learning out of a little bit of chaos or not necessarily knowing the answer to a hard question."

This undoubtedly helps her students as they move into their careers. "As I've [embraced] gray thinking, it has helped me explain to students why there may not be one right medicine for a person."

Dr. Ingrid Thompson (she/her)

Assistant Professor, Public University in the Southeastern United States[1]

Ingrid describes her life before starting her first tenure-track job as a period of being "wrapped up in a chrysalis." In the years leading up to moving to her current city for her teaching job, "I was poking holes in the chrysalis, but I blew it up shortly after moving here." What changed? Having a steady job, with reliable health insurance, allowed her to get the health care she needed for the first time in her life.

You see, Ingrid didn't grow up in an academic family; in fact, she lived in poverty for much of her life, including working in "awful jobs where people treated me like garbage," she says. Those experiences don't define her, and she says they have been instrumental in helping her relate to many of her students, but they are not experiences many of her colleagues share.

Despite its many, many challenges, COVID was the pause in the hurly burly of life that allowed Ingrid's inner work to move from exploration to explosion. "I feel like a totally different person," she says. That work has included different modalities of therapy, working with a nutritionist, and reading. "There isn't one specific tool that was super helpful," she says, "it was learning how to use tools, period." Like many others I interviewed, Ingrid mentioned *Atomic Habits* and its philosophy of "habit stacking," which involves adding a new habit you want to adopt to something you're already doing (Clear 2018). For example, maybe you want to incorporate more stretching but don't remember to do so. Stack that new habit—stretching—on top of something you already do, like eating.

These experiences—of living in poverty, of finding relative stability and safety in a full-time job, of getting better acquainted with her own needs and forming a healthier set of habits—have made the work of teaching feel like something of a relief for Ingrid. Her pedagogy emphasizes the connections between the real world and her teaching (which emphasizes social work and policy advocacy).

Her experiences also mean that the notion of imposter syndrome has never really resonated with Ingrid—or, she admits, maybe it has and she just didn't realize it. Her philosophy is so delightful: "I feel like the world is shitty and awful, so I just work hard. I know all too well that anything can be taken away from you at any time—nothing is guaranteed. I deserve to be here, and I don't know if I'll make it."

Teaching and research come relatively easily to Ingrid, and they are spaces where she thrives professionally. The harder parts of her job, she says, are the internecine politics of committee and service work. "When I first joined committees, I was very earnest and tried to contribute, but I found that caused conflict and just wasn't welcomed." Now that she has more experience, she says she tries to keep her head down and help where she can. "You have to be very purposeful about where you fight."

Bonus: Atlas Green, community college alumnus, in their own words

I was a kid who was almost chewed up and swallowed by the tragic tale poverty weaves into the fabric of many peoples' lives. Financial struggles ruined the relationship I had with my family until the gnashing teeth and volume-torn throats ended with me leaving my home far, far sooner than nearly all of my peers. At age eighteen, a month before my high school graduation, I was homeless and barely stable where I'd landed. There were times when I came very close to caving under that pressure.

After years of battling unchecked mental illnesses and a smothering apathy toward my own care, I was so battle worn and exhausted from fighting everything the world tossed at me. I flickered out, along with my hope. Through sheer luck—being placed in the right class at the right time—I found hope to help me through this time. The incredible kindness of a lovely married couple, Brandon Germany and Kathryn Kiper, saved me.

It started before the homeless mess. I was sixteen and in my junior year of high school. At that time, I was the only source of income for my family, and the job I worked allowed me, on average, about three hours of sleep a night. Food was practically a privilege—one that came infrequently—and tensions were always extremely high in my home. There came a moment in my US History class, taught by Mr. Germany, where my anxiety was teetering out of control. He walked into the class, saw my dire expression, and took a hammer to the dam holding back my tears with a single question: "You okay?"

I can still remember my face scrunching up like a child caught in a lie. The tears were almost as hot as the shame I felt when he escorted me out into the hall to talk. I blundered through an explanation laced with a plea for help . . . or at least a plea for understanding.

Mr. Germany stole a box of tissues from the class next door, and then he changed my life. Before long, Mrs. Kiper joined the fray and became the first strong, intelligent, and unapologetically *her* woman in my life. Together, along with their daughter Madeline, they took my hands and helped me through the rest of high school.

They learned about my situation. They gave me chances to see things I never expected. They urged me to apply to college. When I did the impossible and walked across the high school graduation stage, despite the sudden changes in my life, Mr. Germany stood. His cheers were the first I heard. I was told at my seat that he had been crying during my walk. My first thought was, "Serves him right after making me cry so much!" I never smiled more brightly.

After that, things happened in quick succession. They helped me get my driver's license. I joined them at several family events. With the help of another teacher, Mr. Harrison, they got me a car so I could make it to college.

A straight up CAR!!

I'm writing this about a year since I last saw them in person, but I don't mind. Every mile I put on my car driving to college and every step I took through the hallways on campus are in honor of their efforts. Every A I made, every class I took is another block in the path they helped me get back on. Every day I grow a little happier, and I have never been prouder of myself.

And all it took was two teachers who saw a student crying and thought: Something is really wrong here. How can we support her?

I couldn't have been luckier, and I couldn't be more grateful.

Atlas Green graduated from community college and transferred to a four-year university, where they completed their bachelor's degree. They credit their success to teachers who were attentive to their students and compassionate in their praxis.

Moving into Reflection

In the last four chapters, we've explored the concept of presence, why it matters in learning spaces, and how presence and relationships are the raw materials to build rich learning environments. We've looked at some specific techniques and exercises to build greater presence and foster more meaningful relationships in your classrooms. But the Parker Palmer quote earlier in this book—"We teach who we are. . . . When I do not know myself, I cannot know who my students are" (2007, 2–3)—will motivate the next set of chapters.

You're reading this book because you want to unlock greater learning, greater meaning, and greater connection in your teaching. To do so requires engaging in some inner work around greater knowledge of yourself. Unfortunately, this is not a linear process with a clearly defined beginning and end; this is the work of a lifetime, the process of self-actualization so richly described by Maslow (1998) and Kaufman (2020). I encourage you to approach the next few chapters with a sense of curiosity and wonder. What might you learn about yourself that will make events from your past or present easier to understand? What insights might be unlocked by doing some inner investigation? If it helps, think of this as an anthropologist might: you're going on a quest to deeper self-understanding, because you know doing so will unlock greater insight moving forward. This work is not always easy or comfortable, but it is worth the effort.

Presumably, a life of the mind appealed to you because you already have the prerequisite trait of curiosity. And while higher education rarely encourages introspection—we even eschew the use of the first-person voice in writing!—this process is deeply rewarding. The chapters ahead hope to inspire a virtuous cycle of self-knowledge and improvement. What's good for students is good for us, too. This cycle of continuous improvement is what we most want for our students' learning, so it's only natural that it ought to work for us, too.

OK, ready to get curious? Let's do it!

PART II

TOOLS FOR CULTIVATING SELF-KNOWLEDGE

> The quieter you become, the more you can hear.
>
> Ram Das

In part 1, we explored the *why* for inner work as a professor. In part 2, we'll move into the *how*, exploring several tools for deepening your self-understanding and self-acceptance. But this is not meant to be a theoretical discussion of ethereal topics. Instead, you'll find concrete steps you can take, depending on what you need right now, to become more attuned to yourself and hence more present with others. The goal is simple: by exploring a range of tools, you can take what serves you now and leave the rest. What resonates now may not later, and vice versa. This part is meant to be a resource to which you can return whenever you want to explore the contours of your identity, heart, and soul. When you're feeling adrift, uncertain, or overwhelmed, these tools can help you regain your footing and feel once again like you're charting the course of your own life.

This work is not easy, but it is worth it—much as we might describe the learning and growth we ask of our students. To engage in any effort designed to deepen knowledge, we must be willing to weigh difficult questions and embrace uncertainty. Our existing beliefs may be questioned or even undermined. Ultimately, as is true for our students, the result can be transformative. We can find more meaningful relationships, find greater balance in our work lives, and reduce the impact of stress, burnout, toxic work cultures, and other adversity on our overall well-being.[1]

THERE IS NOTHING WRONG WITH YOU

It's easy to interpret a call for inner work as a call for self-improvement. Let's be really clear that *this book is not designed to make you a better person*. Perhaps you'll come away from engaging in inner reflection feeling like a more self-actualized, transcendent version of yourself. I strongly believe that that person is already inside you, though, and that this work is about unearthing your relationship to him, her, or them.

One of my favorite books, *There Is Nothing Wrong with You*, by Cheri Huber, changed the way I thought about the pursuit of a better, more productive, more fulfilling, happier life. Huber says that chasing these things often implies that there is something deeply wrong, perhaps even pathological, about how we are today. We become a problem that needs solving, trauma that needs overcoming, suffering that needs ending. She writes: "Suffering provides our identity. Identity is maintained in struggle and dissatisfaction, in trying to fix what's wrong. So we are constantly looking for what is wrong, constantly creating new crises so we can rise to the occasion. To ego, that's survival. It is very important that something be wrong so we can continue to survive it" (Huber 2001, 11).

Huber advises us, "Anytime a voice is talking to you that is not talking with love and compassion, don't believe it!" (50). "Self-hate uses self-improvement as self-maintenance," she writes. "As long as you are concerned about improving yourself, you'll always have a self to improve. And you will always suffer" (139).

If you're feeling some defensiveness as you read these quotes, good. That means your ego is jumping into the ring to protect itself. The truth is, our ego wants to run the show. It has good intentions—self-preservation, avoidance of hurt, righteous indignation, all that good stuff—but it is motivated not by connection or growth or happiness, only preserving the status quo. Behind the ego, though, behind that big personality with self-righteous certainty that I AM RIGHT and all challengers must be vanquished? Behind that is the true self, the inner teacher, the inner mentor. She craves the freedom to exist without judgment or argument. She just wants to be accepted and loved, exactly as she is. The ego won't let her, though, not while he's running the show.

The work we're exploring in part 2 of this book is all about turning down the volume on our individual egos and letting our inner selves unfurl. Ultimately, the more you can let that true self out—whatever that might mean to you, which we'll explore—the more you can stop being ruled by the ego-centric need to pathologize every renegade instinct, every Netflix binge, every lazy Sunday morning, every time you don't do the thing, and so forth. Unfurl your genuine self, and you can embrace every moment of doing *and* every moment of not-doing, intentional or otherwise, as exactly what you needed in that moment (see Dore 2022).

Self-acceptance does not mean you quit striving toward your goals. It does mean that you stop thinking the only way to achieve your goals is to punish yourself when you fall short. Huber says, "We've been taught that everything in life makes you either a good person or a bad person. But it's not true, and it never was" (Huber 2001, 190). Western culture teaches us that "our only hope of being good is to punish ourselves when we are bad. We believe beyond doubt that without punishment, bad would win out over good" (8).

There is another way, and it is compassion, starting with compassion for self. "We have a choice," Huber says. "We can live our lives trying to conform to some nebulous standard, or we can live our lives seeing how everything works. When we step back and look at it that way, it is obvious that the attitude of fascination is the only intelligent one to bring to anything" (222). As educators and lifelong learners, this spirit of fascination, of curiosity, of exploration should motivate our work, whether that's academic or personal or both. As you move through the rest of the book, I invite you to embrace these perspectives. There is nothing wrong with you. Unfortunately, too few people are interested in affirming your basic goodness or helping you remember yourself. This book is your invitation to take back that role yourself.

The number of tools you can use for inner exploration is infinite. Truly. Each of us sees the world through the lens of our individual experiences, values, and thoughts, meaning each of us can (and should!) find the unique alchemy of tools that work best for us. In the pages ahead, we'll look at a few that are especially good places to begin. Use this section as an introduction to a variety of tools you might find useful—or not! Take what serves you and leave the rest. Circle back when you find yourself needing ideas on how to discern what's really happening in your mind or in your heart.

Each chapter in this section shares one tool that you might consider as you chart your own inner work journey. The chapter begins with a brief overview of *how* the tool can contribute to your presence, both in and out of the classroom, as well as brief notes on *who* might find it useful. Bear in mind that these tools are not magic bullets; there is no single book or strategy that will suddenly make the challenges in your life manageable or rewarding. Like most things worth doing, they take time. Approach the tools ahead with a curious mind and an open heart. With a deep breath in and out, let's begin.

Chapter 5

MINDFULNESS, OR GETTING QUIET WITH YOURSELF

> The most important work you will ever do is always ahead of you. It is never behind you.
> Stephen R. Covey

Mindfulness and meditation are among the best research-based tools to get this process started. The physical and mental health benefits of mindfulness are well supported by a variety of research studies across a diversity of disciplines. Likely you're both aware of mindfulness practices and feeling at least a little guilty about your imperfect record of putting them into practice. So let's just start with a universal—and biologically rooted—truth: Sitting in meditation is challenging. For everyone. By design. After all, the human psyche craves social connection; the brain was designed, through centuries of evolution, to engage in sorting and ranking constantly. We are not good at isolating ourselves, turning our attention inward,

---

MINDFULNESS

Goal: Mental awareness, self-regulation.

Useful for those who: Have anxious or busy minds; struggle to understand their behaviors or choices.

Connection to teaching: Creating more psychologically safe environments for learners and instructors; generating a deeper understanding of metacognition (and the ability to model it for learners).

and practicing neutrality. We are not good at clearing our minds of thoughts and simply resting in what is. Your brain will not let you do this without a fight, but the good news for us gold-star students is that nobody gets an F in meditation! Your only assignment is to keep trying. (If you are noticing the parallels to a growth mindset, good.)

As is likely the case with you, I have a rather mixed record of adhering to a consistent meditation practice. I go through periods of really committing to a formal practice of sitting in silence and periods of focusing on being as mindful as possible in scattered moments of my days. But regardless of what my practice looks like at any given time, I generally find I stick to the practice most consistently when I lower my expectations. One of the best outcomes of mindfulness practices is our awareness of how deeply *human* we are. When our attention drifts, we are reminded that we are imperfectly human. That humility can deepen our ability to feel empathy for others and shore up our patience with ourselves.

Another key outcome of mindfulness practice is strengthening our capacity for self-regulation—or, put another way, moving more quickly and intentionally out of reactivity. This can not only have a positive impact on the equanimity of our day-to-day lives, especially when a student or colleague challenges us, but it also fosters greater strength in being a co-regulating force when others enter overwhelm. (See introduction.) In this way, we can reduce long-term stress and trauma within our communities by developing our ability to self-regulate.

Too often, we want to pigeonhole mindfulness into a single action—sitting still in silent meditation. We do this to our own detriment, though, as this mindset is unnecessarily restrictive. There are a variety of practices we might consider contemplative, many of which you can consider in figure 5.1, the Tree of Contemplative Practices developed by the Center for the Contemplative Mind in Society. Even this is not an exhaustive collection of practices to deepen your mindfulness, though. You're welcome to download a blank tree to create your own personal tree of practices that serve you.

Today, my meditation practice most often includes pausing midday to soften my gaze out of focus and taking three or five deep breaths. It looks like staring at the wall and letting my mind unfocus for a moment, not thinking about anything in particular. It might include sitting on the floor and petting my dog for a few minutes, or closing my eyes in my desk chair to just see how I'm feeling physically. In short, my "meditation" practice (such as it is) generally looks more like an occasional zone-out, but done intentionally, with purpose.

You may find downloading a meditation app works better for you. (Headspace is particularly popular, as is Insight Timer.) My partner has found the meditation audio clips included with the Mark Williams and Danny Penman book *Mindfulness: An Eight-Week Plan for Finding Peace in a Frantic World* to be enormously helpful. You might also consider some of Dan Harris's work, including the aptly named *Meditation for Fidgety Skeptics*, or Sukey and Elizabeth Novogratz's *Just Sit: A Meditation Guidebook for People Who Know They Should but Don't*. In short, there are a litany of resources to help you find a meditation practice that works for you; don't get discouraged if one does not. Think of the search for a workable, comfortable meditation guide as your first opportunity to practice the neutral acceptance you presumably hope to cultivate through this practice.

As you look over the different modalities and possibilities in the Tree of Contemplative Practices, notice that at root of each of these opportunities is two life-giving resources: awareness and communion/connection. These two sources of life for our human souls are exactly the nourishment this book seeks to amplify in your life. Awareness of your environment, your inner wisdom, and your values fuels mindfulness—and the reverse is also true: engaging in these contemplative practices will deepen the roots of your awareness. Communion and connection provide the socially connective tissue to help us find meaning in our lives and our work. And if we hearken back to the simplistic notion of trauma = overwhelm + isolation, these two resources help us tackle each source of trauma in turn; mindfulness is protective

The Tree of Contemplative Practices

against overwhelm, and community insulates us against feelings of isolation. Thinking back to all we learned in chapter 2, the importance of community becomes a clear and important component of doing this inner exploration. When you pair awareness with communion or connection—and this could be communion or connection with other people, with nature, with a cultural or spiritual tradition, or with your own body—you engage in a contemplative practice.

FIGURE 5.1. The Tree of Contemplative Practices
The practices below are options for filling in the parts of your own tree. Each branch represents a different practice.

Roots	Communion & connection; awareness
Stillness	Meditation; quieting the mind; silence; centering
Ritual/cyclical	Establishing a sacred/personal space; retreats; ceremonies and rituals based in spiritual or cultural traditions
Generative	Gratitude; loving-kindness and compassion meditation; contemplative reading; beholding; visualization
Movement	Walking meditation; labyrinth walking; yoga; dance; aikido; t'ai chi ch'uan
Creative	Music and singing; improvisation; journaling; contemplative arts
Active	Pilgrimages to areas where social justice issues are highlighted; activism, work, and volunteering; vigils and marches; bearing witness
Relational	Deep listening; council circle; storytelling; dialogue

Concept and design by Maia Duerr; illustration by Carrie Bergman. Reprinted with permission from the Center for Contemplative Mind in Society under the Creative Commons Attribution-ShareAlike 4.0 International License.

Try it!

I have found the greatest success with what's called *metta meditation*. The principle here appeals to my sensibilities as a teacher and helper. Essentially, metta meditation aims to direct positive thoughts and kindness toward others; it's sometimes called loving-kindness meditation and appears on the Tree on the limb labeled "generative." As a teacher, I find the focus on directing kindness and acceptance to myself and others—*especially* those with whom I may not have the best or most supportive relationship at the time—to be a good reminder that we are all human, all doing our best at the moment to move forward, and all going to make mistakes. By cultivating a sense of grace and kindness toward those who may be creating agitation in my life, I can focus on my own reaction to their influence and spend less time angsting over why this person insists on making my life harder. And if that sounds like some of the students you've encountered in your career? That's not a coincidence.

Below I've shared my favorite metta meditation script; there are many variations, and I encourage you to find one that resonates with you. To practice, begin by focusing your mind on yourself, and say these words aloud or in your mind. I recommend holding one or both hands over your heart. After you've sent these words directed to yourself, then bring to mind someone you know and love, and repeat the mantra in their direction. Finally, think of someone with whom you have a less positive relationship—maybe someone whom you are estranged from, in conflict with, or have been hurt by. Repeat the mantra in their direction. End with a few deep breaths.

> *(Directed to yourself)*
> May I be happy.
> May I be well.
> May I be safe.
> May I be peaceful and at ease.
>
> *(Directed to others)*
> May you be happy.
> May you be well.
> May you be safe.
> May you be peaceful and at ease.

This meditation practice is especially helpful when you're feeling a surge of negative feelings—toward yourself or others, such as administrators or challenging students. It also cultivates greater empathy, a key ingredient in creating inclusive learning spaces.

Circles of Trust

Several years ago, I was attending a teaching conference when I first heard the name "Parker Palmer," nearly whispered by a speaker in a manner that made clear the reverence with which she held this man and his work. The book she mentioned, *The Courage to Teach*, I had heard of before—many times, in fact—but I hadn't sought it out. Hearing her talk about this man made it sound like she was describing a cult leader or a holy figure. I was certain his work would either be way too woo for the likes of me . . . or, less likely, I'd fall into community with those who revered it.

Turns out, *The Courage to Teach* isn't a recent publication. I hadn't realized. I went to Amazon to look for it, where I found that the tenth anniversary edition was exclusively available from used booksellers—and in 2016, the twentieth anniversary edition wasn't yet out. I was perplexed. Was a book that had allegedly completely changed educators' whole perceptions of their work really some bargain-bin remainder? I was more skeptical than ever, convinced this book would definitely turn out to be a woo-woo tome I'd rehome at my friendly local used bookstore for pennies.

When my well-worn used copy arrived, I shelved it with my pedagogy collection, where it collected dust, staring at me for at least a couple of years. When COVID hit and I retreated into the solace of reading as a coping mechanism, I picked it up and figured it was time to determine which camp I'd fall into. As it turns out, if there were a cult of Parker Palmer, I *would* sign up. (I kind of have, in fact.)

A Quaker who got a PhD in sociology at Berkeley in 1970, Palmer has dedicated his professional life to helping others bridge the gaps of their divided selves. As a co-founder of the Center for Courage and Renewal (CCR), Palmer has inspired hundreds of people from all walks of life, including educators, to commit space and time to inner knowledge explored in community with others.

Most summers, the CCR offers a Heart of Higher Education conference. Prior to 2020, this was often done in person, but the pandemic shifted this conference online from 2021 forward, allowing a more diverse group of educators globally to join and engage in three days of reflection, community, and rejuvenation. I attended in 2021, and it was a needed and nourishing few days with colleagues from literally around the world. I hadn't yet run across the Tree of Contemplative Practices, but one of our exercises was to sketch out our own tree of sorts. That exercise, especially for a decidedly *not*-artistic academic, generated a visual artifact I still look at regularly to remind myself of what grounds me and brings me joy.

CCR prepares people to join Circles of Trust that are guided by a series of touchstones to lay a strong foundation for courageous community. You can find the touchstones in the sidebar below. Each time I turn to the touchstones, a different one stands out to me as something I want to be mindful of that day. I cannot choose a favorite, as they are all powerful and wise, but I confess I do especially love the embrace of silence as a meaningful participant in a conversation and the admonition to turn to wonder, rather than fixing, judging, or advising.

CENTER FOR COURAGE AND RENEWAL TOUCHSTONES

Give and receive welcome. People learn best in hospitable spaces. In this circle we support each other's learning by giving and receiving hospitality.

Be present as fully as possible. Be here with your doubts, fears, and failings as well as your convictions, joys, and successes, your listening as well as your speaking.

What is offered in the circle is by invitation, not demand. This is not a "share or die" event! Do whatever your soul calls for, and know that you do it with support. Your soul knows your needs better than we do.

Speak your truth in ways that respect other people's truth. Our views of reality may differ, but speaking one's truth in a Circle of Trust does not mean interpreting, correcting or debating what others say. Speak from your center to the center of the circle, using "I" statements, trusting people to do their own sifting and winnowing.

No fixing, saving, advising, or correcting. This is one of the hardest guidelines for those of us who like to "help." But it is vital to welcoming the soul, to making space for the inner teacher.

Learn to respond to others with honest, open questions . . . instead of counsel or corrections. With such questions, we help "hear each other into deeper speech."

When the going gets rough, turn to wonder. If you feel judgmental, or defensive, ask yourself:

I wonder what brought them to this belief?

I wonder what they are feeling right now?

I wonder what my reaction teaches me about myself?

Set aside judgment to listen to others—and to yourself—more deeply.

Attend to your own inner teacher. We learn from others, of course. But as we explore poems, stories, questions, and silence in a Circle of Trust, we have a special opportunity to learn from within. So pay close attention to your own reactions and responses, to your most important teacher.

Trust and learn from silence. Silence is a gift in our noisy world, and a way of knowing in itself. Treat silences as a member of the group. After someone has spoken, take time to reflect without immediately filling the space with words.

Observe deep confidentiality. A Circle of Trust depends on knowing that whatever we say will remain with the people [to] whom we chose to say it—whether in small groups or in the large circle—and will never be passed on to others without our explicit permission.

Know that it's possible . . . to leave the circle with whatever it was that you needed when you arrived, and that the seeds planted here can keep growing in the days ahead.

Reprinted with permission from the Center for Courage and Renewal. Learn more at couragerenewal.org.

You may find the programs or resources available from the CCR to be quite helpful in beginning your inner work, given the preponderance of college and university faculty who turn up for these programs. While the contemplative practices explored earlier in this chapter are enormously helpful, for many reasons, we also need community to help us do some of this work, as Parker Palmer reminds us:

- The journey toward inner truth is too taxing to be made solo: lacking support, the solitary traveler soon becomes weary or fearful and is likely to quit the road.
- The path is too deeply hidden to be traveled without company: finding our way involves clues that are subtle and sometimes misleading, requiring the kind of discernment that can happen only in dialogue.
- The destination is too daunting to be achieved alone: we need community to find the courage to venture into the alien lands to which the inner teacher may call us. (Palmer 2004, 26)

Chapter 6

MOVEMENT—CLARITY THROUGH EMBODIMENT

Yoga is the journey of the self, through the self, to the self.

> The Bhagavad Gita

Many years ago, when I was taking my first (of many) tours through graduate school at the University of Arkansas, a good friend of mine got really into yoga. Like, *really* into it. I don't need to say more; you know what I mean. Seemingly overnight, our conversations had more and more nuggets about what had happened last night in class, or how he'd managed to hold a "down dog"—whatever that meant?!—for longer than he had before, or how the teacher had an emergency, so he taught the class. When he'd share about his yoga class, I'd think, "Sounds...interesting...I guess?" I really had no frame of reference.

MOVEMENT PRACTICES

Goal: Embodiment, physical awareness, perception of emotions.

Useful for those who: Have anxious or restless energy; struggle to identify their own emotional or physical states; feel like a brain on a stick (body).

Connection to teaching: Fostering the ability to feel and stay grounded while teaching; greater attunement to nonverbal communication; strengthening emotional intelligence, which smooths the social aspects of learning and working.

But a few years later, after I'd moved to Texas to take what felt like my first real grown-up job, I joined a gym and decided I should see what this yoga craze was all about. I knew nothing about what to expect, other than the faint recollections I had from talking to Eric about his experiences a few years earlier. There were probably important words in front of the word "yoga" in the class name, but I didn't have a reference as to what they meant. This meant I just wandered into a class. To say it was a disaster is putting it mildly. Looking back, I doubt it was a *hot* yoga class, because I would've turned tail and walked right back out of the room. But it was almost certainly a so-called power yoga class. At any rate, it was not any sort of panacea of self-love and warm, fuzzy feelings. Instead, I struggled to understand what on Earth the instructor thought I ought to be able to do with my body. The only part of the class I could keep up with was the nap at the end—I didn't know the word "savasana," only that apparently we were meant to lie on our backs and close our eyes, so "nap" felt like le mot juste. I did not go back. Ever.

And yet, about a decade later, I decided that I ought to become a certified yoga teacher. A yogi I'd become acquainted with in Nashville offered a body-inclusive yoga teacher training, and while I felt like a complete imposter pretending I could be a yoga teacher, the pull to join the training was unmistakable.

I went to yoga teacher training thinking I was going to learn about alignment and yoga postures and how to teach movement classes. What unfolded was something far more expansive. We dove into anatomy and alignment and all the other stuff, sure. We watched a giggle-inducing video by Gil Hedley, called "The Fuzz Speech," about the role of fascia—the connective tissue that exists throughout the body—and its importance in movement.[1] We reviewed the major postures of a yoga practice and talked about creating sequences. All the things you think of when you hear the word "yoga" were definitely part of my training. I learned about the major poses that comprise the movement, or *asana*, of yoga. We discussed modifications, contraindications for different poses (particularly for those who are pregnant), and how to design a yoga sequence for a class.

But yoga is not intended to be a workout style or a means to attain unusual flexibility. It is a whole ecosystem of tools to assist on the journey inward, informed by centuries-old writings and practices. For example, I've taken a deep dive into the *Bhagavad Gita*, a foundational text in yoga philosophy that deeply influenced, among others, Ralph Waldo Emerson, Albert Einstein, and J. Robert Oppenheimer (Syman 2007).

If we want to use movement practices to build greater presence with ourselves and in our learning spaces, we need to do more than perfect a downward-facing dog or contort ourselves into a plow pose or headstand.[2] Instead, we need to find a movement practice—of which yoga is only one option—that grants us a deeper connection to our embodied experience. For some people, that's a sweaty power yoga class; for the rest of us, developing a sense of how and where our bodies are moving requires something a lot less athletic. Developing that embodied experience of our world gives us access to such rich troves of empathy for and interconnectedness with others, though, and it's why I focus on yoga in this chapter.

I especially love Judith Hanson Lasater's description of the goal of yoga: "In its broadest sense, yoga practice is about inviting what is unconscious to the surface so it can be integrated into conscious awareness" (Lasater 2015, 103). At the root of this practice are two strivings: First, the yoga practitioner seeks connection to what they may call God, the universe, or the Source—the state of "total clarity of awareness" (5). Second, the practices that comprise yoga—the eight limbs—are associated with a deeper connection to our sense of being. These are grounded in a moral code called the *yamas* (restraints) and *niyamas* (observances), which comprise two of the eight limbs (5–6).[3] As Adele (2009) writes, this set of ethics "is designed to bring you more and more awareness of not only your body but also your thoughts" (15).

Below, I share a general description of each yama and niyama and how it can apply to your teaching. I encourage you to reflect on how each of these restraints and observances might impact your own teaching practice. What opportunities exist to practice these ethical principles in your own teaching life?

The **yamas**, which regulate our own behaviors as we interact with others and the world, are as follows:

Ahimsa (nonviolence): The emphasis on nonviolence is related both to our relationships with others and our relationship with self. The goal of nonviolence is to live in community with others, sharing in the gifts of humanity, without causing harm to any of us. Or, put succinctly, do the least harm.

Connection to teaching: Education is—or, at least, should be—a liberatory practice. Embracing *ahimsa* in our teaching means working to eliminate harm to students (and colleagues) through our practices. Working with *ahimsa* might involve looking for equity gaps, such as how your class policies and practices advantage some students over others or how your language might express preconceptions or implicit biases.

Satya (truthfulness): The key, of course, is to practice honesty without causing harm to others. Truthfulness is kind, but kind truthfulness requires sensitivity and awareness.

Connection to teaching: As subject-matter experts, we often fancy ourselves especially good at bringing the *satya* to our work. However, we are human and make factual mistakes. Awareness of your past mistakes and a willingness to own up to future ones falls under the umbrella of *satya* practice.

Asteya (non-stealing): The power of *asteya* comes in recognizing that we have a tendency, when unhappy with ourselves or our lives, to reach out and take from others. *Asteya* asks us instead to be content with what we have—and to recognize that we can grow into the person we want to become without taking from others.

Connection to teaching: Educators who have unrecognized or unacknowledged insecurities are at greatest risk of violating the principle of *asteya*—we boost our egos by ensuring others look or feel less competent than we do. How do your course policies penalize students in ways that boost your sense of power over them? Are there ways in which you are trying to assert your authority for the sake of gaining the upper hand? These are spaces where an *asteya* practice is especially powerful.

Brahmacharya (non-excess): Sometimes characterized as having to do only with the pursuit of sexual gratification, *brahmacharya* is best understood as recognizing the sacred in everyday life. Rather than circling on the hamster wheel of accomplishment and striving, *brahmacharya* counsels us to find peace in what we have, to rest in the enoughness of today.

Connection to teaching: Striving for *brahmacharya* can help academics both in and out of the classroom. In our classes, we often feel that there's not enough time to "cover" our material, so we are constantly trying to cram more and more into our limited time with students, often without pausing to ask whether our students are mastering that material.[4] In our professional lives, we are conditioned to hustle for as many publications, honors, and titles as possible to pave a smooth pathway for promotion and tenure. *Brahmacharya* would look like stepping away from that constant striving and instead appreciating all we *have* accomplished and possess in the present moment.

Aparigraha (non-possessiveness): Echoing this tenet of enoughness, *aparigraha* encourages us to remember that material objects and people cannot be truly possessed, only held for a short time. These things can weigh down our lives until we are owned by them, rather than feeling as though we are the owners. *Aparigraha* teaches us to let go of possessiveness and instead embrace the moment as it is, without grasping.

Connection to teaching: To embrace an *aparigraha* practice in education is to understand that we cannot force our students or colleagues to do anything. We are not the bosses of them; even if we have power over them, ultimately they remain human beings with free will. The more you try to control the behavior of another person, the more they will likely resist, taking you further and further from resting in your present self in the present moment. *Aparigraha* in education is the very essence of presence.

The **niyamas**, which relate to our inner world, are:

Saucha (purity): There are many ways that the concept of purity might be pursued in an unhealthy or controlling way. *Saucha* is not that; it instead seeks to find alignment with our values, our inner selves, and our actions, so that we are not engaging in self-deception, manipulation, or ego-driven actions. This might have something to do with the things we put into and do with our bodies, but *saucha* is much more interested in the landscape of our inner lives—our inner dialogues—than it is with the details of what we eat, drink, or do.

Connection to teaching: An educational application of *saucha* might include avoiding the pernicious gossiping and back-channel communications that dominate much of academic life. Rather than engaging in off-the-record conversations and talking around problems, a *saucha* practice would include honest, respectful, compassionate discussion of issues or misunderstandings directly with those involved.[5]

Santosha (contentment): The thing about contentment is that you cannot work for it. Contentment is inherently present only when we step out of the race of striving and wanting. It is staying right here, in this moment—the presence this book is all about finding and encouraging. *Santosha* is inherently in this exact moment, always. It does not look forward and does not reflect backward. It just is. Right now. Without effort.

Connection to teaching: There are no magic tricks to suddenly embody *santosha*, unfortunately. It requires merely staying in the moment, be that during class, with your colleagues, in faculty meetings, or while you're grading. Try to focus on the now, celebrating that you are here, alive, gifted with meaningful work and the company of others.

Tapas (self-discipline): To engage with *tapas* is to face challenge. Sometimes translated as "heat," the word captures the tenacity it requires to sit with challenge or paradox and not try to deflect or resist. *Tapas* means to sit with the challenge without complaint.

Connection to teaching: Sometimes it can feel like all of academic work is *tapas*—staying present to the challenges and paradoxes around us. For example, we want students to learn, grow, and reach their goals, but so much of education seems designed to thwart those efforts. Holding those paradoxes without complaint does not mean we stop trying to improve; however, it does mean that we recognize that the challenge must be met, not ignored.

Svadhyaya (self-study): This entire book could be described as aiming for *svadhyaya*, or self-study. This *niyama* encourages us to look at the stories we tell ourselves and realize they are a construction of reality, not an absolute truth. The ego is the greatest barrier to *svadhyaya*, as it has no interest in examining our perceptions and stories to test out alternatives. The practice of *svadhyaya* helps us see how we change over time.

Connection to teaching: A journaling practice related to your teaching would be one way to strive for *svadhyaya*. The goal is to see the way we're creating stories out of what's happening. Elsewhere, we thought about the assumptions we might make when a student is habitually late to class. Perhaps our instinct is to assume they lack respect for us or our class, and we tell ourselves a story about that, looking down on our student. *Svadhyaya* would encourage us to let go of that story and examine why it was our impulse in reaction to this student behavior. Why are we assuming disrespect? Are there alternative (perhaps more empathetic) possibilities?

Ishvara Pranidhana (surrender): The surrender in *ishvara pranidhana* comes in recognizing that the vastness of the universe is not within our human control. Embracing this *niyama* means letting go of the impulse to fight what is unfolding, instead understanding that nature will do as nature will do, with or without our consent. Our work is to exist in the moment with an open heart.

Connection to teaching: Teaching is rooted in the paradox of wanting to help students learn, grow, and reach their goals while understanding that we cannot do that work for others. The impulse to try to dictate or control students' behaviors is strong. When we practice *ishvara pranidhana*, we surrender the notion that we alone can chart the course of a student's life. Instead, our work is to walk alongside students, remain open to their hearts and aspirations, and hope that they find their own way.

Whew. Are you feeling like these *yamas* and *niyamas* are ... unrealistic to attain? Me too. But that's why we call it a yoga *practice* and not a yoga *accomplishment*. Just as the contours of your inner landscape are always changing, our work to embrace and embody the *yamas* and *niyamas* is a journey without a final destination. You won't ever arrive. But as goals for living a life of joy, contentment, and happiness? These ethical principles are a good place to begin.

Leslie Kaminoff is one of my favorite yoga teachers, writers, and thinkers. He wrote *Yoga Anatomy* with Amy Matthews, an indispensable illustrated guide to the postures that comprise what we think of as yoga. He once said in a workshop at the Asheville Yoga Center I attended: "Yoga is, most fundamentally, a willingness to question in the moment, or *svadhyaya*. 'Is this serving me?' 'Am I stuck in a pattern?' 'Why am I resisting?' Applying [those] questions, in any context, is yoga. *Asana* [movement] is a great way into that questioning, but it's only yoga when that questioning is incorporated. Otherwise, it's just exercise, or stretching, or weight lifting, or meditation" (Kaminoff 2017).

Yoga as a Tool for Empathy

I can hear you asking: so what? Whether you're moving your body for exercise or in the pursuit of yoga ethics, how on Earth might this relate to teaching? Valid questions, perceptive reader. The path between yoga and great teaching might seem like a stretch (pun intended), but I promise it's not. Yoga and other mindful movement practices fundamentally help us register what's happening in our bodies more clearly and more quickly. Two skills are involved in this awareness. One, interoception, is our ability to sense our internal state, a kind of internal barometer of how we're feeling at any given time. Our bodies are constantly sending us these signals, but some of us are more attuned to them than others. The second, proprioception, describes the "sense that allows us to know where our body parts are positioned in space" (Murphy Paul 2021, 85).

I first learned about the relationship of these senses to overall cognitive functioning in Annie Murphy Paul's outstanding book *The Extended Mind* (2021)—required reading, as far as I'm concerned, for anyone who wants to understand how tools (affordances) outside our brain matter boost our ability to learn, perform, and remember.[6] We can develop stronger awareness of our internal states of being through practice—through mindful attention to the signals our bodies are sending to our brains. Doing so has a cascade of positive effects.

Importantly, developing stronger interoception and proprioception can lead to greater empathy for others. The mechanism by which this happens reveals so much about the mind-body connection, which we too often discard as incidental—prone, as we are, to thinking of ourselves as "brains on sticks" (Hrach 2021). In our brains, we have mirror neurons; these cells behave such that our brains "respond equally when we perform an action and when we witness someone else perform the same action" (Winerman 2005). In this way, our brains are generating biochemical responses to the actions of others to make us feel like we're taking those actions, too.

Murphy Paul writes about it in this way:

> The body's interoceptive faculty can . . . bring us into closer contact with *other* people's emotions. That's because the brain, on its own, has no access to the contents of other people's minds, no way to feel what others are feeling. Interpreting others' spoken words and facial expressions may yield only a coolly abstract sense of the emotions that churn within. The body acts as a critical conduit, supplying the brain with the visceral information it lacks. It does so in this way: When interacting with other people, we subtly and unconsciously mimic their facial expressions, gestures, posture, and vocal pitch. Then, via the interoception of our own bodies' signals, we perceive what the other person is feeling *because we feel it in ourselves.* We bring other people's feelings onboard, and the body is the bridge. (Murphy Paul 2021, 40, italics in original)

Imagine one of your students comes to visit your office one day distraught over his inability to understand a tricky concept from class that morning. His face reflects anguish, and his body language is hunched. Your brain will pick up on that nonverbal communication and mirror it in ways you likely won't be conscious of. Perhaps you'll adopt a similar posture or arrange your facial muscles in similar configurations. Your student sees you mirroring their body language and feels understood, seen, cared for.

Meanwhile, you start feeling distraught because your body is signaling to your brain that it's acting like it's distraught. And all of this—all of it!—is happening outside your conscious awareness. Still, it generates empathy in your body, and it solidifies social bonds between us (see Schmidt et al. 2021). It's brilliant, really.

My experiences both practicing and teaching yoga have unquestionably made me a better college professor. Some of the ways I can see the lessons of yoga showing up in my teaching include:

I'm significantly more aware of the energy of a classroom. It's hard to explain exactly how I perceive the energy level in a learning space, but there's no question that I can sense when the bodies in the room are feeling lethargic, restless, or frustrated. By developing my own interoception and proprioception, I've become much more cognizant of the nonverbal communication present around me. This makes me a more aware (more present) instructor.

I'm better able to incorporate accessible movement into my teaching—always with an invitation to opt out, but in nonthreatening ways that invite students to engage more than just their brain matter in learning. Taking thirty seconds to engage in a purposeful stretch or to move in community with others can imbue a learning space with a palpable sense of community.

My equanimity is deeper. I cannot underscore how much studying and embracing yoga philosophy has helped me embrace myself, my students, and this moment *just as it is*. Imagine how different your experience of teaching would be if you weren't constantly battling frustration and disappointment in the failures of your students. I'm not suggesting that I never experience those emotions—of course I do! But I am suggesting that I can move more quickly into a generous view of my students (and colleagues, and self) since I've begun studying yoga philosophy.

Being more aware of my own nonverbal communication means I can better model curiosity-driven behaviors for my students. When I'm grounded, open, and self-aware as a teacher, my students will pick up on that—probably unconsciously, but it will register. Yoga's ability to help me stay embodied and attentive to my own physicality creates greater possibility for my students to perceive me as someone less defensive, more curious and equanimous. That redounds to everyone's benefit.

Finding Your Yoga

Yoga is an incredible tool for sharpening your interoception and proprioception when done mindfully. That last word is critical; if you're moving without careful attention to the sensations happening in your body, it's not yoga—it's exercise. And while there's nothing wrong with exercise—it's quite good!—if we want to use movement to develop greater self-awareness, it must be done intentionally and attentively. Unfortunately, in my experience, there is a strong current of "no pain, no gain" in the way many yoga classes are led.[7] This is valuable only inasmuch as it brings the yogi into a deeper and clearer relationship with her body and its sensations. The key is to find a yoga practice that allows you to maintain your attention to your own body and the sensations it's experiencing in the present moment.

If yoga is something you've not tried before, it can be incredibly daunting to experiment—certainly, my first experience didn't create a yoga evangelist! Here are some suggestions on what to look for in a yoga class, be it in person or online (streaming or videos), synchronous or otherwise (such as recorded practices or apps):

What language does the studio/teacher use? Look for inclusive language that emphasizes accessible classes for all body types and experience levels, such as Dianne Bondy's website: "Yoga benefits all bodies, regardless of their shape, size, age, ethnicity, or ability."

Who is leading the class? Given your personal relationship with your body and your history of body image, how might practicing yoga under this person's instruction reinforce or relax any negative thoughts about yourself?

What kind of yoga are they teaching? Some are more active styles of practice; you'll see them described as vinyasa, ashtanga, or hatha. These styles emphasize steady movement as a pathway to greater embodiment and awareness. Other yoga styles involve less flow and longer, more intentional stretches; look for names like yin, kundalini, or restorative. In these classes, you can expect to spend more time on the floor, holding postures for 5–20 minutes (or more) and getting a deeper stretch while engaging in breathing exercises or meditation-esque silence.

What temperature will make you most comfortable? Many yoga classes now are taught in rooms with the heat turned up—often around 100–104 degrees Fahrenheit. The rationale is that a warmer room allows greater muscular range of movement and engagement. It also means you'll sweat more, which for some yogis is a bonus. Other classes are held at a comfortable room temperature.

Are you comfortable practicing in a room with others? Group yoga classes are terrific if you want to feel a greater connection to community during your yoga practice. For others, the presence of other bodies moving nearby can be distracting and even pull you out of your own mindful practice. The hard-wired, entirely human urge to compare your body's shape with the shapes around you is fierce. Choose a class that is more likely to help you practice with less self-consciousness. This might be a streaming class or yoga video you do on your own, or you could explore taking a private lesson or two with a yoga teacher you feel comfortable with.

What I hope you observe from this discussion is that it's important to create a practice space and mindset that allows you to keep your attention on yourself. Our novelty-seeking brains will drift to look at others, so creating a space where that is either less possible or uninformative is ideal. Obviously, not all yoga classes can be thus constructed, but it's worth keeping this advice in mind when seeking a yoga class (or other movement class) where you want to exercise some mindfulness. You also have total—total!—permission to deviate from any posture suggestions that don't work for you. Any trained teacher leading a yoga (versus an exercise) class should be prepared to help you modify or avoid problematic poses. For example, I loathe downward-facing dog pose and any breathwork that involves holding my breath. When I take a class, I won't even attempt either, no matter what a teacher might cue.

Once your attention can stay on yourself and your practice, yoga is a beautiful way to connect to your somatic intelligence. Regardless of your relationship with your body, it has innate wisdom.

And, by the way, I recommend *not* calling your body an "it," but using whatever pronouns you use. When I think about my body, I think of *her*—she is always trying to tell me something, and I can tap into her wisdom only if I'm listening. Yoga postures can help me listen better, but so can mindfulness (*pratyahara*), meditation (*dhyana*), mindful breathing (*pranayama*), and other contemplative practices. (Refer back to figure 5.1). For next-level exploration of body-based wisdom and healing, you might investigate either "somatic therapy" or "somatic experiencing therapy" with a provider near you. These therapy modalities focus on reconnecting to the body to work through past traumas or anxieties that may still be impacting our mental and emotional well-being.

Try it!

In this section, I describe two embodiment exercises that just about anyone who can stand can try out. If following along with text is challenging, you can access a video version of each exercise on my website, liznorell.com/yoga. Other great beginner-friendly yoga sites are listed at the end of the book.

Find your stance. I was lucky to get to spend a weekend learning from Leslie Kaminoff, a talented yogi mentioned earlier. Leslie's approach to alignment in postures is unique; he focuses on learning how each person's anatomy creates unique expressions of yoga postures, or *asanas*. He introduced me to this exercise. Read through these directions, then try it on your own. If you prefer to listen to the directions, you can find an audio version at my website, liznorell.com/yoga. Find a space where you have several obstacle-free feet in front of and behind you. If possible, do this exercise barefoot or in socks. Begin by standing still, your feet a comfortable distance apart, hands resting at your sides. (If you're familiar, this is *tadasana*, or mountain pose.) Take a few deep breaths and let yourself become aware of your feet, legs, and hips. Notice how they're feeling and whether they are comfortable where you are. Do this without looking at them; just turn your attention (not your gaze) to these areas on your body. Now, close your eyes and take three slow steps forward. Do this mindfully, paying attention to the sensations generated when each foot lands on the ground anew. Pause after three steps, taking a few deep breaths, staying connected to how your feet, legs, and hips are feeling. Now, take three steps backward, eyes remaining closed. Again, pay attention to how your feet respond each time they land on the ground. Once you've arrived back at (roughly) your starting position, focus your attention on your hips. With your eyes still closed, adjust your feet to find whatever stance makes your hips feel most comfortable—so that they're not grasping, tightening, or aching. Play with turning each foot inward or outward, one at a time. Move your feet closer together and farther apart, a little at a time. Bend your knees a teensy bit and then straighten. Keep adjusting until your stance feels comfortable, natural, easy. Now open your eyes and look at your feet. What do you notice? Are they faced forward? Outward? Inward? Do they mirror one another, or does one foot differ from the other? This is an exercise in finding the stance that works with your unique anatomy, in your unique body. If you have a regular yoga practice, this is your natural *tadasana*. Don't feel you must achieve some idealized version of mountain pose; it's not objectively "right" to have your toes touching, or your feet facing directly forward. It's also not necessarily correct to have your feet behaving identically. As Kaminoff says, "We cannot balance an asymmetrical body with a symmetrical practice" (Kaminoff 2017).

Take a moment to imagine how adjusting your stance while teaching might impact the learning environment. This could be as simple as not remaining behind the podium for the entirety of class (entry-level stance experimentation), or as complex as varying how your feet are positioned relative to students. Are your knees locked or slightly bent? How grounded do you feel before you begin a class? Try playing with your stance in class one day and see how the energy of the class (including yours!) might change.

Wake up your feet. This is one of my favorite experiments in body awareness to do in yoga classes. For this exercise, you're going to need a couple of small balls. A tennis ball, bouncy (pinky) ball, or—best—a ball with tiny spikes on it will work.

My favorites are available on Amazon.com and are called spiky massage balls, available in a two-pack for under $10. The first time you do this, use whatever you have handy or can get easily; after you've done this once, you may be persuaded to invest in an inexpensive set of massage balls. (They're great for more than just this exercise.) Once again, we're going to assume a standing *tadasana* pose, or mountain pose. Find your natural stance, hopefully the one you discovered in the last exercise. Slowly let your awareness drift from the soles of your feet, up through your ankles, calves, knees, thighs, hips, trunk, chest, shoulders, arms, hands, neck, and head. As your awareness drifts up, notice any places of tightness, soreness, muscles clenching, or any other sensations. Once you've made it to the crown of your head, take a few deep breaths and notice how your overall balance feels today. You may not notice much here, but see how stable your feet feel, how grounded you're feeling, and whether your body is naturally swaying or adjusting as you stand. If it helps, close your eyes while you tune your attention to those sensations. Once you feel you've got a handle on that, take out your ball and spend at least two minutes rolling it under each foot. You can toggle back and forth between your feet for thirty seconds at a time, or you can do a full two minutes on each foot. Work the ball back and forth, from your toes to your heel, left to right. Use a wall or chair to keep your balance as you apply pressure onto your foot as it rolls over the ball. Once you've finished at least four full minutes of ball rolling, let both feet return to the floor and repeat your *tadasana* from before. As you scan from the soles of your feet, up your body to the crown of your head, notice what feels different this time. Some questions you might ask yourself: How much of my foot feels like it's in direct contact with the floor? Is that more or less than I felt before? How comfortable are my feet? How much is my body swaying now, compared to before? How relaxed is my body? For most people, this exercise jangles awake the nerves and tiny muscles in their feet, and they report the post-ball-rolling stance feels more relaxed, more grounded, and yet more energetic. Because your feet are doing more of the work of grounding you, your core muscles—your abs and back, your glutes and hamstrings—need to engage less, allowing your entire body to relax a bit more. This is not an argument for walking around barefoot on rocks daily, but it is a reminder that our modern lives often allow some of the musculature and nerves designed to make movement easier to go unused much, if not all, of the time.

What might experimenting with your sense of your feet yield in your teaching spaces? I have no idea! Perhaps you're game to try some of these experiments with your students one day in class, or perhaps you'd rather be stealthy in your explorations of your groundedness. But I again invite you to play around with some of this in the context of your teaching spaces, explicitly or quietly. Does your way of interacting with students shift when you have woken up the soles of your feet and can relax your posterior chain—that series of muscles along the back lower half of your body?

Chapter 7

PLAYING BIG

What happens in our inner lives shapes our outer realities.

Tara Mohr

Playing Big is a program, a book, and a framework for thinking about how we behave around our deepest desires. Created by Tara Mohr, the Playing Big model helps women play bigger in their lives—and, importantly, do so on their own terms. Mohr began her career in editorial work after earning a BA in English literature from Yale. She then moved into the business world, consulting with mission-driven organizations after earning her MBA from Stanford. She writes about how those experiences shaped her understanding of how we limit our own opportunities by

---

PLAYING BIG

Goal: Making peace with your inner critic; taking action on your goals.

Useful for those who: Struggle to take the first step toward bigger goals; experience imposter-like feelings; identify as female or nonbinary.

Connection to teaching: Generating empathy for learners who may experience imposter-like feelings, especially those who are first-generation college students, historically minoritized, or otherwise have marginalized identities.

143

listening to the voices that keep us safe—and small—at work. Her book, *Playing Big: Practical Wisdom for Women Who Want to Speak Up, Create, and Lead* (2015), explicitly seeks to help women unearth the fears below the impulses to play smaller.

However, the tools she develops are useful for everyone, not just those who identify as female, in at least a couple of ways: Not only are these tools universally helpful for inner exploration, reflection, and growth, but it's also important for each of us—regardless of our gender identity—to witness how female-identified professionals are systematically encouraged to stay small and compliant with the dominant culture. As we explored in chapter 3, the often toxic culture of higher education creates conditions in which all of us benefit from thinking carefully about our role within this culture.

The central thesis of Tara Mohr's work is that many of us—especially women—resist "playing big," often out of fear.[1] The imposter syndrome, discussed in chapter 1, that so consistently plagues academics (and others) finds plenty of reasons to make our lives, our aspirations, and our work smaller than what our heart yearns for—and our talents are equipped for. Unfortunately, the defense mechanisms our ego builds to protect us from failure and shame mean that we often don't even realize what those aspirations might be.

Instead, we look to the external markers of success defined by the world—you know, kind of like how our students look to the grades we assign as indications of their academic value, rather than determining what they hope their education might mean for their learning or growth. Those external determinants of status and achievement become our pursuit, rather than the things our truest self might find important, meaningful, or rewarding. The more we chase those external validations, the further we move away from knowing and following our own yearnings. Playing big is about seeking reacquaintance with what will truly fulfill our desires for our lives.

There are many ways to engage with Mohr's wisdom. The book is an obvious starting point, but Mohr also offers a Playing Big program, which allows you to work through the material in the book in community with others. For those of us who love a good training program, she also offers a facilitators' training program, usually with a special bonus cohort for those in education who see the applicability of the program to our work. There is a treasure trove of content on her website for those who want to dip their toes in before plunging into a book or program. Regardless of how you might engage with Mohr's work, however, there are several tools in the Playing Big toolkit that have been especially useful for me as I've worked to identify the ways in which I want to play bigger. Below, I sketch out a few . . . but there is much more detail, and many more tools, available in her book. I encourage you to investigate Mohr's work more deeply if any of these resonate for you.

Inner Critic and Inner Mentor

Self-doubt and self-criticism are hallmarks of imposter syndrome, and they spring from an "inner critic" that, for many, sounds like a loop of negative thoughts in our minds. It is all too easy to sketch the inner critic as a petulant demon child who hates everything about us. Sometimes programs or coaches will even suggest creating a cartoonish version of our inner critic, complete with horns and a snarl. Not Mohr, though. What I especially appreciate about her discussion of the inner critic is her recognition that the inner critic's role is a tender one, motivated by vulnerability and fear. Ultimately, the inner critic's job is to keep us from failing, from hurting, from suffering. If we don't take risks, we lose nothing. The inner critic's voice is meant to keep us safe, even if that limits what we might dream or achieve.

One of my most pronounced encounters with my own inner critic came my junior year of high school. (And yes, I'm actually going to tell you a story about the internecine politics of high school clubs, so brace yourself.) I had served as vice president of our Rotary Club–affiliated organization, Interact, that year, which had nicely positioned me to serve as president my senior year. However, for reasons still unknown to me, my very closest high school friend—*who had not even been a member of the club until our junior year*—was persuaded by the outgoing president to run for the office. I was devastated. Betrayed. Petrified of finding out that my friend was more liked than I was. And so, rather than running against someone I feared was more liked, I declined to run. Our friendship suffered. I conceded to being the club's Student Council representative, but I was otherwise fairly inactive in the organization my senior year. I took no risks. I did not lose the election, true, so my inner critic did a great job of keeping my ego safe. But at what cost? In the end, I lost confidence, the opportunity to grow and learn, and a measure of closeness with someone whose friendship I treasured.

My inner critic told me I was unpopular, unlikely to win, and better suited to a lower-profile role. Those messages weren't conceived out of spite, though—they were motivated by fear, by vulnerability, by hurt. Screaming back at the inner critic won't help . . . just as screaming back at someone on the internet will almost certainly only make things worse. Instead, the compassionate response to the inner critic is to acknowledge the fear with which it's leading: "I appreciate your concern, but I'm strong enough to handle disappointment." Had I had access to this wisdom at age seventeen, I might have realized that running for president and failing would have been a far richer, more meaningful experience than refusing to try. By stepping out of the race, I let the voices of fear win and, in so doing, I became even more convinced of my unpopularity and weakness. The inner critic won because fear won.

If there's one thing graduate programs do well across the board, it's amplifying our inner critic. (Return to chapter 3 if you need reminding.) I invite you to look back at your own graduate school experiences and reflect: In what ways did your experiences in graduate school impact the way you think about your work as a scholar and teacher? Do you find yourself, in your work, engaging in critical self-talk about your choices, actions, and results? When you read about a new teaching technique or pedagogical practice, does the idea of giving it a try wake up voices that sound something like: "You can't do this," or "My peers would think less of me if I did this," or "I'm not _____ enough to pull that off"?

If so, it's possible your inner critic is holding you back from growing as an educator. Becoming aware of the voices of the inner critic is a critical first step in loosening their grip on you. The inner critic is not wrong to be afraid; it's just trying to keep you playing safely in your current way of being. But as Susan David so eloquently writes in *Emotional Agility*, playing it safe long-term means engaging in "dead people goals"—depriving yourself of the life-giving effects of trying new things, growing beyond your comfort level, and risking failure on the way to learning (2016). In other words, the inner critic is a challenge to your learning—just as it can be, incidentally, for your students.

GETTING TO KNOW YOUR INNER CRITIC

I was recently on a Zoom call with four colleagues for peer support. Basically, this is a kind of professional learning community (see chapter 3 for more on PLCs). We each had fifteen minutes to share a challenge or question we were facing and to get support—whatever that might look like for us—from the others. One of my colleagues, a brilliant woman, talked about how she was struggling to trust that the world would be able to see what talents and skills she possesses. As she spoke, I was struck by how much negative self-talk I was hearing. I felt like I was hearing directly from her inner critic and not from her full self.

The inner critic is so clever, that one. It's insidious and oh-so-good at pretending to be the voice of reason and not the head of the despair squad. My writing coach and friend Jen Louden likens the inner critic to the "itty bitty shitty committee"—and I confess I just *love* this visual. Whenever I hear Jen talking about the itty bitty shitty committee, I immediately conjure in my mind a team of people sitting at a round conference table, brainstorming on a flip chart ways to destroy my confidence and sense of equanimity. That visual turns out to be quite useful, actually. Tara and Jen both suggest visualizing—in as much detail as possible—your inner critic. You might draw a sketch, find a photo, or craft up a tangible object to represent that part of you that wants to play small and stay safe.

Listening to Your Inner Mentor

But the inner critic isn't the only internal voice that wants to shape us and our actions—it's just the loudest. Mohr describes what she calls our inner mentor, sometimes called the inner teacher (notably by Parker Palmer). The inner mentor is the quieter part of us, the part that knows what we want to do, but is so often drowned out by the rather noisy fearmongering of the inner critic. If, like I once did, you hear the phrase "life coach" and immediately recoil a bit, listen up: The most valuable thing I learned during my own life coaching program was that life coaching—unlike therapy, unlike what you're probably imagining—does not offer advice. Coaches are trained to help clients tap into their own inner wisdom and chart their future paths. Each of these traditions recognizes that underneath all the cultural noise and hustle paradigms, we know ourselves better than anyone else can. Coaches trust that, if you get really quiet and step away from the expectations of others, you can connect to a deep, instinctive sense of what you want. You can uncover what work calls to you, what kinds of feelings you want more of, what your deepest desires are for your life. It just requires turning down the volume on the voices that speak in "shoulds" and "cannots."

I'll be frank with you: The inner mentor isn't going to speak loudly. In fact, if you're used to living with a sassy inner critic, as I am, you may even start to think you are missing the inner mentor. Thankfully, Mohr provides tools to help you connect with this quiet and wise voice inside you. She has a guided meditation and visualization exercise that has been transformational for me. (Other frameworks will call this exercise a "future self" visualization.) Regardless of what it's called, this exercise involves first relaxing fully, then imagining visiting yourself twenty years in the future. It's a short visit, but you ask a few open-ended questions about what your future self wants you to know in the current moment and what she's learned in the last twenty years.

The first time I did this visualization exercise, I was staying at an Airbnb on a farm in Chattanooga, Tennessee. Although I lived only an hour away, I had to be at a morning function to support students participating in a Model United Nations conference, quite early on a Saturday, so I stayed overnight at a rustic cottage on the farm. After wrapping up with my students Friday night, I went back to the cottage, lay back on the cozy bed, turned on the meditation MP3, and closed my eyes. As I've mentioned a few times, I'm pretty skeptical of things that sound woo, and this exercise definitely challenged that. I honestly expected very little. But as I let myself be guided through the meditation, I slowly let my skepticism go and imagined this conversation with my future self unfolding.

Future Liz was living in the house my partner and I had just purchased. She had turned the formal dining room into a welcoming space to sit and talk among stacks and stacks of books. It was cluttered but charming. She said her name was Joy, and she radiated love, gratitude, warmth, and acceptance. When I asked her what I needed to know, she advised me to be patient, confident, and courageous and to love with an open heart. She beamed as she talked about the countless students she had taught over the years and those who had moved on to do amazing things. She gave me a tight hug and bowed in a heartfelt blessing of *namaste*. As I wrapped up the visualization and came back into the present moment, I was astonished to find my cheeks wet with tears. It was a profoundly moving experience. Calm overtook my senses, and I slept unusually peacefully that night, which rarely happens when I'm away from home.

The inner mentor visualization may not be as moving an experience for you, and I've even seen it feel traumatic or overwhelming for others. In other words, this may not be the tool for you in this moment . . . and that's okay. If you are feeling resistant to this visualization, perhaps instead imagine zooming back in time to yourself twenty years earlier. What advice would you give your twenty-years-younger self? What would you suggest that person embrace? What to let go? What will really matter to your future happiness? What isn't so important? And how does that thought experiment help you reorient your perspective on your life now?

The key to this exercise is the perspective we gain when we focus on the things that will impact us long-term. When faced with the minutiae of everyday life, relatively inconsequential decisions can come to feel like weighty choices. Should I go to the disciplinary conference this year? Which journal should I submit my paper to? Am I spending too much time on social media? The inner mentor can give us access to the inner wisdom that allows us to zoom out enough to see the present for what it is. The truth is that very few of our daily moments will linger long. If we can keep our focus on the things that *will* linger, a path unfolds to do the things we find most meaningful. The inner mentor helps shine a light on that path.

Particularly for women in academia, the inner mentor can become your wisest advisor. That's because *you know* what you want—I firmly believe that. You know what you want your life to look like, how you want to feel at work, and how you want to spend your precious time in this life. Unfortunately, though, the notion of claiming those goals as your own is wrought with cultural messages telling us to stay small and quiet and play it safe. The inner critic doesn't want you to have to deal with pushback by challenging the status quo; the inner mentor knows you'll never reach your fullest potential if you don't. The inner mentor–future self visualization exercise has the potential to help clarify your deepest career goals and reassure your inner critic that its worries, while useful, are unnecessary. In an academic landscape rife with challenge, uncertainty, and wobbling mental health, our ability to remain grounded in our own goals and in moving forward on our path is especially challenging. Using this tool is one way to dampen the inner voices rooted in fear.

Hiding

We hide when we're trying to put off something scary. Mohr also calls the urge to hide a kind of "this-before-that" thinking. As the name implies, it pops up when we imagine that there is some accomplishment or milestone we must reach before we can strive for the really big goal. Examples of how I've been touched by this-before-that hiding are: "Once I get my PhD, then I can start researching this other question that's tugging at my interest." or

"After I've been teaching for X years, then I'll have the credibility to write a teaching book." or "I will wait until I've got tenure to try to change the culture at my college." Each of these puts off the work that my heart desperately wants to do, because it's work that scares me. Each of these actions requires a pretty significant intellectual, career, or emotional risk. What if I fail?

Confession: I'm extraordinarily accomplished at hiding. I remember a close friend asking me some twenty years ago, "When are you going to write a novel?" I answered that I needed to live a lot more life before I could do so with credibility or confidence. About a year ago, that same friend reached out to ask if I was there yet. I felt called out. (And also, no, I'm not there yet.) Reading *Playing Big* really acquainted me with my impulse to make excuses for not acting now. It taught me to question that underlying story that I'm not ready enough, credible enough, or experienced enough to do something I know I want to do. Recognizing my skills at hiding pushed me to ask, "What's the worst that can happen?" And then, the worst did.

I am fundamentally a nonconfrontational person, but I recognize in myself the capacity to become quite intransigent when I catch a waft of injustice. Intransigent isn't strong enough, actually; I get abrasive, self-righteous, and quite sarcastic. This is not something I'm proud of, incidentally, but thanks to the inner work I've done over the years, I have begun to be able to see this happening in close to real time. As a community college professor, I was unfortunately given many opportunities to practice noticing my injustice-triggered maladaptation on the loose.

Community college students lead unusually precarious lives; researchers estimate that 29 percent of community college students experience food insecurity and 14 percent experience housing insecurity (CCCSE 2022, 2). Presence with my students means I get above-average exposure to the trials in my students' lives. Sometimes, those trials can be traced back to policies and practices of the institution itself, and that is when I found myself in the trickiest of positions—the ones that could have had the biggest impact on students' lives, but also the ones that jeopardized my standing with college leadership.

In a particularly fraught situation that I will only generally describe here, a dual-enrollment student approached me with concerns about comments made by another professor that had made her uncomfortable. The class was discussing a reading that involved promiscuous activity by a woman, and the professor was asking entirely different questions of the women and the men in the class. My student, a sixteen-year-old female and devout Christian, was appalled by the questions the professor asked the women. The class had taken place on Zoom during the pandemic, and the student had recorded the class conversation on her cell phone. The student approached me to say that she wasn't sure how to proceed, that her parents were incensed, and that she was thinking about sending the video to the local TV news station.

Because the discussion centered on the students' sexual activity, I urged her to file a Title IX complaint. I showed her how to do this and suggested she share the video as part of her complaint. It was in the second half of a semester, and she was worried that filing a complaint would doom her chance to earn a high grade in the class. I assured her that the investigation would be done professionally and that any evidence of retaliation would be handled seriously.

In the end, the professor was found to have acted within their First Amendment–protected discretion, the student earned the only non-A grade of her collegiate career, and she was promised (in writing) the opportunity to switch into a different section of the class—only to have that promise reneged upon because of how late in the semester the investigation wrapped up. She was disappointed, and I was, too—disappointed and angry and disillusioned by the contention routinely made that our college centered student well-being and inclusion.

It was quite some time later when this incident came back to haunt me. In my tenure year, the chief academic officer (CAO) of the college recommended I be denied tenure because of my actions in this incident. In the recommendation, the CAO wrote, "One occasion I can speak about is when she referred a student who had an issue with an instructor to the college judicial officer instead of to the faculty member or the [division] dean. While Dr.

Norell's desire to help students is commendable, there is an organizational hierarchy and professional relationships to recognize and develop. Dr. Norell is not new to the College, so she should be aware of this hierarchy." My advocacy for the student, which adhered to the mandated annual Title IX training, was weaponized to deny me tenure.

This might invite the question of whether hiding is a strategy worth embracing in the fragile pre-tenure years of a college teaching career. Only you and your conscience can answer that question, but I have no regrets. My experience advocating for this student and working to create a culture of genuine care at my college was rooted in the values and priorities I had clarified through my own inner work journey. Had I failed to stand up for the student as I did—had I ignored the mandatory reporter requirements of my role—I would have violated my own conscience. This is the power of seeing your hiding tendencies for what they are. Yes, they seek to protect you—but, in so doing, they stand in the way of living out your values and conscience.

Another way hiding manifests might resonate for you, too—it's what Mohr calls "evermore education." Maybe I just need to get this one other degree, you might say. Oh, I saw an interesting certificate program on Facebook the other day—maybe I should do that? So many of my friends and colleagues fall victim to the evermore education impulse. I can't tell you how many graduate certificates and second doctorates I've considered. I can tell you that I've probably weighed obtaining every social science or education-adjacent master's degree that exists. My friends talk about taking courses in freelance writing or user-experience research. Perhaps you can identify with these impulses, too. Evermore education is just another way to delay the bigger actions we yearn to take, the ones fear holds us back from taking, with what feels like an indefensible decision to learn and grow. Incidentally, falling down a Google rabbit hole is a small-scale way that evermore education can manifest. Sorry to call you out like that.

If evermore education, or hiding in general, is something you recognize in your own life, consider this alternative: Maybe you already know enough. Maybe your unique experiences and perspective are enough to get started. Maybe you don't need to accomplish something else or obtain more education before you try. Maybe the worst thing isn't actually the worst thing. Maybe inaction is actually the thing you'll regret most later on.

This book is for faculty who want to experience more meaningful work. But for those who seek to exit academia, these fears can be particularly strong. Translating academic experience outside of our ecosystem is neither obvious nor confidence-inspiring. Chapter 3 deals more directly with academic culture. Here, I'll simply encourage you to adopt a strengths-based mindset over a deficit-oriented one.[2]

Leaping

This leads directly into the last of Mohr's tools that I'll share here, one she calls leaping. The defining characteristics of a leap are that it:

- Connects to something around which you want to play bigger.
- Will allow you to gather more information on an unknown part of that thing.
- Can be described with a short phrase.
- Could be finished within 1–2 weeks.
- Makes you feel the kind of fluttery, because-I-am-so-excited fear (and not the heavy sense-of-doom kind of fear).
- Puts you and your work in front of your intended audience.

Leaping, in short, requires us to take a small but meaningful step—a leap!—toward our ultimate goals. When I wanted to write this book, my initial leap looked like signing up for a week-long writing retreat with writing coach Jen Louden. I wrote about 15,000 disorganized, stream-of-consciousness words that week, and I began to feel, for the first time, the chains of imposter syndrome loosening. (For more on imposter syndrome, revisit the sidebar in chapter 1.) And then the academic year began, and my pages fell lower and lower in my list of recently opened Google docs. My next leap came when, facing some challenging and frustrating

COVID-related changes in my campus work, I decided to devote less energy to fighting unwinnable battles and more energy to this book. I signed up for another writing group with Jen, one that had me sending five or six pages of writing each week to a peer for structured feedback. Each of these leaps helped me learn what the writing process would look like for me, how it might integrate into my life as a professor, how to recognize the fluttery fear of potential, and how to put me closer to my intended audience. Those leaps were critical in getting this book into your hands; I'm completely convinced you wouldn't be reading this had I not taken those leaps.

What sort of leap would help you make small but significant progress toward your goals? Think of this as your growth edge—that next step that you haven't taken before, that feels a wee bit scary, but that you objectively have the skills and knowledge to take. What is your growth edge right now? Do you want to try out a new pedagogical framework or teaching tool? Want to explore a new vein of research? Lead a study abroad? Attend a specialized conference? Sit quietly with this thought for a while, asking yourself what possibility on the horizon gives you that frisson of excited energy, the kind that makes your skin feel fizzy and your mind whirl with possibility. Some of the possibilities that spring to mind probably make you feel a deep sense of insecurity or fear—and that's okay. Those aren't where you'll find your leap. Instead, home in on the possibilities that feel *just* out of your current reach, the ones that you know you'll do *someday* but haven't yet found the right time for. The ones that will put you into closer touch with the work you really, *really* want to do. Choose one of those, and then figure out a smaller version of that goal, something you could do in a couple of weeks, and test out the possibilities. It's not a Superman-sized leap over tall buildings; think of this as a hopscotch-sized leap, from one square to the next (possibly skipping a square, if you want to get fancy).

Try it!

Choose one (or more!) of the prompts below and do some reflective writing/journaling on it. Set it aside and come back later—perhaps later in the same day, tomorrow, or in a few days. What Playing Big strategies might help you move forward with what you unearthed?

- Sketch out what your ideal day looks like. Answer questions like:
  - What time do I get up? What are my morning rituals?
  - What kind of work do I do during the day? How much am I interacting with others, and who are those people?
  - What does the rhythm of this day feel like? How would it feel to inhabit that rhythm?
  - What evening rituals close out my day? What time do I go to bed? How do I feel—emotionally and physically—at the end of the day?
- What dreams might I have for my career, but they feel so impossible that I won't even allow myself to consider them? Why am I so convinced they're impossible? Do I have evidence for that impossibility?
- In what ways are you holding yourself back from taking action toward your goals because you feel like you need to do something else first? Are you engaging in the evermore education trap? How would you fill in this gap: I need more _____ before I can pursue my goals (e.g., education, job security/tenure, practice, time, money, maturity)?

Chapter 8

WHO AM I? AS SEEN THROUGH THE ENNEAGRAM

> If we can allow ourselves to be gentle with ourselves no matter what our feelings may be, we have the chance of discovering the very deep roots of who we are.
>
> Fred Rogers

If you are a psychologist, chances are good the chapter title has already got your blood pressure spiking. Charitably, research psychologists consider popular personality typing tests about as useful as they do astrology (e.g., Geher 2021), learning styles (Furey 2020), and other pseudo-science-y trends.[1] To be fair, there is not a lot of rigorous research on personality that finds its way into the *Cosmo*-quiz-laden pop psychology books available on your local

---

PERSONALITY FRAMEWORKS

Goal: Understanding the ego and its instincts; awareness of behavioral patterns.

Useful for those who: Want to deepen understanding of how the ego shapes their instinctive behaviors, particularly when under stress; crave a framework for understanding the self/ego.

Connection to teaching: Understanding how the ego influences our mindset toward, and reactions to, learners; creating opportunities for meeting learners with more grace.

bookstore shelves.[2] This chapter will not seek to debunk decades of psychological research—that's decidedly not the purpose of this book, nor do I fancy myself capable of writing such a thing. Neither will this chapter advise you to change your entire life based on the results of any personality test.

Instead, this chapter seeks to use an increasingly popular tool, the Enneagram, as a lens to help you dive into how your ego impacts your behavior, particularly in times of stress. The Enneagram doesn't diagnose or prescribe. It's a tool that helps us understand what our ego's go-to defense mechanisms are—because once we understand those instinctual reactions, we can watch them happen in real time and, if we choose, make a different choice. Unfortunately, though, our egos are usually hard at work outside our conscious awareness. This isn't because we're raging jerks, but because the ego is powerful. As researcher Scott Barry Kaufman writes, "I define the ego as *that aspect of the self that has the incessant need to see itself in a positive light.* A noisy ego spends so much time defending the self as if it were a real thing, and then doing whatever it takes to assert itself, that it often inhibits the very goals it is most striving for" (Kaufman 2018, italics in original). The Enneagram makes the hidden mechanisms of the ego more readily visible. It is like a decoder ring for the cryptic messages of our instinctive behavior. It is a potentially useful tool for quieting the ego. This matters for our work here because a quieter ego allows for a more present you.

I'll talk more in the chapter ahead about the limited scientific, peer-reviewed research about the Enneagram. For now, let me tell you a story. At a recent dinner I attended, one of my colleagues mentioned the Enneagram, as he knows I am an Enneafan (a word I just made up, but I think it works). Another colleague at our table of seven said, "Oh, I KNOW you're not bringing up a personality test at dinner with a psychologist!" Perhaps what I've said above will convince the skeptical to dive in here. And if not, please thumb ahead to chapter 9 now. It's a good one, filled with evidence-based psychology that will make your heart much happier and lower your hackles. Promise.

Exploring the Enneagram

While there is an entire cottage industry of personality testing and profiling, few of these tools go much beyond providing a snapshot of the contours of your personality. As Jim McPartlin writes, "The biggest reason I champion the Enneagram over all other [systems] is its driving message: *You are fine just as you are*. But *being* is not the same as *knowing*" (McPartlin 2021, 19). "The Enneagram does *not* attempt to change you," he continues. "It will, however, illuminate your patterns and help build on strengths that serve you well, while teaching you how to let go of those that don't" (19–20). This has been my experience as well.

Like every teenaged girl I knew, I lived for the *Cosmo* quiz that would tell me something fascinating (and probably cryptically positive) about myself. The summer I turned seventeen, I was first exposed to the Myers-Briggs Type Indicator (MBTI) test at a six-week academic camp for honors students in my state. I was captivated reading the description of my MBTI type (INFJ, if you're curious). I felt deeply seen and understood, something we all crave. And yes, I was definitely falling victim to two related effects—the Barnum Effect, which describes the tendency for "people [to] accept general personality interpretations as accurate descriptions of their own unique personalities" and the Forer Effect (Dickson and Kelly 1985).[3] These personality descriptions are often vague, double-headed, generally applicable, and favorable. When I first read the description for my alleged MBTI type, I certainly felt that someone had peered deeply into the inner recesses of *my* soul and understood something about me that nobody else had ever seen.

It's a little precious, right? The problem, as I now see it, is that I had no clear path forward once I'd discovered this information. Short of passing out a one-sheeter about my INFJness to everyone in my life, how would this knowledge help me? Perhaps it might create a sense of inner psychological safety, in that I wouldn't see some of my quirks as inherently bad or wrong. But there was no path for growth out of the MBTI.

In many ways, the popular discourse around the Enneagram can be just as superficial as my initial exposure to the MBTI.

At the dinner I mentioned earlier, three of the seven of us had a sense of our dominant type, and so our four clueless dining companions heard us saying things like, "I'm a one and my husband is a four." "Oh, wow. I bet that's tricky, isn't it?" As though the Enneagram could uniquely explain why two people in a marriage experience challenges around effective communication. (insert eyeroll) When the Enneagram comes up in groups of people who think they know their type, it can quickly become an impenetrable and exclusionary conversation that sounds an awful lot like a cult (Montell 2021). Wings! Arrows! Subtypes! Instincts! There's a whole lingo.

This can all be true *and* the Enneagram can be helpful. As I've learned more, I've come to see the utility behind the framework. That's because the Enneagram can be used to help us cultivate greater awareness, acceptance, and growth. While the Enneagram does not ask you to change anything about yourself, awareness of your default patterns of behavior can allow you to make a different choice, rather than falling back on your comfortable routines, particularly when stressed.

While the Enneagram is not specifically designed for or by faith communities, the embrace of the Enneagram among American Christians has led to an explosion in its popularity in recent years. The publication of *The Road Back to You* in 2016 brought this framework into popular consciousness. Its author, Ian Morgan Cron, is an Episcopalian priest, and his use of an explicitly Christian lens to apply the Enneagram continues to attract readers and students.

The roots of the Enneagram date back millennia, with the popular understanding of this framework emerging around 1900 with the work of George Gurdjieff (McPartlin 2021, 13). In the 1950s, Oscar Ichazo began incorporating lessons from the Enneagram into modern psychology in his work at the Arica Wisdom School in Chile (Hook et al. 2020, 866). Claudio Naranjo, a student of Ichazo's, translated his teacher's lessons into existing Western psychological systems, especially those related to diagnostic criteria and "psychodynamic theories of character structure." While academic research on the validity and reliability of the Enneagram is sparse, it does exist. Meta-analyses like Daniels et al. (2018) and Hook et al. (2020) suggest that the existing evidence of the model's utility merits further scholarly study. In particular, Hook et al. (2020) find that the Enneagram dovetails nicely with theories of attachment style. The authors also link the Enneagram's focus on breaking negative cycles of self-sabotage by pursuing ego-motivated coping mechanisms with "psychodynamic models such as Time-Limited Dynamic Therapy" (869; see also Levenson 2017). Daniels et al. (2018) explain that the Enneagram helps facilitate personal development through "an increase in awareness and empathy and less identification with ego" (232). Hook et al. (2020) surmise that "a clear understanding of Enneagram personality development, then, suggests that it is more of a psychodynamically informed theory of character structure and growth than a static personality trait theory or typology." They further conclude, "Research provides initial evidence that the Enneagram can be a helpful tool for promoting personal and spiritual growth" (879).

A growing body of research in health science education recommends using tools like the Enneagram to meet students' professional requirements. To maintain accreditation status, for example, Doctor of Pharmacy (PharmD) programs are expected to help students meet the following standard: "4.1. Self-awareness—The graduate is able to examine and reflect on personal knowledge, skills, abilities, beliefs, biases, motivation, and emotions that could enhance or limit personal and professional growth" (ACPE 2016, 2). Childs-Kean, Edwards, and Smith (2020) examine a variety of personality frameworks that might boost PharmD students' ability to engage in personal reflection and development in meaningful ways.

Did that quick overview of scholarly research persuade you? Maybe not. But despite all the skepticism the first few pages of this chapter may have engendered, I fundamentally believe that this way of looking at your larger patterns of behavior, especially your teaching behaviors, can be enormously helpful in cultivating presence in and out of the classroom. A foundational principle of Enneagram teachings is that each of us contains aspects of all nine types, but that we default to one type, or our "dominant" type, particularly when we're feeling stress or pressure. It's less that we are one cluster of traits and more that we interact with the world in particular ways, with particular goals, and with particular needs.

The Enneagram gives us nine "types"—really, nine ways of interacting with the world or (as Jerome Lubbe [2020] describes it) nine energies. Each ego type has a core desired feeling, a core fear, and a particular response to stress or setbacks. No person is exclusively one type, but we're especially good at or comfortable with our dominant type's ego-preservation strategies.

The hard-core scientists among us will object that there is no scientifically valid test to determine your dominant type—and they're right. I've heard Enneagram typing described as an art, a process—and not even a clear, linear process at that. You might be tempted to think of this as a weakness of the framework; however, I see it as a strength, a reason to trust this framework more than your run-of-the-mill *Cosmo* quiz. Rather than presenting the Enneagram as a one-size-fits-all tool and reductive filter for all human behavior, those who embrace this framework understand that our ego is going to complicate any effort to see beneath its loud voice with clarity. The more you engage in self-study, the more clearly you can see yourself, the good and the less-good, and not just the pristine image of self that your ego wants the world (including you) to perceive. In other words, the fact that no Enneagram test can perfectly predict your dominant type allows us to engage in an individualized process of inner inquiry and learning, rather than accepting a single view of our inner life without doing any work ourselves.

So how do you get started? The best advice I can give you is to take a test or two (see the resources at the end of this book) and hold the conclusions lightly. As you get deeper into your own self-exploration, you may find—as I have, many times—that your initial hypothesis is probably a misreading of your own experiences and patterns of behavior. This is expected. Welcome this as another invitation to practice a growth mindset.

You'll find some of my favorite Enneagram books and resources in the Additional Resources section. However, I also want to share some basics of the Enneagram with you here, to spark your curiosity. In truth, you don't need an actual test because—as my psychology professor friend Emily reminds me regularly—these things aren't scientific in any scholarly sense of the word, anyway. You can read the descriptions and suggestions below and see what feels like a reasonable working hypothesis for you. You'll find a lot of information available freely online, and there is a burgeoning number of Enneagram coaches, writers, and thinkers out there who can help you dive more deeply if you're interested.

Dimensions of the Enneagram

Briefly, it's worth explaining how a few of the building blocks of the Enneagram work. Here are two dimensions that you'll see used in Enneagram books and resources frequently:

Passions: The way we use the word "passion" in everyday life isn't how the Enneagram framework uses it, so you'll be forgiven for getting tripped up here. In the Enneagram world, a passion is something you are obsessed with, something that drives your behavior, particularly when you're under stress. It's not something you love deeply; it's something that consumes your thinking in a detrimental way. For example, the passion of Type Twos is pride. We don't love being proud, but we are deeply invested in seeing ourselves as good people with only the best of intentions (even when we do not have the best of intentions). We'll push back on any insinuation that we are not inherently good people, because that quality is our passion—meaning we cannot let it go.

Core desires: Each Enneagram type has some emotion or state of being they desperately want to achieve. For the Nines, that desire is inner stability. My partner is a Nine, and he becomes physically uncomfortable with conflict of any kind, to the point that if it's left unresolved, he will become physically ill. The **core fear** of each type is the flip side of the **core desire**; it's the quality or state of being each type wants to avoid most. So the core desire of a Three is to feel valuable and worthwhile, and the core fear of the Three is being worthless.

Understanding the Nine Types

Below, I provide a short summary of each type. This summary is based on years of study, reading, and experience with each of the nine types. James Baldwin said, "You cannot fix what you will not face." For me, the Enneagram is an indispensable tool for identifying what I'm not facing—but that, if faced, I could "fix," not by changing my fundamental nature, but by making a different choice in the moment.

Type 1: The Perfectionist

Sometimes also called: The Reformer, The Idealist

Ones want to get everything capital-R Right, first and foremost. They have very strong feelings about the proper way to do something, and they get easily frustrated when others make different choices. Ones have especially active inner critics; they are extremely hard on themselves, unwilling to forgive any oversight or accident they make. They live a life of rules. Because of their perfectionistic tendencies, they are especially bad at allowing others to help them or do something for them. For that reason, they are at especially high risk of overwork and burnout. Despite having very loud and very mean inner critics, they are especially sensitive to criticism.

- Core fear: Being "bad," corrupt, unredeemable, or chaotic
- Core desire: Being "good," aligned with God or the sacred, having integrity
- Passion: Resentment—a continual frustration and dissatisfaction with oneself and the world

Type 2: The Helper

Sometimes also called: The Giver, The Mentor

Twos are natural servants. They thrive in service positions and may gravitate toward teaching because of its orientation to others. They freely give love, compassion, empathy, and grace to others, often without precondition. The world is quite willing to take advantage of their sweetness and generosity. In fact, when Twos remain relatively unaware, they will do almost anything for anyone if it means they will be seen positively and appreciated. At higher levels of awareness, Twos set boundaries on their giving and value their own emotional and mental health equally to that of others. They crave recognition and appreciation.

- Core fear: Being without love
- Core desire: Being loved and being a source of love
- Passion: Pride—pride in one's virtue, to deny one's own needs or suffering

Type 3: The Achiever

Sometimes also called: The Performer, The Motivator

Threes live and die by their accomplishments. They are constantly chasing recognition and gold stars, defining their self-worth through what they have managed to achieve. Threes sincerely want to be the best they can be—which is a good quality! But taken to the extreme, Threes lose sight of their inherent value and become engulfed by their egos.

- Core fear: Being worthless and deficient
- Core desire: Feeling valuable and worthwhile
- Passion: Vanity—efforts make the ego, not one's true self, feel good

Type 4: The Individualist

Sometimes also called: The Romantic, The Original

Fours typically have artistic, romantic souls that look for creative outlets and deeper meaning. They often feel as though there's something missing from their lives—if only they can figure out what that is, then they'll finally be happy and fulfilled. They crave self-understanding and exploration. Often artists, writers, creators, or performers, Fours are deep individuals who are not content with surface-level conversations for long. Depth is their jam.

- Core fear: Having no identity or significance
- Core desire: Finding one's true self and significance
- Passion: Envy—something fundamental is missing

Type 5: The Investigator

Sometimes also called: The Observer, The Thinker

Fives feel like the world may overwhelm them at any moment. They are deeply introspective and curious about the world, and they have quick, intelligent minds. Their natural curiosity often excites them, leading them to learn a lot and often invent an entirely new way to handle a complex problem. They are whimsical, idiosyncratic, and independent. Fives are the most likely to feel like they weren't just born in the wrong country or wrong era, but that they were born on the wrong planet. When at lower levels of awareness, Fives can be withdrawn and impassive. At higher levels of awareness, though, they recognize that true presence comes from contact with others.

- Core fear: Being unable to know what is real and true
- Core desire: Understanding reality
- Passion: Avarice—too much interaction may bring catastrophic depletion

Type 6: The Loyalist

Sometimes also known as: The Skeptic, The Trooper

Sixes plan everything. They have backup plans, and backup plans for those backup plans. They are concerned about being caught unprepared. You might be a Six if you twist René Descartes's classic proposition as, "I'm anxious, therefore I am." You want a Six in the exit row when a plane malfunctions; they've studied the emergency pamphlet and will be poised under pressure. They see themselves as providing stability and security within their spheres, troubleshooting problems and finding solutions. However, this constant vigilance is exhausting, and Sixes are highly vulnerable to burnout because of it. Their dedication to others and their natural talents at building community mean they are drawn to professions like teaching. In times of uncertainty, though, Sixes may be especially at risk of extreme stress.

- Core fear: Being lost, without orientation
- Core desire: Finding a trustworthy orientation so they are secure
- Passion: Fear—of things not happening now; doubting or worrying about future events

Type 7: The Individualist

Sometimes also known as: The Epicure, The Visionary

Sevens are joy come alive. They crave novelty, adventure, and adrenaline. This restlessness comes from classic FOMO—the fear of missing out. They sense they do not have joy within themselves, so they're constantly looking for it outside of themselves. Because of their constant pursuit of the new and exciting, Sevens can be mistaken as childish—but they are not. Instead, they are child-*like* in their enthusiasm for living. Sevens are fun to be around, usually, unless you're trying to get them to look within themselves. The ego of a Seven wants to do literally anything other than examine itself. As generalists with excitement about a range of things, Sevens are often accomplished achievers and do many things well.

- Core fear: Deprivation, being in pain
- Core desire: Feeling alive and without pain
- Passion: Gluttony—the insatiable desire to fill up on every pleasure life can give

Type Eight: The Challenger

Sometimes also called: The Champion, The Protector, The Boss

Just as you know when you're in the presence of a Seven (because they are so boundlessly fun), you will know when you're around an Eight. They are fierce advocates who aren't afraid of a necessary fight. They've learned to stand up when something feels wrong or violates their values. Deeply principled and resourceful, they are often the change-makers in society. Activism and advocacy come naturally to them, and they are drawn to leadership roles. They naturally protect and provide for those in their circles. Eights have a can-do attitude and are determined to find a solution to any problem you might bring them.

- Core fear: Being without life (being impotent)
- Core desire: Being alive, strong, and powerful
- Passion: Lust—the constant need for intensity, control, and self-exertion

Type Nine: The Peacemaker

Sometimes also called: The Harmonizer, The Mediator

Nines abhor conflict. They want everyone around them to be content, if not happy, all of the time—and certainly happy with them. Nines will bend over backward to ensure nobody is disappointed in them. They worry that conflict will mean disconnection, and nothing feels scarier to a Nine than being without connection to others. To be around a Nine is to feel safe, trusted, and appreciated. They do not demand others change or become someone else; instead, they are serene and accepting of others. Nines are often unselfconscious and unpretentious. They're genuinely nice people who are easy to be around. Because they abhor conflict, they're often quite good at mediating challenges—but only if the parties don't become hostile or aggressive, which will cause the Nine deep distress.

- Core fear: Being fragmented, disconnected, and cut off from everything

- Core desire: Having wholeness and inner stability
- Passion: Sloth/disengagement—a desire to be unaffected by life

Understanding My Two-ness

As a tool for self-expression, the Enneagram has provided me with incredibly rich insights and powerful tools to maintain greater presence in every sphere of my life, including—and perhaps especially—with my students. To give you a sense of how that plays out, I'll share a bit about my own journey with the Enneagram. At a retreat for women held in the Blue Ridge Mountains of north Georgia, I went to an optional workshop on getting to know yourself better. The entire workshop was an introduction to the Enneagram, describing the nine types and giving us a quick exercise to try to identify our dominant type. For some, this quick test was a challenge; for me, it could not have been easier. I quickly formed a working hypothesis of my dominant type—I'm super-efficient in Two energy, as Lubbe (2020) would say. Twos are called the "Helpers," and when I turned to the short description of the Two, I read things like, "Twos essentially feel that they are worthy insofar as they are helpful to others. Love is their highest ideal."

I wasn't overwhelmed by what I read, honestly; I'm somewhat inured to reading descriptions of my personality or behavior and identifying with what I'm reading. (Those Barnum and Forer Effects are real, y'all!) What really struck me in this initial exposure to the Enneagram, though, was the somewhat casual observation our facilitator made, saying Twos often feel like they have to hustle for love by imposing their helpfulness on others. Nobody's ever said it to me quite like that, but I was intrigued. I filed this away, but I didn't do much more exploration then.

About ten months later, I started a life coach training program, even though the phrase "life coach" made me so uncomfortable that I wasn't capable of saying it without a smirk. All I knew was that I wanted to do it anyway. (Perhaps a touch of the "evermore education" was at play? See chapter 7.) I had to be away from my obligations at work for three days before classes began, so I had to get permission from my dean and provost. In seeking that permission, I said that I wasn't totally sure *how* this program would benefit me, my students, and the college, but that I was sure it would. Truer words were never spoken.

As part of my program, I was required to complete sixty hours of coaching over the course of nine months. In practical terms, this meant that my co-trainees and I arranged for several coaching swaps a week . . . and that I became the beneficiary of *a lot* of coaching myself. There was one peer, with whom I swapped a few times, who was especially great at cutting through my instinct to hold myself in high positive regard. (This is true for all types, but it's a core part of a Two's identity.) She asked tough questions, ones that wouldn't allow me to hide behind my veil of virtue. One question still—several years later—haunts me; it went something like this: "If you are forcing your help on others because you want them to love you, aren't you just bullying them into loving you? And is that really *love*?"

I hadn't been terribly impacted by my first glance at the Enneagram framework, but that question shook me. It allowed me to see how my instincts, the ones that flowed from a place of genuine care for others and a genuine desire to leave a positive mark on the world, were undergirded by fear. The central fear of a Two is that we are unloved and unlovable; by helping others, we can feel appreciated in a way that temporarily soothes that fear. My entire teaching career, seen through this lens, could be described as a way to boost my own ego, a bypass around presence, a way to placate my anxieties.

By coming to this realization, I could begin seeing my impulses in action. When a student came to me with an issue they were struggling with, I could sense that helper instinct rising, celebrating the opportunity to feel useful. In that moment, I could leap directly into problem-solving mode, thinking about what I could do or say to ease the student's burden. Doing so would ensure my ego got a little boost—*Look at how helpful you are! You are such a good person, Liz!*—and I'd feel more confident the student would have positive regard for me, their super-helpful-and-caring professor. But I could also choose to step back a little, focus my attention on the student himself or herself, and ask more questions. To, essentially, put on my coaching hat and give the student space to talk more. That doesn't mean I would never again try to help—far from it. But it *does* mean that my first impulse could be paused while I gave the student space to determine what *they* could do to make life easier. If they needed my help, they would ask.

Try it!

My impulse is to design a self-exploration plan for every type—but I know that's the Two instinct in me arising. Instead, I encourage you to reflect on the descriptions above and see if one or two sound particularly familiar. Then Google that Enneagram type and start chasing rabbits down holes, as little or as much as you like. It's worthwhile to keep these questions in mind:

- What does my ego get out of avoiding my basic fear?
- What if my ego is wrong, and I *can* handle tackling my fears head on?
- What if I already have everything I need?
- What could I do differently next time I notice myself avoiding something out of fear?

Chapter 9

CONFRONTING OUR BIASES

Do the best you can until you know better. Then, when you know better, do better.

Maya Angelou

This chapter is a bit different. For starters, this chapter doesn't ask you to cultivate a self-care practice or dive into understanding your personality in isolation. Instead, it aims to shine a light on the ways our brains trick us out of challenging our long-held beliefs. No question, this can be uncomfortable.

What's more, this chapter might unintentionally seem to imply that the work of confronting our biases is entirely the responsibility of the individual. Instead, I see surfacing and addressing bias to be a both/and scenario. Friends know I'm

---

UNCONSCIOUS BIASES

Goal: Unearthing cultural roots of cognitive shortcuts; understanding their impact on behavior.

Useful for those who: Want to adopt a more inclusive, equitable, culturally relevant mindset; are ready to confront cultural biases that may be influencing them.

Connection to teaching: Fostering a more inclusive classroom environment; understanding how, when, and why some learners fail to achieve their goals.

fond of saying, possibly ad nauseum, that we cannot solve systemic problems with individual action (for all the reasons discussed in the imposter syndrome sidebar in chapter 1). *And,* as the Margaret Mead quote reminds me often, "Never doubt that a small group of thoughtful committed individuals can change the world. In fact, it's the only thing that ever has." As with most pithy quotes, Mead's obscures the very real work of social movements and organizing, but it nevertheless points to the power each of us has to influence the thinking and actions of those nearby.

You're likely reading this book because you've already done some of this work. Higher education professionals who pick up this book are unlikely to be novices when it comes to understanding how bias can influence our interactions with one another. I encourage you to try to set your ego aside as you read. Your ego is going to get defensive, and that's both expected and okay. If it helps, think about a myth about your discipline that really gets your goat. For me, it's the notion that if we'd just implement term limits, corruption in government would magically vanish. (Ahem. It wouldn't.) And oh! How I wish I could wave a magic wand and change the entire country's mind on this. But I can't. Digging into this chapter's brief exploration of cognitive biases helps us know *why* and *how* to do better. Let's make Maya Angelou proud.

An Assignment

I have an assignment for you. You're a good student—you're a professor, after all!—so I'm going to trust you to do your homework before proceeding with this section. I need you to go read the *Oatmeal*'s comic that begins, "You're not going to believe what I'm about to tell you." It's cited in the references (Inman 2023), and it's far more effective at introducing this topic in a way that won't send your adrenal system into *as* high of an alert state as any words I could use. (There is a rated-G version and a *definitely-not-rated-G* version. Choose the one that aligns with your tolerance for swearing.)

Hmmm. Are you still here? I really mean it—go read that comic now. I'll wait.

drumming fingers
staring out window
taking a drink of water—hydration is important!
quick stretch—motion is lotion!

Okay, I'm going to take it on faith that you've done as I've asked. And whoa! How much of that information was new to you? I know I had a few moments of scratching my head, metaphorically, and wanting to do some extra-thorough checking of those sources. (And if you're wondering *What kind of comic has sources?* Then you just outed yourself as a homework-skipper, and I want you to remember this moment the next time one of your students *claims* they totally did the reading before class, even though every morsel of memory of that reading seems to have escaped them. Because you just did the same thing, friend. No judgment. Just an observation.)

The backfire effect is potent. We don't even notice it happening, we just sit back and let the waves of our righteous indignation crash over us, enjoying the incredibly satisfying sense that we were right all along. I mean, it really does feel AMAZING to be right, doesn't it?

Except . . . friends, I'm sorry, it's just so, so dangerous. And as your friendly neighborhood political psychologist, I feel duty-bound to tell you that the extent to which you're hurting discourse in this country is directly proportional to how often you feel that satisfying sense that you were right all along. Because the fact is, our brains are absolute misers. Their willingness to be generous with thinking energy makes a sloth look downright frenetic. Our brains take shortcuts all the time. If they were cars navigating a cross-country drive, you can bet they'd be the ones taking shortcuts through cow-strewn fields to shave off thirty seconds.

Put bluntly: your brain doesn't want to admit it might be wrong, and this is dangerous. It's a common, understandable, efficient, and entirely human preference for taking the easy way out. It's not like your brain is lazy; it is keeping you alive, day after day, after all. It just wants to hold as much energy as possible in reserve, you know, in case you get in a life-endangering pickle. The brain is really the Enneagram 5 of our physiology, in other words. (I couldn't resist.)

I'm deliberately being punchy here because any time you decide to examine your biases, it's going to get uncomfortable quickly. So please, try to lay down your defensiveness. Take a few breaths. Maybe do a *metta* meditation (chapter 5) and make the object of your focus your ego. She's SO dramatic, and all that drama has probably worn her out, so perhaps invite her to go take a nap for this section.

Why You Should Care

As I ended a recent semester, I met with a night class of students for the last time. It was a melancholic evening, as the last day of class always seems to be for me. I get attached to my students and to the community we build, and it's sad to know that we will never again be together in a space like that. At the end of class, as students were packing up to leave, I offered a hug to anyone who wanted one. That's when Eric (not his real name) approached me. We had a powerful interaction wherein it became clear that Eric was used to being disregarded or censored by the authority figures in his life.

A bit about this student: While he had no formal or institutionally facilitated accommodations that I knew about, Eric displayed the classic behaviors of neurodivergence—possibly autism, possibly ADHD, possibly both (AuDHD, it's sometimes called). He would routinely stand in the middle of a class meeting, pace around, walk out the door for a few moments, and then come back, and he always—always—had something to contribute to any topic of discussion. He was smart, perceptive, and well-informed, but his verbal and nonverbal behaviors were of the sort that get labeled as disruptive. They didn't bother me, and in an effort to create a space where my students could just be themselves, I never mentioned them.

A week after class ended, I was reviewing the short student videos I assigned as a final reflection for the semester. I call these "impact statements," and the goal is to capture in a 4–6-minute video what during our time together had the biggest impact on them. One student, after reflecting on the course material, surprised me when she included a reflection on Eric's behavior the first night of class. She was sitting in the same general area as he was, and she described his frequent movements and comments as disruptive—but not annoying, she added. She said she kept waiting for me to say something, to ask him to be quieter or move around less. The fact that I didn't shocked her.

As this peer continued to reflect, she said she realized that she had some repetitive behaviors that others might find disruptive, like her tendency to click a pen repetitively or to shift in her chair audibly. She also shared that when she was younger, she was the child in her classes who was called out for being disruptive and was punished frequently for doing so. In thinking through this, she realized nothing Eric was doing was bad, that I was giving him space to exist without correction. "Stuff like that made me think that when someone is doing something different to what is normally allowed in the classroom, you immediately think that they're a bad student or have bad behavior or something," she said, "but seeing you be so patient and kind towards someone ... I saw that, and I appreciated that." I like to think this student had a moment of healing as she thought through this experience. I hope that her noticing that, instead of censuring or reacting to Eric's behavior, I just remained present to his thoughts and ideas, without commenting on his behaviors, spurs more mindful attention to how she interacts with others.

This experience reminded me of the power of our biases to impact our nonverbal, sometimes even unconscious behaviors in ways that may harm our students. Left unexamined, our biases can undermine any other inner work we take on. When our intentions don't engage with our biases, we may send conflicting messages to our students (and colleagues), which can undermine trust.

Everyone Is Biased

I think back to Madeline Dore's (2022) observation that, in some ways, we resemble sponges. Sometimes we're in a period of absorbing—like when I spent several months just reading and thinking and coalescing my ideas for this book—and sometimes we're in a period of squeezing—like when I tried to write this entire book in the span of three months. (Unsuccessfully, I hasten to add.) Our biases come from absorbing the cultures we live in and move through. We could try to resist them, but they absolutely surround us, and they're going to seep into our sponge. And then we encounter someone or something novel, and we can't help but squeeze out some reactions that are rooted in that culture. I'm willing to admit I've probably tortured this metaphor—but I think you understand the point. The cultural messages we receive become part of our automatic thoughts, the ones that happen before we bother to examine them.

Again, this does not make you a bad person. It makes you normal, human, and efficient—and also sometimes wrong. But to err is human, and our responsibility is only to observe, learn, and try to do better.

There are a host of cognitive biases worth acquainting yourself with, because they're every bit as common as the backfire effect and, potentially, as damaging to our work as educators. There are terrific resources for doing so, including Wikipedia's regularly updated "List of Cognitive Biases" and the Cognitive Bias Codex you can download from the Wikimedia Commons. (I know of at least one campus library with a poster-sized framed version of that image.) Here are a few that strike me as particularly helpful for us as educators:

Bandwagon effect: When lots of people believe something to be true, you're far more likely to trust it than the alternative. In other words, common wisdom makes us all less smart, in that we are far less likely to examine the evidence for these common beliefs than less-popular ones. Want to know why this should matter to you? Here's one reason: Neuromyths. You can find terrific resources online from cognitive scientists and researchers that will go into the details of why a student's preferred learning style doesn't impact their learning, or how we don't only use 10 percent of our brains.[1] There is a fabulous questionnaire you can download and share with your students and colleagues from

Pooja K. Agarwal and Patrice M. Bain's book, *Powerful Teaching: Unleash the Science of Learning* (2019), and the website they built to support the book, available at powerfulteaching.org.

Status quo bias: We dislike change—the devil you know and all that. Particularly for educators who have been at it for a while, the notion of making radical changes to the way we do things can be destabilizing and threatening. This can sometimes show up as the impulse to shoot down a younger colleague's ideas by saying something like, "We tried that X years ago, and it didn't work." Rosenberg's entire book is basically an indictment of the status quo bias in higher education (2023).

Confirmation bias: When we believe something to be true, even if it's just a hunch, we will readily accept any information that confirms our hunch without much examination. Conversely, we'll be quite skeptical of any contradictory evidence, digging deeply to find a methodological issue or other error to explain that evidence away as anomalous. This shows up in our relationships with colleagues and students. Say, for example, you suspect that your student John is cheating on his exams, or that Alice is chronically late to class because she's undisciplined. Any evidence that John has performed much better than earlier in the semester will make you more certain something nefarious is afoot, just as Alice's falling asleep during class will reinforce your perception of her laziness. What if, instead, John is simply working hard and improving? Or maybe Alice has recently lost her housing and is living on a friend's couch, begging rides to campus from anyone who can offer them? You have already settled on an initial guess, and you're unlikely to look for evidence that you're wrong. What's more, your initial guess will shape how you interact with John and Alice in potentially harmful ways.

Fundamental attribution error: This cognitive bias has to do with the difference between how we explain our mistakes versus those made by others. We tend to think of ourselves as competent, well-intentioned people whose errors are generally because of circumstances. I didn't miss a deadline because I'm poorly organized or easily distracted; I was too busy doing important work and it slipped my mind—could've happened to anyone in my circumstances. But when it comes to judging the errors made by others, we tend to think their failures are the result of personal qualities. John did poorly on the first exam because he didn't study hard enough, and Alice comes late to class because she lacks discipline. In other words, we assume our mistakes are oversights, whereas the mistakes of others are character flaws.

Dunning-Kruger effect: The last cognitive bias worth noting in this very condensed list is one that I suspect we have all experienced—not that we'd readily admit it. The Dunning-Kruger effect occurs when we are overconfident of our skills or knowledge when we actually know relatively little about a topic. The opposite can also be true, that we underestimate our skills or understanding when we are experts—though this latter case isn't as commonly observed as the former. Ultimately, the Dunning-Kruger effect can be the result of poor metacognitive skills, and as a result it's likely to show up in your students, particularly those who are already at higher risk of challenges in your classes—the first-generation, minoritized, or otherwise less privileged students you teach.

The Thorny Bias—Race

Regardless of how you might identify politically or ideologically, each of us has a responsibility to confront the historical reality of the United States' treatment of indigenous and minority populations. Simply put, there are students in your classrooms who are carrying the weight of our shared history, and if you want to experience true connection and play a part in the transformation of their lives, you must do this work. There is no shortcutting the awkwardness or pain it may bring you; however, I can testify that this work has the power to transform entire communities in positive ways. I hope this section will convince you of the imperative necessity of pushing through the discomfort.

Let me be really clear about the fact that I am a White woman who has lived a fairly comfortable life filled with privileges, ones I have largely taken for granted. Only in recent years have I been able to see those privileges for what they are. I'm not an expert on racial justice, anti-racism, or social justice. I'm a student of these topics, every bit as much as I suspect you might be. My advocacy for this work has sprung directly from my participation in communities of practice. I've read, listened to the wisdom and experience of others, and tried to approach this with the most open mind and open heart I can. We are living with centuries of persecution of entire communities, and we are not going to address, in any meaningful way, the problems springing from history's long shadow if we work in isolation. This is a shared history, and it must be a shared process of reconciliation and healing.

Many years ago, a colleague who primarily teaches in our paralegal program made a somewhat off-handed remark to me about a book he had just read, *Just Mercy* (Stevenson 2014). "Have you ever considered using that in your American government course?" he asked. I confessed that I hadn't heard of the book or its author, Bryan Stevenson, but I made a note to look it up later. That summer, I was recruited to teach a five-week summer bridge course at a nearby regional university. This grant-funded course included about fifty students, identified based largely on their incoming ACT scores, who were seen as being at risk of academic struggles in their first semester of college. During that time, the students would take two courses concurrently, engage in community-building activities, and earn a weekly stipend for completing the requirements. The goal, based on a persuasive body of evidence, was to create a learning community that would give these students a network of support when the fall semester began. All I knew about these students was what I've shared in this paragraph. I would be meeting with them three times a week for five weeks; the other two weekdays, they'd be completing work online and independently. I knew I needed to think creatively about how to create a sense of community and investment among these students, and I assumed that I would have a rather diverse set of bodies, minds, and hearts in the room.

Remembering the conversation with my paralegal studies colleague, I decided to abandon any textbook for the course and instead assign *Just Mercy*. This meant I had to read the book, too, which I did in the two weeks before our course began. Like many of my students in the years to come, my first reading of the book was, in many ways, the proverbial lifting of the veil on my ignorance of racial inequities and the legacy of slavery in our country.

My heart broke so many times while reading the book. There was a single short sentence about halfway through—I won't repeat it here, because I don't want to say anything to convince you not to read the book—that so shook me, I had to put the book down for a solid week before I could circle back.[2]

While many of the students in my summer bridge class described themselves as not liking to read, I asked them to give the book at least four chapters before they gave up on it. We read a few chapters at a time, and then every week or so, we'd make a big circle in the classroom and spend about an hour going around the circle to share reactions. I asked each student to share one scene or moment from the book that left an impression on them. It could've been something that surprised them, shocked them, took an emotional toll, or felt relatable. Just share one thing. As we went around the room of about twenty-five students for the first time, there were a few scenes that came up repeatedly, but, for the most part, each student had reacted to something different. Only one confessed she hadn't read any of the book yet, saying, "I just really hate reading and I don't see the point." (She later turned out to be one of the book's biggest fans.)

The experience was powerful, for me *and* for the students. I had asked them to keep a weekly journal, reflecting on what we did in each class. They would turn them in on the last day of the week, and I'd read them over the weekend and return them on Monday. The impact of these circle chats was clear. Even among those students who were relatively quiet during class time, they were honest and raw in their journals. Some shared stories about how scenes from the book paralleled their own experiences. Others expressed shock that the degree of racial discrimination portrayed in this book was in the relatively recent past. Students noted that we were meeting less than five hours away from where the stories in the book took place. For that reason, the students could identify with much in the book, no matter what their race or personal experiences.

Although unintentional at the time, the incorporation of *Just Mercy* into my American government course marked the beginning of my efforts to shine a light on issues of racial injustice in my courses.[3] At the end of each semester, I have asked my students whether they believe the book is relevant to our course; the overwhelming majority says yes. I poll them on whether I should look for something different to read, and I've had many students (dozens) threaten to hunt me down if I ever assign something different. "Everyone needs to read this book," they tell me emphatically. I've now assigned it to more than a thousand undergraduate students, and only one told me she thought it was boring or a waste of her time. Those who assign books in college classes will recognize that this *simply does not happen*; there are always students who complain about reading assignments. Whatever magical talents Bryan Stevenson has—and I'm convinced they are many—count among them his ability to write a book that students almost universally treasure.

Part of the reason I have appreciated *Just Mercy* is its narrative style. Research tells us that storytelling has deep resonance with the human psyche (Cron 2012; Gottschall 2012). Stevenson's masterful weaving of minor characters into the narrative arc emphasizes the many faces of racial injustice in America today. It touches the young and old, across the range of neurological talents, of many races and economic statuses. Students almost always find someone in the book to whom they can relate, regardless of their backgrounds. The narrative presentation of information about the criminal justice system allows students to cultivate empathy for the characters and for Stevenson himself.

When thinking about how you might incorporate more race-conscious materials or lessons into your courses, my experiences suggest this is a useful lens for doing so. As this chapter has suggested, that process begins with your own exploration of how America's racist past impacts your understanding, your behavior, and your language. There is no quick way to unpack these historical influences; you must do the reading, do the self-examination, and have the difficult conversations that allow you to become more aware of and present to your complicated cultural understandings. Know that this work will be challenging, indeed threatening, to the way you see yourself and your world. Plunge ahead anyway, as it will give you the tools and the confidence to help your students do the same.

Try it!

This is tender, vulnerable self-exploration—there's a reason I made it the final tool in this toolkit! Be gentle with yourself. Remember: *We all have biases.* Your biases do not make you a bad person; they make you human. We cannot fix systemic problems with individual adjustments, but we can become aware of how systems impact us. That process means we have an opportunity, if we choose to take it, to make a different choice when we see those systems operating on us.

Project Implicit

Harvard's Project Implicit is a rich trove of analyses that you can explore to surface some of your own implicit/subconscious biases. The tests are based on the Implicit Association Test (IAT), a method of measuring differential response times based on things that are culturally preferred versus things that run counter to the dominant culture. The test moves too quickly for your self-monitoring and self-regulating impulses to ensure you look "unbiased." Again, this does not make you a bad person. It does help shine a light on the automatic, unconscious ways your brain works. Knowing this alone won't change those beliefs, but your work to surface those unconscious biases can help you work on ensuring they don't become your default choices. In other words, by shining a light on your instinctive responses, you can know when to pause and question whether you're making a cognitive choice or resting on your cognitive defaults.

We will all fall victim to the cognitive biases explored in the first part of this chapter—it's an entirely human reaction. Here are some questions that can slow down your thinking, giving you time to check your default assumptions:

- *What evidence would persuade me that I'm wrong?* If you struggle to answer this one, chances are good you're experiencing confirmation bias.
- *What feels threatening about an alternative explanation?* If you're feeling very destabilized by the possibility that your

beliefs are incorrect, you may be falling into the backfire effect or confirmation bias.
- *How would others react if I had a different perspective?* If it feels quite threatening to imagine disagreeing with your colleagues, there's a good chance you're falling into a bandwagon effect.
- *Why am I reacting in this way to someone's behavior?* If you're getting frustrated, angry, or dismissive because of someone else's behavior—*especially* if that person is a student!—it's worth asking what assumptions you're making about the behavior. Otherwise, you risk making a fundamental attribution error.
- *How much do I really know about this topic?* When you feel the impulse to make a stringent statement of fact, check yourself: are you really an expert, or have you just acquired a familiarity with the topic? The Dunning-Kruger effect is one of the hardest to spot in our own thinking, but it's worth checking yourself.

The American Academy of Family Physicians (AAFP) recommends eight strategies for reducing biases, using the acronym IMPLICIT (Maryville University 2022)[4]:

- **Introspection:** Using tools like those at Project Implicit or by engaging in self-study, identify what biases you have.
- **Mindfulness:** Identifying those biases is an important step, because once you're aware of them, you can become more mindful of how and when they might impact your behavior. Keep in mind that this is more likely when you're feeling pressured or stressed. Exercise the mindfulness tools we explored in chapter 5—pause, take a few breaths, and check in with yourself—when you're feeling that pressure.
- **Perspective-taking:** Put yourself in the shoes of people with other identities or cultures. How would your experience of a situation change if you were standing in their shoes?
- **Learn to slow down:** The goal here is to interrupt your automatic reactions and assumptions (as we did with the *Oatmeal* comic exercise at the start of this chapter). When

you're in conversation with or considering a person with a different identity than yours, before jumping to a stereotype, pause to remember all the people you've known personally who share this identity. Think about how different and nuanced each of them is. Keep this in mind as you consider behaviors or qualities of others.
- **Individualization:** Instead of thinking about how a person shares traits with others in their identity groups, focus on how they are unique. What traits do you share with this person?
- **Check your messaging:** Take a close—perhaps uncomfortably close—look at how you're using language in your syllabus, in your assignments, and in class. Are you unintentionally or implicitly communicating harmful messages about expectations? What about how you talk with colleagues who have different identities or backgrounds than you? If you have a trusted friend or colleague, perhaps ask for feedback about how you use language and whether there are opportunities to be more inclusive. Just make sure you're not demanding others do emotional labor to educate you or asking people you don't know well to act in ways that may feel professionally risky. A good practice is to make a request and invite the person to say no.
- **Institutionalize fairness:** Work within your own systems to promote policies, practices, and cultures that emphasize equitable practices. Review your existing policies, procedures, and campus climate and identify a small number (two or three, perhaps) areas where you could make improvements in your inclusivity.
- **Take two:** By this, the AAFP means you're not going to get everything right the first time you try. Give yourself and others the grace to wobble at first, and then reflect, adjust, and try again. You've been steeped in your culture, with all of its inherent and implicit biases, your entire life. You cannot unwind that overnight, or really ever. What you can do is keep trying to be a little bit better each day. I'm reminded of our Constitution's Preamble, where the Founding

Fathers set out a goal of creating a "more perfect union." That recognition that we'd never achieve perfection, but that we'd continue to strive toward the goal of betterment, is a useful lens for viewing this work.

Have the Hard Conversations

In her book, *So You Want to Talk About Race,* Ijeoma Oluo shares a few principles to keep in mind when you begin having conversations about race—though these principles will apply to difficult conversations on other topics, too (Oluo 2018, 45–48). They are:

- **State your intentions.** Make sure you're explicit about what the goal of the conversation is, and make sure your conversational partner(s) will go along with that goal.
- **Don't let emotions hijack the conversation.** If you can keep that goal in mind, you'll be less likely to let defensiveness—I stress, *a totally natural response*—interfere with that goal.
- **Do your research.** Please don't ask someone else to educate you on something you could easily Google. Instead, do your research first, then start the conversation. If you realize you are in unfamiliar territory, hit pause and do some more research before proceeding. This is especially important in conversations with people of color about race.
- **Beware of oppressing other groups.** It's easy to shift the blame onto other groups (e.g., southerners, the uneducated). Don't fall into the trap of absolving your own implicit biases by blaming or oppressing some other group.
- **Defensiveness is a sign to get curious.** When you start to feel those entirely natural feelings of defensiveness arise, get curious. What is triggering your defensiveness? What feels threatening?
- **Don't police the tone of others.** Others discussing difficult issues with you are probably just as uncomfortable and defensive as you likely feel. Don't force them to further self-monitor by ensuring you are comfortable with their tone or facial expressions and body language.

- **White folks, monitor how often you refer to yourself.** Conversations about race and other bias-involved topics are about *systems*, not *individuals*. Your personal feelings will get involved, but they are not the point. Pay attention if you start using personal pronouns (I, me) frequently—it's a sign you're dwelling on your own experience and not the system itself.
- **Try to be better, not right.** There is no "winning" a conversation about topics that involve minoritized groups. It's not a debate; no points are scored; no winner is crowned. The opponent in any discussion of bias is systemic discrimination, not a person.
- **Do not demand these conversations from members of minoritized groups.** As discussed earlier in this chapter, it is patently unfair to require the people who have historically been oppressed to educate others about the ways in which the system oppresses. You need to do that work, not outsource it to someone already traumatized by systemic discrimination, including racism.

CONCLUSION

A Roadmap Forward

> Start where you are. Use what you have. Do what you can.
>
> Arthur Ashe

In this final chapter, I've laid out a few questions to get you started on your own path forward to greater self-awareness, self-understanding, and presence. There is no one right path forward, only the one that works for you—or, barring that, the one that you set upon, realize you've made a wrong turn, reroute as best you can without a GPS to admonish you, and travel along for the rest of your days. In truth, the scenic route is often far more enjoyable if you can let yourself enjoy it. It's true on road trips and it's true with inner work.

In the preceding pages, I've offered up metaphors of sailing and battles—to capture the journey toward transcendence and the challenges along the way (respectively). In this concluding chapter, my goal is to help you envision what the seas ahead look like for your sailboat (your innermost self) as you prepare to chart a course forward. Will your seas be rough or gentle? Will you stay in shallow depths near the shore or plunge into deeper waters? I'll stop belaboring the metaphor (well, soon), but that's our goal here.

Your sailboat and your journey are yours alone—nobody else gets to decide which way your bow points, and while others can introduce obstacles along the course, you are the pilot. I can't know what journey is right for you, so in this chapter I hand off the hard work to you, capable reader. To help guide you in getting started on your own path forward to greater self-awareness, self-understanding, and presence, I offer a series of questions. Reflect (or journal) on the ones that resonate for you in this moment. During times of uncertainty or struggle, feel free to come back and peruse the questions. Perhaps something new will strike you, or perhaps revisiting your thoughts from an earlier time (i.e., your journal) can help reorient you.

In that spirit, the resources and questions below are only meant to get you started. You might choose one and go for a walk-and-talk with a trusted friend or colleague. Or maybe you'll just let these marinate in your mind, whirring in the background while you're bustling to and fro in the motions of your everyday life. If you start to worry that you're off course, I suggest you pull to mind the quote at the top of the chapter from Arthur Ashe. Above all, remember that your life is short and precious and, most of all, *yours*. Do what serves *you*, your values, and your life's work.

Questions to Reflect on the Present

- What student behaviors upset me the most? Once identified, try to determine *why* these behaviors bother me. What assumptions am I making about the motivations behind these behaviors? Is it possible there might be different explanations for these behaviors?
- What behaviors among my colleagues upset me the most? Once identified, try to determine *why* these behaviors bother me. What assumptions am I making about the motivations behind these behaviors? Is it possible there might be different explanations for these behaviors?
- What myth about my discipline makes me want to scream? Why is this myth so charged for me? What am I doing to dispel the myth? What could I do?
- What thoughts race through my head before I fall asleep? What thoughts arise as soon as I wake up?
- What challenges, issues, and/or concerns are causing me the most stress right now?
- When was the last time I felt genuinely proud of something I'd done or said?

- When do I feel uncomfortable? Describe the environment, feelings, or people who inspire those feelings. Explore what about that situation gives rise to feelings of discomfort.
- What puts me on the defensive? In what circumstances do I feel defensiveness arising? Is it predictable or seemingly at random?
- What feels most motivating right now? What makes me feel so excited to pursue that?

Questions to Explore Your Hopes for Your Future

- Ten or twenty years from now, what do I hope my former students think about my class and my teaching?
- What would my colleagues say about my contributions to the department, institution, or their lives if I died suddenly next month?
- What are the biggest worries I have about my future?
- If I knew I was going to die one year from today, how would I spend that time?
- How do I want others to feel when they're around me? When have I felt that way around others, and what did they do to make me feel that way?
- Would I do [something I want to do] if nobody would ever find out I did it? Or is my ego seeking recognition?

Questions to Find a New Perspective

- When did I last learn something meaningful from my students? From my colleagues? What circumstances allowed me to learn from them?
- What's the most interesting thing I've learned outside of a classroom? What circumstances helped me learn that thing? Are there ways to replicate that exploration or learning in my classrooms or with my students?
- When was the last time I read something from outside my discipline? Are there ways that might inform my research or teaching? Whose recommendations might

I seek to expand my understanding of the issues I care most about?
- What do I currently take for granted in my life?
- What perceived failures in my past have turned out to be blessings in disguise?
- If I could go back to my high school graduation day, what would I tell my teenage self?
- What has most surprised me about my life so far?
- When was the last time I changed my mind about something? What led to the change of perspective?

Questions to Spark Possibility

- What's the discipline least like mine? What could I learn from an expert in that discipline? How might the theories or philosophies of that field inform my work?
- If my teaching style was an animal, what would it be? What behaviors does my teaching embody? Is that what I want it to look like?
- What mantra do I want to embody in my life?
- What would I do if I knew I could not fail?
- If I could go back to being eighteen and start my adult life over, what decisions would I keep and what would I change? Would I end up in (roughly) the same place?

Questions to Encourage Gratitude

- What challenges did my students have to conquer to attend class today? What obstacles stood in the way of their completing this [paper, homework, reading, exam]?
- Will I ever be in a room with these specific people again? How many will walk out the door and live an entire life without ever contacting me again? What might I miss out on by not being in touch with them?
- What's a small act of kindness once shown toward me that I have never forgotten?

- When am I at my happiest? What am I doing and with whom?
- What can I do this week to add good to others' lives?

Creating a Plan

Below you'll find four steps to incorporating the strategies and ideas from the preceding chapters into an action plan.

Step 1: Discernment, or determining what purpose and values are most important to you. This is an important step, because it gives you the compass for setting your course.

Identify your "why" by using the template and examples from Simon Sinek (p. 46). Try to use as few words as possible.

What is your inner critic saying about your dreams? Use the section on pages 145–50 to try to identify what fears are under those messages from the inner critic.

What values matter most to you in your teaching and in your career? Consider engaging with Brené Brown's values exercise to identify a handful of words that capture your deepest value commitments, available in the resources section of her website (Brown 2022).

Need some clarity around what you desire most deeply? Jennifer Louden has a wonderful set of journal prompts to "liberate and clarify your desires" as a companion resource to her excellent book *Why Bother? Discover the Desire for What's Next* (Louden 2020). Visit her website and look for the PDF download under the "Desire" section.

Step 2: Inventory, or reflecting on your life as it is *right now*. How are you spending your time? What projects, tasks, or people consume the biggest shares of your attention and care? For now, simply *observe*. Collect data. This is not the time to judge what you find; you're merely seeking information.

Consider tracking your time in thirty-minute chunks (or you can go for smaller chunks if you've got the bandwidth to do so) for a day or two. You might look at Clark (2018) for an example of this—though be warned that Clark did this for a full month. (Who has that kind of time?!) Look back over your tracker and see where you're giving your time.

If you're feeling *really brave*, you could do something similar with your devices (phones, computers, tablets). For example, you might download your browser history for a particular period to see what sites you spent your time on. Use your phone's tools to see what apps you use most and for how long.

Look over your sent emails or outbound text messages and see who's getting your digital attention. Are these students? Colleagues? People outside of work? Alumni? Friends? Partners?

For the bravest of us, you might ask your closest friend(s) and partner(s) to give you feedback on what you seem most preoccupied with. You could ask them what you talk about most, what tone you take, what your mood seems to be, or what they've noticed you spend big shares of your time on. Only ask for this feedback if you're prepared to get a subjective but useful perspective on your priorities. It might sting a bit.

Step 3: Evaluation, or comparing steps 1 and 2. This is tricky, and you might be tempted to get really judgy about whether you're meeting your ostensible priorities. Chances are high that you are not—and that's *entirely normal*. Try not to let this affect your mood. Remember Maya Angelou's quote from chapter 9: "Do the best you can until you know better. Then, when you know better, do better." We cannot change the past, so there's no reason to spend time dwelling on what you've already done. Right now—this moment—is the only thing under your immediate influence.

Celebrate the wins: Where are you doing a good job of living your values? What is working for you?

Look—*kindly, please!*—at the mismatches: Why are the time drains getting so much of your attention? What about them feels harder to resist? Why aren't the priorities getting more of your time? What about them feels easier to disregard?

Step 4: Mapping, or charting your path. What could this look like?

Borrow from *Atomic Habits* (Clear 2018), and frame your priorities (step 1) as who you are—your identity. It's not enough to say, "I want to spend more time with my kids," because that's (in James Clear's language) outcome-focused. Instead, think about who you are: "I am someone who makes spending time with her kids a priority." And then create plans to do that.

Make space for regular reflection. What have you learned about yourself by reading this book and reflecting on its messages? Where are the places in your life you'd like to exercise more intentionality? How can you incorporate time into your routines that will allow for more of that reflection on your deeper purpose and values? Does that look like blocking off time regularly, or planning a weekly, monthly, quarterly, or annual time to step out of the day-to-day hustle so you can examine your core priorities and your actions?

A Final Note

If it's good for our students, it's probably good for us, too—and vice versa. It's a theme I've returned to many times in the pages of this book. As we journey to becoming more present professors, it's imperative that we remember the power of community. This work can be done in isolation, yes, but it will be *so much more meaningful* if you do it with others you trust and whose company you enjoy. Find the people who occupy your work shelters, and engage them with questions, reflections, and explorations from this book. Create a group text thread, or a standing meeting, or some other way to check in regularly.

Set loose your brilliant authentic sail. I can't wait to see you out on the high seas soon.

NOTES

Chapter 1

1. The use of the word "authentic" to describe a person's presentation of self is not without its problems. As Beer (2020) cautions, "Although most people would define authenticity as acting in accordance with your idiosyncratic set of values and qualities, research has shown that people feel most authentic when they conform to a particular set of socially approved qualities, such as being extroverted, emotionally stable, conscientious, intellectual and agreeable." In other words, what we consider *authentic self* may just be another iteration of presentation of self. Nevertheless, throughout this book I use the word "authentic" to describe a presentation of self that is consistent with the one we embody when we are our least guarded, most present selves. This aligns with Kernis and Goldman's (2004) definition of authenticity, as shared in Schlegel et al. (2009, 2–3): "the unimpeded functioning of one's true self in daily life." Schlegel et al. (2009) report that Kernis and Goldman "have found that self-reported authenticity is positively related to such important outcomes as self-actualization, self-concept clarity, and self-esteem, and negatively related to psychological distress" (2–3).

2. The expectation that women will smile in social situations is largely cultural—and, in many instances in modern American culture, quite problematic. A meta-analysis of the research on gender differences in smiling underscores that women do, indeed, smile more often than men (LaFrance, Hecht, and Paluck 2003); however, the authors also demonstrate that the gendered differences in smiling frequency are highly contingent on social groups and social factors. Nevertheless,

I point out the research here only to suggest that my interpretation of whether a woman smiled at me is a well-documented cultural phenomenon but problematic in the gendered burden it places on women to do the emotional labor of maintaining smooth social interactions.

3. I've changed some names in anecdotes throughout the book to anonymize those who did not give permission to discuss their experiences. In this case, "Noah" was not a friend and moved to another state before I began writing this manuscript, so I could not obtain permission.

4. We have scant data on the prevalence of imposter syndrome, also known by the less-pejorative imposter phenomenon, in higher education. *The Chronicle of Higher Education* reported on a study in the mid-1980s that estimated that about 70 percent of people—across all genders and walks of life—had felt like imposters for at least some of their careers (Gravois 2007). As a *HigherEdJobs* piece points out, "The higher up you climb in your career the more susceptible you are to this condition, so it's actually even more likely that higher education professionals think of themselves as imposters" (Zackal 2020).

5. This paragraph is about your own self-acceptance and belonging, but please pause and consider how this applies to your students, too.

6. A note here for those who may be feeling some resistance around all this fuzzy language. As a social scientist, I'm vaguely uncomfortable with ethereal topics that sound a bit "woo." However, I'm also persuaded by ample research on embodied cognition showing that thinking is not limited to the brain. In the same way that you will be able to sense when someone sitting next to you is angry, you will sometimes just intuitively know things without having a conscious understanding of how or why you came to know them. For excellent reviews of this research, see Cavanagh (2016), Hrach (2021), and Murphy Paul (2021).

7. Like other anecdotes involving students, this is not the student's actual name.

Chapter 2

Note on the epigraph: Jesse Stommel challenged educators to summarize their pedagogy in four words. His own entry was: "Start by trusting students," which he tweeted on April 30, 2016. *The Chronicle of Higher Education* investigated in its October 27, 2019, article, "Forget Grades and Turnitin. Start Trusting Students," by Beckie Supiano.

1. Of course, there's science behind this, too. While it's fair to say that a high-protein or complex carbohydrate snack would provide a more

stable and lasting improvement to cognitive function, there is ample evidence demonstrating the brain boost we get after consuming food. For example, Kanarek and Swinney (1990) demonstrate that sugary snacks boosted cognitive performance relative to low-calorie, non-caffeinated alternatives. This was particularly true when the cognitive tasks required sustained attention.

2. I confess, I'm an unrepentant agent of chaos when it comes to classroom furniture layouts. If I must rearrange the furniture to meet my class's needs, then I have no guilt about leaving the room in our configuration. This is sometimes met with frustration by colleagues who teach in classrooms immediately after me. Why is the tidy arrangement of desks into rows the norm? Why should it be? And why should those of us who make more engaging layouts be compelled to return the furniture to meet someone else's needs when nobody ever bothered to ask us about ours?

3. This quote has been ascribed to the Dalai Lama, Kurt Vonnegut, and others. It is so common in our popular discourse that it's difficult to know who said it first—but we could all stand to be reminded of the sentiment regularly.

4. I thank Tom Tobin for reminding me of this on Twitter while I was writing this chapter.

Chapter 3

1. Any qualitative research effort will first be interrogated for how its participants were selected. I made a modest effort to prevent collecting only those voices that I knew agreed with me in a few ways. First, I asked many academic friends—about fifty—to share the name(s) of the professor(s) that had the biggest impact on them as students. I contacted each of the faculty members named by those friends. Second, I looked for active academic Twitter users who regularly posted about pedagogy, specifically with sensitivity to care for students. I generated a list of about two dozen faculty members from that effort, each of whom I contacted as well. In the end, I met with two faculty members in person, twelve via Zoom, and one by phone. The others either did not respond or declined. The interviews included in the next chapter were chosen for the diversity of experiences each colleague described. I make no claims about the representativeness of my sample of interviews and sources, only that their experiences provide many different perspectives on the culture of academia as a monolith.

2. In the interest of fairness, higher education leaders have an impossible job. As Brian Rosenberg's book makes clear, "shared governance" often just means change—certainly anything beyond incremental change—is impossible (2023, 99). In a world where the financial and enrollment challenges besetting non–Ivy League institutions look bleaker by the day, the impulse to work around often intransigent tenured faculty is logical. A better approach would almost certainly be to work together, but these existential threats make genuinely open-minded collaboration nigh on impossible.

3. In a moment that reinforced how the line between satire and reality is often blurry, Lorenzo Lorenzo-Luaces tweeted the following in early 2023: "I'm a scientist who publishes 17 amazing papers and 1 major grant a week. Are there a lot of contextual factors outside my control that contribute to my success? IDK probably. In this thread, I focus on a tiny factor under my control. And yours! See, it's all about mindset 1/327" Sadly, many thought he was being serious, which is the most disappointing indictment of hustle culture in academia that I can fathom.

4. The seemingly indefatigable Regan A. R. Gurung published a short but powerful piece that collects a lot of evidence to combat this hardass instinct. See Gurung (2023) to dig into that research.

5. I *will NOT* use the *r*-word. See this site for resources: https://tll.mit.edu/rigor-as-inclusive-practice/.

6. For more on this, see Cia Verschelden's work on *Bandwidth Recovery*. In addition to her two books on the topic, her website has a wealth of resources, including videos explaining key concepts.

7. Allow me to strongly endorse the strategy of befriending a current or former kindergarten or early childhood educator. They have the *best* ideas for student engagement that will accomplish so many goals—they'll keep you and your students physically and mentally engaged, they'll tap into that inherent joy of learning we felt in our younger years, and they'll shake things up by ensuring your class is a space of vitality. I remember two students a few years ago who approached me on the last day of the semester. One said, "I really struggled with this class because I never knew what we would be doing in class that day." The other said, "I *loved* this class—I never knew what we'd be up to next!" Both were right, and making sure you find that delicate balance between providing enough structure for the students made nervous by uncertainty while also keeping things engaging and a wee bit surprising is a very hard thing to do. It's worth it, though.

8. In the interest of full disclosure, I have previously served as a member of the advisory board for the Teaching Professor Online Conference.

9. Full disclosure: I have a master's degree in library science and *could* have become an academic librarian. Many of my closest friends are librarians. Thus, I am not unbiased on this matter.

Chapter 4

1. I have anonymized this profile at the request of the subject. Due to the sensitive personal matters they discussed and their pre-tenure status, they did not want their identity, discipline, or institution identified. "Ingrid Thompson" is an alias.

Part II

1. Just remember: Your inner work won't fix broken or toxic systems.

Chapter 6

1. Hedley's theories about the role of fascia and its relative importance in movement are not without detractors. However, since "The Fuzz Speech" had its heyday, scientists have argued that the network of fluid-filled spaces throughout the body, the "interstitium," should rightly be called its own organ (Rettner 2018). Fascia is another name for this system (Jampolis 2018).

2. The yoga teacher in me implores you NOT to attempt this without an experienced—and *insured*—yoga teacher around. Please.

3. The other six limbs are *asana* (postures, what we typically think of when we hear the word "yoga"), *pranayama* (mindful breathing), *pratyahara* (turning inward), *dharana* (concentration), *dhyana* (meditation, or de-concentration), and *samadhi* (a state of unity, or pure bliss). (Adele 2009, 15; see also Shah 2020)

4. Allow me to state without qualification how much I loathe the concept of material "coverage."

5. Chapter 3 deals with the culture of higher education. After reading that chapter, or even as you're reading this one, you might think that this *saucha* practice sounds implausible given our institutional contexts.

Bear in mind this: You cannot exercise *saucha*—or, indeed, any of the *yamas* and *niyamas*—in a space lacking in psychological safety.

6. For a teaching-focused look at the principles in Murphy Paul's book, be sure you also look at Susan Hrach's book, *Minding Bodies* (2021), available from West Virginia University Press.

7. As a person who is almost never cold, I strongly believe that "hot yoga" is objectively painful and violates the principle of *ahimsa*, but that's just my perspective. *Namaste*.

Chapter 7

1. In explaining what she means by this, Mohr writes, "[*Playing Big*] is a practical guide to moving past self-doubt and creating what you most want to create—whether in your career, in your community, or in a passion you pursue outside of work. It's not about the old-school notion of playing big—more money, more prestigious title, a bigger empire, or fame. It's about you living with a sense of greater freedom to express your voice and pursue your aspirations" (Mohr 2015, xii).

2. This is yet another example of a major theme of this book: what's good for students is good for us, too. A strengths-based approach is backed by evidence of its utility in working with students, and it can rightly be seen as a natural extension of adopting a growth mindset. In the pedagogical literature, a strengths-based mindset is discussed as a component of a framework called Appreciative Inquiry (AI). The AI Commons site describes it thusly: "At its heart, AI is about the search for the best in people, their organizations, and the strengths-filled, opportunity-rich world around them. AI is not so much a shift in the methods and models of organizational change, but AI is a fundamental shift in the overall perspective taken throughout the entire change process to 'see' the wholeness of the human system and to 'inquire' into that system's strengths, possibilities, and successes" (Stavros, Godwin, and Cooperrider 2015).

Chapter 8

1. Lindeman (1998) explores why we are willing to embrace pseudoscientific phenomena. Her explanation rests on two key observations: humans are motivated to understand themselves and the world, and it is cognitively demanding to interrogate the scientific basis for every idea in our crowded information landscape.

2. There is rigorous scientific work on personality, though. The most comprehensive is the framework of the Big Five personality traits, which are extroversion, agreeableness, openness, conscientiousness, and neuroticism (e.g., John and Srivastava 1999; John, Naumann, and Soto 2008; McCrae and Costa 1999).

3. The Barnum Effect is named for P. T. Barnum, the showman at the center of the circus company bearing his name, who was sometimes said to have a "a little something for everyone" (Dickson and Kelly 1985, 367). This phenomenon is sometimes referred to as the Forer Effect, after the psychologist best known for describing it, Bertram Forer.

Chapter 9

1. A 2020 meta-analysis by Newton and Salvi found that a majority of teachers, including brand-new educators, believe that matching teaching strategies to perceived student learning styles will yield greater learning. The 37 studies the authors evaluated (representing more than 15,000 educators across 18 countries) found the incidence of self-reported belief in matching teaching to learning styles to range from 58 to 97.6 percent, with a weighted percentage across the studies of 89.1 percent. They also found no evidence that this belief has declined in recent years.

2. It's on page 153, if you want to look it up later, about Ian Manuel.

3. As I write this, the state where I live (Tennessee) is making these conversations legally risky for college faculty. At a recent conference roundtable, a fellow political scientist from California asked if the American Political Science Association needed to start a legal defense fund for those of us from such states. Sadly, the answer is a resounding yes.

BIBLIOGRAPHY

Accreditation Council for Pharmacy Education (ACPE). 2016. "Accreditation Standards and Key Elements for the Professional Program in Pharmacy Leading to the Doctor of Pharmacy Degree." https://www.acpe-accredit.org/pdf/Standards2016FINAL2022.pdf.

Adele, Deborah. 2009. *The Yamas and Niyamas: Exploring Yoga's Ethical Practice*. Duluth, MN: On-Word Bound Books.

Agarwal, Pooja K., and Patrice M. Bain. 2019. *Powerful Teaching: Unleashing the Science of Learning*. San Francisco: Jossey-Bass.

Association of College and Research Libraries. 2018. *Standards for Libraries in Higher Education*. https://www.ala.org/acrl/standards/standardslibraries.

American Psychological Association. 2022. "Unconditional Positive Regard." APA Dictionary of Psychology. https://dictionary.apa.org/unconditional-positive-regard.

Banerjee, Amitav, U. B. Chitnis, S. L. Jadhav, J. S. Bhawalkar, and S. Chaudhury. 2009. "Hypothesis Testing, Type I and Type II Errors." *Industrial Psychology Journal* 18 (2): 127–31.

Basile, Vincent, and Flávio S. Azevedo. 2022. "Ideology in the Mirror: A Loving (Self) Critique of Our Equity and Social Justice Efforts in STEM Education." *Science Education* 106: 1084–86.

Beer, Jennifer. 2020. "The Inconvenient Truth about Your 'Authentic' Self." *Scientific American*. https://blogs.scientificamerican.com/observations/the-inconvenient-truth-about-your-authentic-self, March 5, 2020.

Begeer, Sander, Saloua El Bouk, Wafaa Boussaid, Mark Meerum Terwogt, and Hans M. Koot. 2009. "Underdiagnosis and Referral Bias of Autism in Ethnic Minorities." *Journal of Autism and Developmental Disorders* 39: 142–48.

Benjamin, Ruha. 2022. *Viral Justice: How We Grow the World We Want.* Princeton, NJ: Princeton University Press.

Berdahl, Loleen. 2023. "How to Capture the Power of Imposter Syndrome." *Academia Made Easier* [Substack newsletter], January 9, 2023.

Berg, Maggie, and Barbara K. Seeber. 2017. *The Slow Professor: Challenging the Culture of Speed in the Academy.* Toronto: University of Toronto Press.

Blum, Susan. 2020. *Ungrading: Why Rating Students Undermines Learning (and What to Do Instead).* Morgantown: West Virginia University Press.

Bowler, Kate. 2021. *No Cure for Being Human (and Other Truths I Need to Hear).* New York: Random House.

Brookfield, Stephen D. 2015. *The Skillful Teacher: On Technique, Trust, and Responsiveness in the Classroom.* San Francisco: Jossey-Bass.

Brookfield, Stephen D. 2017. *Becoming a Critically Reflective Teacher*, 2nd ed. San Francisco: Jossey-Bass.

Brown, Brené. 2010. *The Gifts of Imperfection: Let Go of Who You Think You're Supposed to Be and Embrace Who You Are.* Center City, MN.: Hazelden Publishing.

Brown, Brené. 2012. *Daring Greatly: How the Courage to Be Vulnerable Transforms the Way We Live, Love, Parent, and Lead.* Garden City, NY: Avery.

Brown, Brené. 2013. "Brené Brown on Empathy." RSA, December 10, 2013. https://www.youtube.com/watch?v=1Evwgu369Jw.

Brown, Brené. 2015. *Rising Strong: The Reckoning. The Rumble. The Revolution.* New York: Random House.

Brown, Brené. 2017a. *Braving the Wilderness: The Quest for True Belonging and the Courage to Stand Alone.* New York: Random House.

Brown, Brené. 2017b. "Daring Classrooms." SXSWedu, April 7, 2017. https://www.youtube.com/watch?v=DVD8YRgA-ck.

Brown, Brené. 2023. "Dare to Lead List of Values." https://brenebrown.com/resources/dare-to-lead-list-of-values/.

Brown, Peter C., Henry L. Roediger III, and Mark A. McDaniel. 2014. *Make It Stick: The Science of Successful Learning.* Cambridge, MA: Belknap Press.

Cavanagh, Sarah Rose. 2016. *The Spark of Learning: Energizing the College Classroom with the Science of Emotion.* Morgantown: West Virginia University Press.

Cavanagh, Sarah Rose. 2023. "Will Mandated Mental-Health Breaks Do More Harm than Good?" *Chronicle of Higher Education*, February 28, 2023. https://www.chronicle.com/article/will-mandated-mental-health-breaks-do-more-harm-than-good.

CCCSE. 2022. *Mission Critical: The Role of Community Colleges in Meeting Students' Basic Needs*. http://www.cccse.org/NR22.

Chacko, Sheaba. 2023. "It's Not You, It's What Happened to You." TEDx Talks, January 25, 2023. https://www.youtube.com/watch?v=2nlSDozD8Gk.

Challenger, Melanie. 2021. *How to Be Animal: A New History of What It Means to Be Human*. New York: Penguin Books.

Chestnut, Beatrice, and Uranio Paes. 2021. *The Enneagram Guide to Waking Up: Find Your Path, Face Your Shadow, Discover Your True Self*. Charlottesville, VA: Hampton Roads Publishing Company.

Childs-Kean, Lindsay, Mary Edwards, and Mary Douglass Smith. 2020. "Use of Personality Frameworks in Health Science Education." *American Journal of Pharmaceutical Education* 84 (8): 1085–94.

Clark, Dorie. 2018. "Track Your Time for 30 Days. What You Learn Might Surprise You." *Harvard Business Review*, April 11, 2018. https://hbr.org/2018/04/track-your-time-for-30-days-what-you-learn-might-surprise-you.

Clarke Gray, Brenna. 2022. "The University Cannot Love You: Gendered Labour, Burnout, and the Covid-19 Pivot to Digital." In *Feminist Critical Digital Pedagogy: An Open Book*, edited by Suzan Koseoglu and George Veletsianos. EdTech Books. https://edtechbooks.org/feminist_digital_ped/zXHDRJAq.

Clear, James. 2018. *Atomic Habits: An Easy and Proven Way to Build Good Habits and Break Bad Ones*. Garden City, NY: Avery.

Cleveland Clinic. 2024. "Neurodivergent." Accessed March 9, 2024. https://my.clevelandclinic.org/health/symptoms/23154-neurodivergent.

Council on Foreign Relations. 2024. Model Diplomacy site, https://modeldiplomacy.cfr.org/.

Cox, Milton D. 2004. "Introduction to Faculty Learning Communities." *New Directions for Teaching and Learning*, 97 (Spring 2004): 5–23.

Cozolino, Louis, and Susan Sprokay. 2006. "Neuroscience and Adult Learning: New Directions for Adult and Continuing Education." *Neuroscience and Adult Learning* 110 (Summer 2006): 11–19. https://doi.org/10.1002/ace.214.

Cron, Lisa. 2012. *Wired for Story: The Writer's Guide to Using Brain Science to Hook Readers from the Very First Sentence*. Berkeley, CA: Ten Speed Press.

Cuddy, Amy. 2012. "Your Body Language May Shape Who You Are." TEDGlobal, June 2012. https://www.ted.com/talks/amy_cuddy_your _body_language_may_shape_who_you_are.

Cuddy, Amy. 2018. *Presence: Bringing Your Boldest Self to Your Biggest Challenges*. New York: Little, Brown Spark.

Cunningham, Heather V., and Susanne Tabur. 2012. "Learning Space Attributes: Reflections on Academic Library Design and Its Use." *Journal of Learning Spaces* 1 (2). https://libjournal.uncg.edu/jls/issue/view/44.

Csikszentmihályi, Mihály. 2008. *Flow: The Psychology of Optimal Experience*. New York: Harper Perennial.

Csikszentmihályi, Mihály, Sami Abuhamdeh, and Jeanne Nakamura. 2005. "Flow." In *Handbook of Competence and Motivation*, edited by Andrew J. Elliot and Carol S. Dweck, 598–698. New York: Guilford Press.

Dahlkild, Nan. 2011. "The Emergence and Challenge of the Modern Library Building: Ideal Types, Model Libraries, and Guidelines, from the Enlightenment to the Experience Economy." *Library Trends* 60 (1): 11–42.

Daniel Tatum, Beverly. 2017. *Why Are All the Black Kids Sitting Together in the Cafeteria?: And Other Conversations About Race*, 20th anniversary ed. New York: Basic Books.

Daniels, David, Terry Saracino, Meghan Fraley, Jennifer Christian, and Seth Pardo. 2018. "Advancing Ego Development in Adulthood through Study of the Enneagram System of Personality." *Journal of Adult Development* 25: 229–41.

David, Susan. 2016. *Emotional Agility: Get Unstuck, Embrace Change, and Thrive in Work and Life*. Garden City, NY: Avery.

Davis, Carolyn. 2020. "How Institutions Protect Racists—#BLM Guest Post." *The Professor Is In*, July 16, 2020. https://theprofessorisin.com/2020/07/16/institutions-protect-racists-blm/.

Dickson, D. H., and I. W. Kelly. 1985. "The 'Barnum Effect' in Personality Assessment: A Review of the Literature." *Psychological Reports* 57: 367–82.

Donahoe, Emily Pitts. 2023. "Introducing the Progress Tracker." *Unmaking the Grade* [Substack newsletter]. https://emilypittsdonahoe.substack.com/.

Dore, Madeleine. 2022. *I Didn't Do the Thing Today: Letting Go of Productivity Guilt.* Garden City, NY: Avery.

Duhigg, Charles. 2016. "What Google Learned from Its Quest to Build the Perfect Team." *New York Times Magazine*, February 25, 2016. https://danmoser.github.io/static/google_perfect_team_comments-Moser.pdf.

Edmondson, Amy C., and Zhike Lei. 2014. "Psychological Safety: The History, Renaissance, and Future of an Interpersonal Construct." *The Annual Review of Organizational Psychology and Organizational Behavior* 1: 23–43.

Emdin, Christopher. 2016. *For White Folks Who Teach in the Hood . . . and the Rest of Y'all Too: Reality Pedagogy and Urban Education.* Boston: Beacon Press.

Emdin, Christopher. 2021. *Rachetdemic: Reimagining Academic Success.* Boston: Beacon Press.

Engel, Debra, and Karen Antell. 2004. "The Life of the Mind: A Study of Faculty Spaces in Academic Libraries." *College & Research Libraries* 65 (1): 8–26.

Felten, Peter, and Leo M. Lambert. 2020. *Relationship-Rich Education: How Human Connections Drive Success in College.* Baltimore: Johns Hopkins University Press.

Fosslien, Liz, and Mollie West Duffy. 2019. *No Hard Feelings: The Secret Power of Embracing Emotions at Work.* New York: Portfolio/Penguin.

Frederickson, Barbara L. 2013. *Love 2.0: Creating Happiness and Health in Moments of Connection.* New York: Plume.

Friere, Paolo. (1970) 2018. *Pedagogy of the Oppressed.* New York: Herder and Herder.

Furey, William. 2020. "The Stubborn Myth of 'Learning Styles'—State Teacher-License Prep Materials Peddle a Debunked Theory." *Education Next* 20 (3): 8–12. https://www.educationnext.org/stubborn-myth-learning-styles-state-teacher-license-prep-materials-debunked-theory/.

Gannon, Kevin. 2020. *Radical Hope: A Teaching Manifesto.* Morgantown: West Virginia University Press.

Gannon, Kevin. 2021. "The Data Is In: Performative Hardassery Is Not Good Teaching." *The Tattooed Professor*, September 16, 2021. https://thetattooedprof.com/2021/09/16/the-data-is-in-performative-hardassery-is-not-good-teaching/.

Gibson, Amelia N., Renate L. Chancellor, Nicole A. Cooke, Sarah Paul Dahlen, Shari A. Lee, and Yasmeen L. Shorish. 2017. "Libraries on the Frontlines: Neutrality and Social Justice." *Equality, Diversity and Inclusion: An International Journal* 36 (8): 751–66.

Glowacki-Dudka, Michelle, and Michael P. Brown. 2013. "Professional Development through Faculty Learning Communities." *New Horizons in Adult Education and Human Resource Development* 21 (1–2): 29–39.

Goffman, Erving. 1959. *The Presentation of Self in Everyday Life.* New York: Anchor Books.

Gottschall, Jonathan. 2012. *The Storytelling Animal: How Stories Make Us Human.* New York: Houghton Mifflin Harcourt.

Gravois, John. 2007. "You're Not Fooling Anyone." *Chronicle of Higher Education* 54 (11). https://www.chronicle.com/article/youre-not-fooling-anyone/.

Gurung, Regan A. R. 2023. "Hitting Your Sweet Spot: The Fine Balance of Being Flexible." *The Teaching Professor*, March 6, 2023. https://www.researchgate.net/publication/369992180_Hitting_Your_Sweet_Spot_The_Fine_Balance_of_Being_Flexible.

Hammond, Zaretta. 2015. *Culturally Responsive Teaching and the Brain: Promoting Authentic Engagement and Rigor among Culturally and Linguistically Diverse Students.* Thousand Oaks, CA: Corwin.

Hammonds, Keith H. 2000. "You Can Do Anything—But Not Everything." *Fast Company* 30 (April 2000). https://www.fastcompany.com/40384/you-can-do-anything-not-everything.

Hare, Brian, and Vanessa Woods. 2020. *Survival of the Friendliest: Understanding Our Origins and Rediscovering Our Common Humanity.* New York: Random House.

Harris, Dan. 2018. *Meditation for Fidgety Skeptics: A 10% Happier How-To Book.* New York: Spiegel and Grau.

Hedley, Gil. 2009. "The Fuzz Speech." Ask Gil about Anatomy, February 7, 2009. https://www.youtube.com/watch?v=_FtSP-tkSug&t=1s.

Hogan, Kelly A., and Viji Sathy. 2022. *Inclusive Teaching: Strategies for Promoting Equity in the College Classroom.* Morgantown: West Virginia University Press.

Holstead, Carol E. 2022. "Why Students are Skipping Class So Often, and How to Bring Them Back." *Chronicle of Higher Education*, September 1, 2022. https://www.chronicle.com/article/why-students-are-skipping-class-so-often-and-how-to-bring-them-back.

Hook, Joshua N., Todd W. Hall, Don E. Davis, Daryl R. Van Tongeren, and Mackenzie Conner. 2020. "The Enneagram: A Systematic Review of the Literature and Directions for Future Research." *Journal of Clinical Psychology* 77 (4): 865–83.

hooks, bell. 1994. *Teaching to Transgress: Education as the Practice of Freedom.* New York: Routledge.

hooks, bell. 2003. *Teaching Community: A Pedagogy of Hope.* New York: Routledge.

Hrach, Susan. 2021. *Minding Bodies: How Physical Space, Sensation, and Movement Affect Learning.* Morgantown: West Virginia University Press.

Huber, Cheri. 2001. *There Is Nothing Wrong with You: Going beyond Self-Hate.* USA: Keep it Simple Books.

Inman, Matthew. 2023. "You're Not Going to Believe What I'm About to Tell You." *The Oatmeal.* https://theoatmeal.com/comics/believe.

Irish, Bradley J. 2023. "How to Make Room for Neurodivergent Professors." *Chronicle of Higher Education,* March 2, 2023. https://www.chronicle.com/article/how-to-make-room-for-neurodivergent-professors.

Jampolis, Melina. 2018. "The Real Science behind Fascia Ailments." *CNN.com,* November 8, 2018. https://www.cnn.com/2018/11/08/health/fascia-blasting-explainer-exercise-jampolis/index.html.

Jaremka, Lisa M., Joshua M. Ackerman, Bertram Gawronski, Nicholas O. Rule, Kate Sweeny, Linda R. Tropp, Molly A. Metz, Ludwin Molina, William S. Ryan, and S. Brooke Vick. 2020. "Common Academic Experiences No One Talks About: Repeated Rejection, Imposter Syndrome, and Burnout." *Perspectives on Psychological Science* 15 (3): 519–43.

John, Oliver P., Laura P. Naumann, and Christopher J. Soto. 2008. "Paradigm Shift to the Integrative Big-Five Trait Taxonomy: History, Measurement, and Conceptual Issues." In *Handbook of Personality: Theory and Research,* edited by Oliver P. John, R. W. Robins, and L. A. Pervin, 114–58. New York: Guilford Press.

John, Oliver P., and Sanjay Srivastava. 1999. "The Big Five Trait Taxonomy: History, Measurement, and Theoretical Perspectives." In *Handbook of Personality: Theory and Research,* edited by L. A. Pervin and Oliver P. John, 102–38. New York: Guilford Press.

Kahneman, Daniel. 2011. *Thinking, Fast and Slow.* New York: Farrar, Straus and Giroux.

Kaminoff, Leslie. 2017. "Yoga Anatomy and the Breath." Workshop delivered at the Asheville Yoga Center, September 15–17, 2017.

Kaminoff, Leslie, and Amy Matthews. 2021. *Yoga Anatomy,* 3rd ed. Champaign, IL: Human Kinetics.

Kanarek, Robin B., and David Swinney. 1990. "Effects of Food Snacks on Cognitive Performance in Male College Students." *Appetite* 14 (1): 15–27.

Kaufman, Scott Barry. 2018. "Why Quieting the Ego Strengthens Your Best Self." SBK Blog, May 21, 2018. https://scottbarrykaufman.com/quieting-ego-strengthens-best-self/.

Kaufman, Scott Barry. 2020. *Transcend: The New Science of Self-Actualization*. New York: TarcherPerigee.

Kaufman, Scott Barry. "Sailboat Metaphor." ScottBarryKaufman.com. Accessed March 7, 2024, https://scottbarrykaufman.com/sailboat-metaphor/.

Kelley, Ann, and Sue Marriott. 2018. "How Good Boundaries Actually Bring Us Closer, with Guest Juliane Taylor Shore." *Therapist Uncensored* podcast episode 81, https://therapistuncensored.com/episodes/tu81-how-good-boundaries-actually-bring-us-closer-with-guest-juliane-taylor-shore/.

Kelsky, Karen (@ProfessorIsIn). 2022. "I created a new Crowdsource Survey, this time on scholars leaving academia. In a few hours it has gotten 85+ responses." Twitter, May 11, 2022. https://twitter.com/professorisin/status/1524575981477908480.

Kelsky, Karen. 2023. "Professor Is Out: Crowdsource Survey on Scholars Leaving Academia." Available as a Google spreadsheet: https://docs.google.com/spreadsheets/d/1IrGobdMzAo2Mj7KThJyltVs8HFSGo9topxClG-b4ROY/edit?usp=sharing.

Kernis, Michael H., and Brian M. Goldman. 2004. "Authenticity, Social Motivation, and Psychological Adjustment." In *Social Motivation: Conscious and Unconscious Processes*, edited by Joseph P. Forgas, Kipling D. Williams, and Simon M. Laham, 210–27. New York: Cambridge University Press.

Koenig, Rebecca. 2019. "'Academic Capitalism' Is Reshaping Faculty Life. What Does that Mean?" *EdSurge*, November 25, 2019. https://www.edsurge.com/news/2019-11-25-academic-capitalism-is-reshaping-faculty-life-what-does-that-mean.

Kranich, Nancy C. 2020. "Libraries and Democracy Revisited." *Library Quarterly: Information, Communication, Policy* 90 (1): 121–53.

Kreitzer, Mary Jo. 2022. "Why Personal Relationships Are Important." *Taking Charge of Your Health and Wellbeing*. https://www.takingcharge.csh.umn.edu/why-personal-relationships-are-important.

Krishnamurti, Jiddu. 1974. *On Education*. Ojai, CA.: Krishnamurti Foundation of America. https://jiddu-krishnamurti.net/en/krishnamurti-on-education.

LaFrance, Marianna, Marvin A. Hecht, and Elizabeth Levy Paluck. 2003. "The Contingent Smile: A Meta-analysis of Sex Differences in Smiling." *Psychological Bulletin* 129 (2): 305–34.

Lang, James. 2021. *Small Teaching: Everyday Lessons from the Science of Learning*, 2nd ed. Hoboken, NJ: Jossey-Bass.

Larremore, Daniel. 2022. "Waterman Lecture: Trends in US Faculty Hiring and Retention: A Study of Prestige, Diversity, and Inequality." National Science Foundation News, October 21, 2022. https://www.youtube.com/watch?v=tvJMtfuxJgo.

Lasater, Judith. 2015. *Living Your Yoga: Finding the Spiritual in Everyday Life*. Berkeley, CA: Rodmell Press.

Leffingwell, Hannah. 2023. "The Academic Career is Broken." *Chronicle of Higher Education*, January 19, 2023. https://new.nsf.gov/od/honorary-awards/waterman.

Levenson, Hannah. 2017. *Brief Dynamic Theory*, 2nd ed. Washington, DC: American Psychological Association.

Lindeman, Marjaana. 1998. "Motivation, Cognition, and Neuroscience." *Scandinavian Journal of Psychology* 39 (4): 257–65.

Louden, Jennifer. 2020. *Why Bother? Discover the Desire for What's Next*. Vancouver: Page Two.

Louden, Jennifer. 2022. https://jenniferlouden.com.

Love, Bettina. 2019. *We Want to Do More Than Survive: Abolitionist Teaching and the Pursuit of Educational Freedom*. Boston: Beacon Press.

Lubbe, Jerome D. 2020. *The Brain-Based Enneagram: You Are Not a Number*. Amherst, NY: Books Unplugged.

Lukasik, Karolina M., Otto Waris, Anna Soveri, Minna Lehtonen, and Matti Laine. 2019. "The Relationship of Anxiety and Stress with Working Memory Performance in a Large Non-depressed Sample." *Frontiers in Psychology* 10 (4). https://doi.org/10.3389/fpsyg.2019.00004.

Lundberg, Carol A. 2003. "The Influence of Time-Limitations, Faculty, and Peer Relationships on Adult Student Learning: A Causal Model." *Journal of Higher Education* 74 (6): 665–88.

Lundberg, Carol A. 2014. "Peers and Faculty as Predictors of Learning for Community College Students." *Community College Review* 42 (2): 79–98.

Lux, Vera, Robert J. Snyder, and Colleen Boff. 2016. "Why Users Come to the Library: A Case Study of Library and Non-Library Units." *Journal of Academic Librarianship* 42 (2): 109–17.

Manson, Mark. 2024. "7 Strange Questions that Help You Find Your Life Purpose." Accessed March 9, 2024. https://markmanson.net/life-purpose.

Marfice, Christina. 2021. "Everything You Need to Know About the Inbox Zero Method." *Superhuman Labs*, November 3, 2021. https://blog.superhuman.com/inbox-zero-method/.

Martin, Dimple J. 2023. "Professional Learning Communities: A Meaningful Approach to Faculty Professional Development." *Faculty Focus*, March 22, 2023. https://www.facultyfocus.com/articles/academic-leadership/professional-learning-communities-a-meaningful-approach-to-faculty-professional-development/.

Maryville University. 2022. "How to Identify and Overcome Your Implicit Bias." https://online.maryville.edu/blog/addressing-implicit-bias/.

Maslow, Abraham H. 1998. *Toward a Psychology of Being*, 3rd edition. New York: Wiley.

Mayne, Laura. 2022. "Why Boundaries Are Important." Twitter thread, November 25, 2022. https://twitter.com/LauraJaneMayne/status/1596134293231009797.

Mayo, Liz. 2023. "Women Do Higher Ed's Chores. That Must Change." *Chronicle of Higher Education*, February 13, 2023. https://www.chronicle.com/article/women-do-higher-eds-chores-that-must-change.

McCrae, Robert R., and Paul T. Costa Jr. 1999. "A Five Factor Theory of Personality." In *Handbook of Personality: Theory and Research*, edited by L. A. Pervin and Oliver P. John, 139–53. New York: Guilford Press.

McDevitt, Neale. 2006. "Unmasking the Imposter Phenomenon." *McGill Reporter* 38 (17). http://www.reporter-archive.mcgill.ca/38/17/zorn/index.html.

McMurtrie, Beth. 2022. "A 'Stunning' Level of Student Disconnection." *Chronicle of Higher Education*, April 5, 2022. https://www.chronicle.com/article/a-stunning-level-of-student-disconnection.

McMurtrie, Beth. 2023. "Teaching in an Age of 'Militant Apathy.'" *Chronicle of Higher Education*, February 15, 2023. https://www.chronicle.com/article/teaching-in-an-age-of-militant-apathy.

McPartlin, Jim. 2021. *The Enneagram at Work: Unlocking the Power of Type to Lead and Succeed*. New York: St. Martin's Essentials.

McQuaid, Goldie A., Kevin A. Pelphrey, Susan Y. Bookheimer, Mirella Dapretto, Sara J. Webb, Raphael A. Bernier, James C. McPartland, John D. Van Horn, and Gregory L. Wallace. 2021. "The Gap between

IQ and Adaptive Functioning in Autism Spectrum Disorder: Disentangling Diagnostic and Sex Differences." *Autism* 25 (6): 1565–79.

Mohr, Tara. 2015. *Playing Big: Practical Wisdom for Women Who Want to Speak Up, Create, and Lead.* Garden City, NY: Avery.

Montell, Amanda. 2021. *Cultish: The Language of Fanaticism.* New York: HarperCollins Publishers.

Murphy Paul, Annie. 2021. *The Extended Mind: The Power of Thinking Outside the Brain.* Boston: Houghton Mifflin Harcourt.

Murthy, Vivek H. T. 2020. *Together: The Healing Power of Human Connection in a Sometimes Lonely World.* New York: HarperCollins Publishers.

Nagoski, Emily, and Amelia Nagoski. 2020. *Burnout: The Secret to Unlocking the Stress Cycle.* New York: Ballantine Books.

National Science Foundation. 2024. "The Alan T. Waterman Award." Accessed March 9, 2024. https://new.nsf.gov/od/honorary-awards/waterman.

Neuhaus, Jessamyn. 2019. *Geeky Pedagogy: A Guide for Intellectuals, Introverts, and Nerds Who Want to Be Effective Teachers.* Morgantown: West Virginia University Press.

Newton, Philip M., and Atharva Salvi. 2020. "How Common is Belief in the Learning Styles Neuromyth, and Does It Matter? A Pragmatic Systematic Review." *Frontiers in Education* 5: December 2020.

Nicolas, Sarah. 2018. "50 of Our Favorite Library Quotes About How Awesome Libraries Are." *Book Riot*, March 8, 2018. https://bookriot.com/library-quotes/.

Norell, Liz. 2023. "Writing as a Tool for Teamwork." *Inside Higher Ed*, November 21, 2023. https://www.insidehighered.com/opinion/blogs/just-visiting/2023/11/21/writing-has-lots-uses-beyond-producing-text.

Novogratz, Sukey and Elizabeth. 2017. *Just Sit: A Meditation Guidebook for People Who Know They Should but Don't.* New York: Harper Wave.

Nunn, Lisa M. 2021. *College Belonging: How First-Year and First-Generation Students Navigate Campus Life.* New Brunswick, NJ: Rutgers University Press.

Olou, Ijeoma. 2018. *So You Want to Talk About Race.* New York: Seal Press.

Osterman, Karen F. 2000. "Students' Need for Belonging in the School Community." *Review of Educational Research* 70 (3), 323–67.

Palmer, Parker. 2004. *A Hidden Wholeness: The Journey toward an Undivided Life.* San Francisco: Jossey-Bass.

Palmer, Parker. 2007. *The Courage to Teach: Exploring the Inner Landscape of a Teacher's Life*, 10th anniversary ed. San Francisco: John Wiley and Sons.

Parker, Priya. 2018. *The Art of Gathering*. New York: Riverhead Books.

Parker, Priya. 2020. "Together Apart." *New York Times*. https://www.priyaparker.com/together-apart.

Philipson, Ilene. 2002. *Married to the Job: Why We Live to Work and What We Can Do about It*. New York: The Free Press.

[The] Professor Is Out Facebook group. https://www.facebook.com/groups/professorisout.

Remen, Rachel Naomi. 1996. "In the Service of Life." *Noetic Sciences Review*, Spring 1996. https://palousemindfulness.com/docs/remen-service.pdf.

Rettner, Rachael. 2018. "Meet Your Interstitium, a Newfound 'Organ.'" *Scientific American*, March 27, 2018. https://www.scientificamerican.com/article/meet-your-interstitium-a-newfound-organ/.

Rosenberg, Brian. 2022. "Higher Ed's Prestige Paralysis." *Chronicle of Higher Education*, November 22, 2022. https://www.chronicle.com/article/higher-eds-prestige-paralysis.

Rosenberg, Brian. 2023. *"Whatever It Is, I'm Against It": Resistance to Change in Higher Education*. Cambridge, MA: Harvard University Press.

Russell, Joyce E. A. 2014. "Career Coach: The Power of Using a Name." *Washington Post*, January 12, 2014. https://www.washingtonpost.com/business/capitalbusiness/career-coach-the-power-of-using-a-name/2014/01/10/8ca03da0-787e-11e3-8963-b4b654bcc9b2_story.html.

Sbarra, David A., and James A. Coan. 2018. "Relationships and Health: The Critical Role of Affective Science." *Emotion Review* 10 (1). https://doi.org/10.1177/1754073917696584.

Schiano, Bill. 2021. "Give Your Brain a Break: Course Design Tips to Avoid Feeling Overwhelmed." *Harvard Business Publishing Education*. https://hbsp.harvard.edu/inspiring-minds/course-design-tips-to-avoid-feeling-overwhelmed.

Schlegel, Rebecca J., Joshua A. Hicks, Jamie Arndt, and Laura King. 2009. "Thine Own Self: True Self-Concept Accessibility and Meaning in Life." *Journal of Personal and Social Psychology* 96 (2): 473–90. doi:10.1037/a0014060.

Schmidt, Claire. 2023. "6 Ways to Maintain Healthy Company Culture." *Forbes*, February 27, 2023. https://www.forbes.com/sites/forbeshumanresourcescouncil/2023/02/27/6-ways-to-maintain-healthy-company-culture/.

Schmidt, Isabell, Tuomas Rutanen, Roberto S. Luciani, and Corinne Jola. 2021. "Feeling for the Other with Ease: Prospective Actors Show High Levels of Emotion Recognition and Report Above Average Empathic Concern, but Do Not Experience Strong Distress." *Frontiers in Psychology* 12. https://doi.org/10.3389/fpsyg.2021.543846.

Schuman, Rebecca. 2022. "Beating Yourself Up is Labor, But It's Not Work." *Chronicle of Higher Education*, November 8, 2022. https://www.chronicle.com/article/beating-yourself-up-is-labor-but-its-not-work.

Schwartz, Harriet L. 2019. *Connected Teaching: Relationship, Power, and Mattering in Higher Education*. Sterling, VA: Stylus Publishing.

Scott, Kim. 2019. *Radical Candor: Be a Kick-ass Boss without Losing Your Humanity*. New York: St. Martin's Press.

Shah, Sejal. 2020. "How to Make the Yamas and Niyamas Work for You in the Modern World." *Art of Living*. https://www.artofliving.org/us-en/yoga/beginners/yamas-niyamas.

Sides, John. 2022. "The Monkey Cage." https://johnsides.org/the-monkey-cage/.

Sinek, Simon. 2017. *Find Your Why: A Practical Guide for Discovering Purpose for You and Your Team*. New York: Portfolio/Penguin.

Sinek, Simon. 2019. "If You Want to Be Successful in Life, Master This One Skill." Impact Theory. October 15, 2019. https://www.youtube.com/watch?v=V2K4VqkfRaM.

Sinek, Simon. 2019. *The Infinite Game*. New York: Portfolio/Penguin.

Sinek, Simon (@SimonSinek). 2024. "About." LinkedIn. https://www.linkedin.com/in/simonsinek/.

Stanovich, Keith E., and Richard F. West. 2000. "Individual Differences in Reasoning: Implications for the Rationality Debate?" *Behavioral and Brain Sciences* 23 (5): 645–65. https://doi.org/10.1017/S0140525X00003435.

Stavros, Jacqueline, Lindsey Godwin, and David Cooperrider. 2015. "Appreciative Inquiry: Organization Development and the Strengths Revolution." In *Practicing Organization Development: A Guide to Leading Change and Transformation*, 4th ed., edited by William Rothwell, Roland Sullivan, and Jacqueline Stavros, 96–116. Hoboken, NJ: John Wiley and Sons. https://doi.org/10.1002/9781119176626.ch6.

Stevenson, Bryan. 2014. *Just Mercy: A Story of Justice and Redemption*. New York: Spiegel and Grau.

Stommel, Jesse (@Jessifer). 2016. "Start by trusting students. #4wordpedagogy" Twitter, April 30, 2016. https://twitter.com/Jessifer/status/726424167420145664.

Supiano, Beckie. 2019. "Forget Grades and Turnitin. Start Trusting Students." *Chronicle of Higher Education*, October 27, 2019. https://www.chronicle.com/article/forget-grades-and-turnitin-start-trusting-students/.

Supiano, Beckie, and Karin Fischer. 2023. "Connecting in the Classroom and Beyond." *Chronicle of Higher Education*, February 23, 2023. https://www.chronicle.com/report/free/connecting-in-the-classroom-and-beyond.

Svich, Caridad, ed. 2016. *Audience Revolution: Dispatches from the Field*. New York: Theatre Communications Group.

Syman, Stefanie. 2007. "Bhagavad Gita: The Timeless First Book of Yoga." *Yoga Journal*, October 1, 2007. https://www.yogajournal.com/yoga-101/spirituality/first-book-yoga/.

Tagg, John. 2019. *The Instruction Myth: Why Higher Education Is Hard to Change, and How to Change It*. New Brunswick, NJ: Rutgers University Press.

Tinnell, Teresa L., Patricia A. S. Ralston, Thomas R. Tretter, and Mary E. Mills. 2019. "Sustaining Pedagogical Change via Faculty Learning Community." *International Journal of STEM Education* 6 (26): 1–16.

Tobin, Thomas J., and Kirsten T. Behling. 2018. *Reach Everyone, Teach Everyone: Universal Design for Learning in Higher Education*. Morgantown: West Virginia University Press.

Tompkins, Jane. 1990. "Pedagogy of the Distressed." *College English* 52 (6): 653–60.

Tulshyan, Ruchika, and Jodi-Ann Burey. 2021a. "End Imposter Syndrome in Your Workplace." *Harvard Business Review*, July 14, 2021. https://hbr.org/2021/07/end-imposter-syndrome-in-your-workplace.

Tulshyan, Ruchika, and Jodi-Ann Burey. 2021b. "Stop Telling Women They Have Imposter Syndrome." *Harvard Business Review*, February 11, 2012. https://hbr.org/2021/02/stop-telling-women-they-have-imposter-syndrome.

van der Kolk, Bessel. 2014. *The Body Keeps the Score: Brain, Mind, and Body in the Healing of Trauma*. New York: Penguin Books.

van der Kolk, Bessel. 2023. "The Body Keeps the Score." Opening keynote at the Institute for Trauma, Adversity, and Resilience in Higher Education virtual event, "Trauma and Resilience in Higher Education: Naming the Urgency, Envisioning Change, Sharing Tools." April 26, 2023.

Verschelden, Cia. 2024. *Bandwidth Recovery*. Accessed March 9, 2024. https://bandwidthrecovery.org/.

Wicker, Alden. 2017. "Conscious Consumerism Is a Lie. Here's a Better Way to Help Save the World." *Quartz*, March 1, 2017. https://qz.com/920561/conscious-consumerism-is-a-lie-heres-a-better-way-to-help-save-the-world.

Wilcox, Christina S. 2020. *Take Care of Your Type: An Enneagram Guide to Self-Care*. New York: Tiller Press.

Wilkerson, Isabel. 2020. *Caste: The Origins of Our Discontents*. New York: Random House.

Williams, Mark, and Danny Penman. 2011. *Mindfulness: An Eight-Week Plan for Finding Peace in a Frantic World*. New York: Rodale.

Williams, Tom. 2022. "Four in 10 Higher Education Staff Say They'll Quit in Five Years." *Times Higher Education*, November 10, 2022. https://www.timeshighereducation.com/news/four-10-higher-education-staff-say-theyll-quit-five-years.

Winerman, Lea. 2005. "The Mind's Mirror." *Monitor on Psychology* 36 (9): 48. https://www.apa.org/monitor/oct05/mirror.

Winter, Richard. 2009. "Academic Manager or Managed Academic? Academic Identity Schisms in Higher Education." *Journal of Higher Education Policy and Management* 31 (2): 121–31.

Wright, Mary C. 2023. *Centers for Teaching and Learning: The New Landscape in Higher Education*. Baltimore: Johns Hopkins University Press.

Yagoda, Ben. 2018. "Your Lying Mind: The Cognitive Biases Tricking Your Brain." *The Atlantic*, September 2018. https://www.theatlantic.com/magazine/archive/2018/09/cognitive-bias/565775/.

Zackal, Justin. 2020. "Three-Step Guide to Overcoming Imposter Syndrome." *HigherEdJobs*, October 14, 2020. https://www.higheredjobs.com/Articles/articleDisplay.cfm?ID=2469.

Additional Resources

Mindfulness Resources

Dr. Kristin Neff's Self-Compassion guided practices and exercises: https://self-compassion.org/category/exercises

Free library of mindfulness practices: https://www.freemindfulness.org/download

Headspace app (for guided meditations): https://www.headspace.com/ (free to start, then monthly or annual fee)

InsightTimer app: https://insighttimer.com/ (free and paid options)

Books

10% Happier, Dan Harris
The Miracle of Mindfulness, Thich Nhat Hanh

Yoga Resources

Yoga International, with classes (videos) and articles: https://yogainternational.com/ (free to try; ongoing access requires fee)
Accessible/adaptable yoga teachers:
Anna Guest-Jelley (CurvyYoga.com): book, video, blog articles, online yoga studio (with fee/subscription)
Dianne Bondy (diannebondyyoga.com): books, videos, YouTube channel, online yoga studio (with fee/subscription)
Amber Karnes (bodypositiveyoga.com): online yoga studio (with fee/subscription), free videos on YouTube
Jessamyn Stanley (jessamynstanley.com): book, free videos on YouTube and Instagram, online yoga studio (with fee/subscription)
Yoga with Adriene: YouTube channel (https://www.youtube.com/@yogawithadriene)

Books

Living Your Yoga, Judith Hanson Lasater
The Yamas and the Niyamas, Deborah Adele
Eastern Body, Western Mind, Anodea Judith

Enneagram Resources

Enneagram Institute: type descriptions, RHETI test (fee), classes finder (https://www.enneagraminstitute.com/)
Chestnut Paes Enneagram Academy: type/subtype descriptions, Compass test (fee), training online (https://cpenneagram.com/)
Free Enneagram test (from Eclectic Energies): https://www.eclecticenergies.com/enneagram/test (choose the Classic test)

Books

The Wisdom of the Enneagram, Don Richard Riso & Russ Hudson
The Complete Enneagram, Beatrice Chestnut
The Enneagram Guide to Waking UP, by Beatrice Chestnut and Uranio Paes
The Road Back to You, Ian Morgan Cron
The Enneagram Made Easy, Elizabeth Wagele and Renee Baron
The Enneagram at Work, Jim McPartlin

Implicit Bias Resources

Maryville University has a comprehensive and accessible list of strategies, tools, and ideas for tackling our own implicit biases: https://online.maryville.edu/blog/addressing-implicit-bias/

Project IMPLICIT, Harvard's online resource of implicit association tests (IATs) to gauge the unconscious biases you hold: https://implicit.harvard.edu/implicit/

Books

Think Again: The Power of Knowing What You Don't Know, by Adam Grant

Hivemind: The New Science of Tribalism in Our Divided World, by Sarah Rose Cavanagh

Biased: Uncovering the Hidden Prejudice That Shapes What We See, Think, and Do, by Jennifer Eberhardt

Whistling Vivaldi: And Other Clues to How Stereotypes Shape Us, by Claude Steele

The End of Bias: A Beginning, by Jessica Nordell

Blindspot: Hidden Biases of Good People, by Mahzarin Banaji and Anthony Greenwald

Resources to Bring It All Together

Mark Manson's seven strange questions to help you find your purpose (see Manson 2024) provide a different entry point to these often ephemeral and large questions. I especially love question #2: What's true about you today that would make your eight-year-old self cry? Answering this question can help you tap into things you loved doing earlier in life that perhaps deserve a revisit. He also has a free 29-page guide called "What the Hell Are You Doing with Your Life?" that you can download at https://markmanson.net/downloads/life-purpose-ebook.

Brené Brown's Daring Classrooms site has a multitude of resources to create more humane, supportive learning environments. Find the Daring Classrooms Hub at https://brenebrown.com/hubs/daring-classrooms-hub/.

INDEX

Italicized references indicate illustrations.

able-bodied, 24, 70
acceptance, 34, 35, 78, 113, 115, 119, 121, 149, 160, 168, 196
Accreditation Council for Pharmacy Education (ACPE), 161
acting/improv, 95, 105, 121
active learning, 3, 36, 80
Adele, Deborah, 129, 199, 218
adjunct/contingent faculty, 6, 9–10, 20, 54, 56, 60, 61, 64, 66, 81, 96, 100, 101
administration, 56, 60, 77, 122
adrenaline, 2, 49, 167, 173
advocacy, 21, 59, 107, 109, 121, 153, 168, 179
affirmation, 29, 32, 115
Agarwal, Pooja K., 178
agency, 1, 13, 46, 49, 103
Alan T. Waterman Award, 63
Alexander, Bryan, 88
American Psychological Association, 78
Anechiarico, Frank, 68
Angelou, Maya, 172–73, 193
Antell, Karen, 86
anthropology, 51, 94, 95, 112
anxiety, 10–11, 21, 23, 25, 29, 41, 48, 54, 68, 72, 94, 101, 105, 110, 117, 127, 139, 167, 170, 182, 200

appreciation (or lack thereof), 26, 34, 45, 61, 77, 131, 145–46, 165, 168, 170, 176
Arizona State University, 75
Ashe, Arthur, 188–89
assessments/assignments, 3, 4, 45, 47, 48, 59, 105, 118, 173, 175, 180, 182, 185
Association of College and Research Libraries, 85
assumptions, 21, 95, 133, 183–84, 189
attendance, 28, 69
attention, 7, 13, 14, 16, 21, 22, 23, 26–28, 37, 50, 77, 89, 98, 108, 111, 117, 118, 125, 134, 137–41, 171, 176, 178, 192, 193
authenticity, 1, 5, 7, 8, 12, 15–18, 20, 23–25, 29, 34, 37, 49, 50, 97, 98, 100, 103, 107, 115, 194
authority, 11, 56, 66, 67, 71, 72, 99, 101, 130, 175, 195
awareness (incl. of self), 5, 17, 34, 46, 88, 108, 112, 113, 117–21, 127, 129, 130, 134, 136, 137, 140–41, 157–58, 160–61, 165–66, 183, 188
Azevedo, Flávio S., 57

backfire effect, 174, 177, 184
Bain, Patrice M., 178
Baldwin, James, 88, 164

221

bandwagon effect, 177, 184
Banerjee, Amitav, 44
Barcroft, Julie, 93–94
Barnum Effect, 159, 169, 201
barriers/obstacles, 20, 41, 72, 133, 188, 199, 201
Basile, Vincent, 57
Bass, Randy, 31
Begeer, Sander, 75
behavior, 2, 12, 17, 21, 27, 39, 51, 62, 66, 67, 78, 94, 101, 117, 130–31, 133, 136, 157–58, 160–63, 169, 172, 175–76, 182, 184–85, 189, 191
Behling, Kirsten T., 80
Belcher, Wendy Laura, 64
belonging, 11, 19, 22–23, 25, 27, 34–39, 48–49, 51, 57–58, 65, 82–83, 89, 136, 196; cognitive, 32
Benjamin, Ruha, 56, 74
Bentley University, 13
Berdahl, Loleen, 24
Berg, Maggie, 55, 56, 65
Bhagavad Gita, 127, 129
biases, 24, 71, 161, 172–87, 219; implicit, 5, 70–71, 130, 219
biology, 51, 135
Blum, Susan, 94–96
boundaries, 60, 90, 96, 165
Bowler, Kate, 56
Boynton, Petra, 57
brain, 2, 3, 33, 75, 98, 99, 104, 117–19, 127, 134–36, 138, 172, 174–75, 177, 183, 196–97
breathing, 10, 64, 72, 85, 116, 119, 122, 138–41, 175, 184, 199
Brookfield, Stephen D, 32, 49
Brown, Brené, 22–23, 50–51, 94, 192, 219
Brown, Michael P., 82
Brunell, Tom, 59
Bullard, Holly, 96–97
bullying/hazing, 38, 58–59, 71, 76–77, 170
Burey, Jodi-Ann, 24–25
burnout/exhaustion, 3–4, 14, 64, 110, 113, 118, 164, 167
business, 37, 46, 48, 51, 93, 143

care/caring, 33, 34, 49, 78, 135, 153, 170
career, 56, 58, 60, 68, 100, 151, 153, 192, 200
Carnegie, Dale, 43
caste, 62, 70
Cavanagh, Sarah Rose, 31, 68–69, 97–98, 196, 219
CCCSE, 151
celebration, 33, 35, 48, 65, 90, 132, 170, 193
Center for Courage and Renewal, 125–26
center for teaching (CTL), 6, 69, 78–81, 102
certainty/uncertainty, 10–12, 23, 27, 29, 30, 50, 57–58, 113–14, 150, 167, 189, 198, 200
Chacko, Sheaba, 3
challenge, 6, 7, 14–17, 32–33, 36, 40, 43–44, 50, 52, 55, 57, 59, 66, 68–69, 75–76, 78, 81, 87–88, 93, 101, 109, 114, 116–18, 122, 132, 147, 149, 150, 154, 160, 168–69, 172, 179, 182, 188, 189, 191, 198
Challenger, Melanie, 52
change, 1, 17, 21, 24, 39, 46, 61, 90, 104, 106, 111, 114, 123, 133, 140, 151, 155, 158–60, 168, 173, 178, 183–84, 191, 193, 198, 200
Chattanooga State Community College, 93
Chew, Stephen, 100
childcare, 43, 60
Childs-Kean, Lindsay, 161
choice, 13, 44–45, 69, 117, 158, 164, 183
Chronicle of Higher Education, 61, 63, 68, 69, 75, 196
Clark, Dorie, 192
Clarke Gray, Brenna, 72
Clear, James, 109, 193–94
Cleveland Clinic, 75
coach/coaching, 3, 6, 33, 38, 55, 145, 147–48, 154, 163, 169–71
Coan, James A., 37
cogenerative dialog, 45–46

cognitive load/cognitive bandwidth, 13, 14, 22–23, 32, 73, 192
cognitive resources, 14–15, 134, 172, 177, 183, 196, 197
collaboration, 18, 47, 52, 85, 87, 90
comfort/discomfort, 6, 11, 14, 25–29, 33, 44, 52, 60, 71, 72, 74, 80, 96, 99, 112, 119, 138–41, 147, 152, 160, 162–63, 169, 172, 175, 179, 185–86, 190
community, 6, 26–27, 35–36, 38–39, 48, 56, 68–69, 74, 78, 81–82, 84, 86, 89–92, 94–95, 99, 103–5, 118, 120, 123–24, 126, 130, 136, 138, 145, 160, 167, 175, 179–80, 194, 200
community college, 1, 9, 61–62, 64, 93, 110–11, 151
community of practice/faculty learning communities, 6, 78, 81–83, 147, 180
compassion, 29, 33, 40, 111, 114–15, 121, 146, 217
competition, 23, 51–52
concentration, 2, 13–14, 36, 69, 199
concern/worry, 22, 28, 43, 104, 150, 167, 189, 190
conferences, 64, 78, 83–84, 97, 104, 123, 150
confidence, 10–11, 46–47, 50, 58, 66, 68–69, 77, 96, 99, 102, 107, 146–47, 149, 151, 153–54, 170, 179, 182
confirmation bias, 11, 23, 178, 183–84
connection, 16–19, 26–28, 30–32, 36–38, 40, 43, 50, 69, 82, 89–90, 97–98, 101, 106, 112, 117, 119–21, 129, 138, 168, 179
conscience, 44, 153
conscious/unconscious, 2, 17, 21, 50, 53, 64, 73, 129, 135–36, 153, 158, 168, 172, 176, 177, 183, 196, 219
control, 49, 96, 108, 131, 133, 168, 198
conversation, 50, 132, 185
co-regulation, 1–3, 118
corporate, 24, 55, 56, 57, 77
cortisol, 2, 49
Costa, Karen, 44

courage/bravery, 22, 30, 48, 50, 124, 126, 149, 193
Covey, Stephen, 117
COVID, 4, 68, 72, 87, 93, 98, 104, 106–7, 109, 123, 152, 155
Cox, Milton D., 83
Cozolino, Louis, 31
criminal justice/prison/justice-involved, 93, 182
crisis, 44, 60, 88
criticism, 16, 47, 60, 145, 164
Cron, Ian Morgan, 160, 218
Cron, Lisa, 182
Csikszentmihályi, Mihály, 36
Cuddy, Amy, 7
cult/cultish, 50, 123
culturally responsive teaching, 40
culture, 1, 4, 5, 6, 8, 15, 23, 24, 25, 34, 40, 48, 50, 51, 54–91, 94, 100, 113, 144, 148, 150, 151, 153, 172, 177, 183, 185, 195–96, 199; toxic, 76–77, 99, 100, 113, 144
Cunningham, Heather V., 87
curiosity, 28, 59, 86, 112, 115, 116, 124, 136, 137, 163, 166, 186

Dahlkild, Nan, 86
Daniel Tatum, Beverly, 70
Das, Ram, 12
David, Susan, 147
Davis, Carolyn, 73
Dean College, 99
default mode network, 98
departments/disciplines/disciplinary, 12, 23, 58.59, 61, 64, 66, 104, 150, 190
Descartes, Rene, 166
desire, 37, 143–44, 148, 162–69, 192
Dickson, D. H., 159
disability, 5, 24, 70, 71, 175
Discord, 41–43
discussions, 26, 28, 33, 47, 80, 88, 90, 175, 181, 187
diversity, 45, 76, 79, 86, 89, 123, 180, 197
divided life, 34, 123
dogs, 51, 98, 119

224 INDEX

Donahoe, Emily Pitts, 45
Dore, Madeleine, 115, 176
dramaturgical model, 12
Duhigg, Charles, 47
Duke University, 51
Dunning-Kruger Effect, 179, 184

ecosystem/environment, 40, 69, 119, 140, 154, 172, 190
Edmondson, Amy C., 47
EdSurge, 56
efficiency, 49, 55–57
ego, 19, 76, 114, 115, 130, 131, 144, 146, 157, 158, 162, 165, 167, 170, 171–73, 175, 190
Einstein, Albert, 129
elitism/prestige, 62–66, 70, 72
email, 41, 193
embodiment, 5, 25, 86, 127–42, 196
Emdin, Christopher, 23–24, 45, 65
Emerson, Ralph Waldo, 129
emotional labor, 72, 96, 185, 196
emotions, 1, 34, 78, 122, 127, 129, 135, 136, 151, 152, 161, 181, 186, 187, 190
empathy, 29, 51, 93, 118, 122, 129, 133, 134, 135, 143, 161, 165, 182
encouragement, 32, 90
engagement/disengagement, 23, 28, 31, 32, 35, 36, 48, 67, 68, 78, 106, 124, 138, 194, 198
Engel, Debra, 86
English, 36, 93, 99
Enneagram, 5, 94, 107, 108, 157–71, 175, 218
equity, 73, 76, 78, 130, 172
Erikson, Eric, 101
ethics, 88, 129–33
evolution, 12, 51, 67, 117
excitement, 35, 155, 190
exercise/sports, 35, 41, 98, 109, 129, 134, 137
expectations, 33, 45, 118, 185
experience, 49, 99, 116, 181
exploration/experiments, 16, 115, 142, 149, 190, 194
extroverted, 106, 195, 201

Faber, Liz, 99–100
facilities/furniture, 34, 36, 42, 89, 197
faculty development/faculty developers, 78, 97
failure/mistakes, 15, 33, 35, 36, 40, 47, 48, 50, 122, 130, 136, 144, 145, 172
fear, 67, 68, 69, 71, 124, 144–48, 150, 153, 154, 163–71, 178, 179, 191, 192
feedback, 3, 49, 155, 185, 193
Felten, Peter, 31
first-generation students, 71, 143, 179
Fisher, 48
flexibility/inflexibility, 67, 69, 75, 93
food insecurity, 110, 151
Forer Effect, 159, 169, 201
Fosslien, Liz, 47–48
Fournier, Eric, 100–102
Frederickson, Barbara L, 37
freedom, 45, 69, 114, 131, 200
Friere, Paolo, 36
frustration, 39, 136, 184, 197
fundamental attribution error, 178, 184
funding/money/pay, 56, 96, 110
Furey, William, 157
Fuzz Speech, The, 128, 199

Gannon, Kevin, 31, 39, 58, 67
gender/gender identity, 24, 54, 60, 66, 70, 72, 73, 143, 144, 152; women, 4, 54, 60, 75, 101, 143, 147, 195–96
Georgetown University, 31
George Washington University, 32, 63, 90
Gibson, Amelia N., 86
Glazier, Rebecca, 48
Glowacki-Dudka, Michelle, 82
goals, 115, 132, 133, 143, 154–56, 172
Goffman, Erving, 12, 13, 16
Gottschall, Jonathan, 182
grades, 33, 39, 40, 94, 95, 101, 105, 132, 144, 152
graduate school, 38, 40, 58–62, 63, 66, 70, 74, 100, 101, 105, 106, 127, 146
graduate students, 55, 63, 74
graduation, 52, 111, 191

INDEX

Grant, Adam, 52, 219
gratitude, 18, 121, 149, 191
Green, Atlas, 110–11
growth, 16, 38, 52, 114, 132, 133, 146, 147, 159, 160, 161
Gurdjeff, George, 160

habits/rituals, 89
Hammond, Zaretta, 40, 49, 55
Hare, Brian, 51–52
harm, 130, 176, 178, 185
Harris, Dan, 119, 218
Hartberg, Yasha, 102–3
Harvard Business Review, 24
healing, 18, 20, 38, 76, 105, 139, 176, 180
health /wellness, 37, 57, 65, 77, 108, 131, 139; mental, 68–69, 102, 110, 165
heart, 65, 113, 116, 117, 122, 133, 144, 151, 158, 180, 181
Hedley, Gil, 128, 199
help/helping professions, 17, 133, 164–65
Herman, Jennifer, 69
hiding, 32, 150–54
hierarchy, 52, 69, 71, 72, 74, 76–77, 103, 153
history, 36, 54, 110, 179–80
Hogan, Kelly A., 70
Holstead, Carol E., 69
Hook, Joshua N., 160–61
hooks, bell, 7, 69, 71, 73, 77
hope, 31, 39, 52, 77, 79, 110, 144, 156, 190, 200
hospitality/welcome, 34, 42, 48, 67, 78, 89, 124
housing insecurity, 151, 178
Huber, Cheri, 114–15
human, 1, 17, 40, 49, 57, 76, 96, 99, 122, 130, 133, 138, 174, 177, 183
hustle, 3, 57, 60, 65, 72, 77, 148, 169, 194, 198

Ichazo, Oscar, 160
identity, 5, 26, 38, 46, 54, 65, 69, 70, 74, 95, 100, 101, 114, 170, 184, 185, 193; minoritized/marginalized, 5, 49, 60, 61, 64, 66, 69, 70–76, 92, 143, 179, 187
illness, 10, 20, 37, 43, 68, 110
imposter syndrome/phenomenon, 5, 8, 23, 24, 29, 50, 58, 71, 77, 95, 99, 102, 103, 105, 109, 128, 130, 143, 145, 154, 173, 196
impression management, 9, 12, 16, 25, 29, 68
inclusion, 25, 76, 78, 122, 136, 172, 185
independence, 46, 74, 75, 166
inequality, 17, 18, 19, 74
influence, 1, 39, 122, 129, 157, 173, 182, 193
Inman, Matthew, 173, 184
inner critic, 11, 143, 145–48, 150, 164, 192
inner mentor/inner teacher, 114, 125, 126, 145, 148–150
inner work, 1, 6, 34, 51, 53, 63, 66, 70, 72, 92, 94, 96, 99, 104, 112, 114–16, 126, 132, 133, 136, 144, 151, 161, 162, 173, 176, 182, 184, 188
insecurity, 11, 12, 23, 27, 52, 67, 72, 101, 130, 155
instincts/impulses, 2, 38, 52–53, 64, 67, 115, 133, 148, 157, 158, 170, 183, 184
Institute for Trauma, Adversity, and Resilience in Higher Education, 1
intention, 44, 48, 88, 90, 119, 176, 184, 186, 194
interoception, 134, 135, 137
introverted, 26, 71, 103, 104
invitation/invite, 49, 136, 138
Irish, Bradley J., 75
isolation/solitude, 3, 38, 68, 87, 117, 119, 120

James Madison University, 68
Jaremka, Lisa M., 59
job market (academic), 9, 59, 63, 64, 67
journaling, 40, 96, 99, 102, 181, 189
joy, 19, 124, 133, 167, 194, 198
judgment, 18, 23, 42, 124, 125

K-12 education, 39, 198
Kahneman, Daniel, 13–14
Kaminoff, Leslie, 134, 139–40
Kasle, Jill, 32–33
Kaufman, Scott Barry, 15, 16, 37, 112, 158
Kelley, Ann, 3
Kelly, I.W., 159
Kelsky, Karen, 38, 55
kindness, 103, 110, 121–22, 130, 191
Koenig, Rebecca, 56
Kranich, Nancy C., 86
Kreitzer, Mary Jo, 37
Krishnamurti, Jiddu, 31
Krisoff, Derek, 39

Lambert, Leo M., 35
Lang, James, 32, 39
Larremore, Daniel, 63
LaSalle University, 106
Lasater, Judith Hanson, 129, 218
leadership, 26–29, 50, 62, 152–53, 168
leaping, 154–56
learning management systems (LMS), 42, 88–89
Leffingwell, Hannah, 66
Lei, Zhike, 47
Levenson, Hannah, 47, 161
library/librarians, 41, 78, 84–87, 199
listening, 29, 124
Louden, Jennifer, 147, 154–55, 192
love, 16, 35, 114, 115, 122, 128, 149, 165, 167, 170
Love, Bettina, 70
Lubbe, Jerome D., 162, 169
Lundberg, Carol A., 31
Lux, Vera, 87
lying/cheating, 44, 131, 178

manipulation, 60, 131
Marriott, Sue, 3
Martin, Dimple J., 83
Maryville University, 184–86
Maslow, Abraham, 15, 17, 37, 112
MassBay Community College, 1
Matthews, Amy, 134

Mayne, Laura, 59–60
Mayo, Liz, 61
McCarthy, Seán, 68
McClure, Kevin, 56
McDevitt, Neale, 23
McMurtrie, Beth, 68, 69
McQuaid, Goldie A., 75
McPartlin, Jim, 159–60, 218
Mead, Margaret, 173
meditation, 5, 105, 117–26, 139, 148, 149, 175, 199
meetings/gatherings, 9, 27, 32, 41, 87–88, 132, 175, 181, 194
mentor, 23, 41, 59, 62, 64, 70, 72, 101, 150
metacognition, 102, 117, 179
Miller, Michelle, 39
mindful, 5, 52, 72, 87, 117–26, 134, 137–39, 176, 184, 199, 217–18
mindset, 104, 118, 138, 154, 157, 172, 198; growth of, 33, 118, 162, 200
minefields, 5, 54, 57–77, 91
Mohr, Tara, 5, 143–56, 200
Montell, Amanda, 160
Mother Teresa, 19
motivation, 32, 67, 69, 115, 161, 190, 200
Murphy Paul, Annie, 134–35, 196, 200
Murthy, Vivek H., 38
music, 35, 105
myths, 14, 51, 103, 173, 177, 189; learning styles, 157, 177, 201

Nagoski, Emily, 4
Nagsoki, Amelia, 4
names (students'), 41, 42, 43
Naranjo, Claudia, 160
Neuhaus, Jessamyn, 103–4
neurodivergent, 24, 75–76, 175; attention deficit-hyperactivity disorder (ADHD), 75, 175; autism, 75–76, 175; bipolar, 75; Down syndrome, 75; obsessive-compulsive disorder (OCD), 75
neurotypical, 24, 70, 75–76
New York Times, 47, 87

Nicolas, Sarah, 84
nonverbal communication, 7, 14, 25, 127, 135, 136, 175–76, 186
norms, 47, 72, 75, 90
Novogratz, Elizabeth, 119
Novogratz, Sukey, 119
Nunn, Lisa M., 48

office (faculty), 33, 34, 41, 42, 135
Oklahoma University Health Science Center, 107
Olou, Ijeoma, 186–87
onboarding (first day), 29, 41, 48, 82, 89
Oppenheimer, J. Robert, 129
opportunity, 1, 45, 48, 70, 82, 85, 119, 125, 146, 152, 170, 183, 200
Osterman, Karen F., 48
overwhelm, 2–4, 13, 45, 68, 80, 85, 113, 118–20, 149, 166

Palmer, Parker, 34, 49, 50, 64, 67, 68, 95, 102, 112, 123, 126, 148
Parker, Priya, 34, 87–91
passion, 56, 98, 106, 163–69, 200
pedagogy, 33, 39, 40, 78, 99, 104, 109, 123, 146, 155, 197, 200
Penman, Danny, 119
perfection/imperfection, 102, 108, 164
performative hardassery, 58, 66–69
persona, teaching, 8, 17, 103, 191
personality, 12, 157, 169, 172, 201; tests, 107, 158, 159
Pharmacy Education (PharmEd), 107–8, 161
Philipson, Ilene, 46
Playing Big (Mohr), 5, 143–56, 200
policy, 44, 72, 75, 130, 151, 185
political science, 10, 26, 28, 58–59, 173–74, 181, 185, 201
positionality, 5, 54, 61
Poulos, Christopher, 104–6
power, 2, 49, 69, 71, 92, 96, 100, 124, 130, 131
practice (noun), 118, 120, 126, 128, 141

practice (verb), 35, 122, 134
precarity/poverty, 60, 70, 74, 109; students, 28, 110, 151, 178
presentation of self, 12, 13, 16, 35
Prevost, Shelley, 33
privilege, 70–76, 107, 179
productivity, 57, 65, 102
promotion, 10, 61, 81, 83, 131
pronouns, 43, 139, 187
proprioception, 134–35, 137
psychology/psychological, 77, 97, 157, 158, 160, 163, 174; safety, 6, 16, 25, 34, 47, 48, 57, 78, 117, 159, 200
publication/publishing, 59–60, 64
purpose, 16, 27, 38, 39, 52, 60, 87, 89, 91, 110, 119, 194

race, anti-racism, 73, 179; discrimination based on, 24, 71, 73, 103, 179–82, 186–87; people of color, 4, 54, 61; White, 45, 60, 66, 70, 73, 74, 187
reactivity, 25, 118, 122, 125, 184
reflection, 44, 53, 95, 101, 102, 106, 111, 112, 114, 124, 125, 144, 146, 156, 161, 171, 176, 181, 185, 189, 192, 194
regulation, 3, 117
relationships, 5, 17, 18, 25, 27, 30, 31, 37, 38, 39, 45, 51, 53, 58, 92, 103, 105, 110, 113, 114, 122, 137, 146, 178
relevance, 45, 69, 182
Remen, Rachel Naomi, 17, 18–20
research, 58, 59, 97, 98, 104–6, 155, 157, 158, 160, 161, 186, 190, 196, 197
resistance, 38, 49, 52, 131, 134, 136, 149
respect, 52, 71, 124, 133
Rettner, Rachael, [199]
Rexing, Christen, 106–7
risks, 47, 145, 146, 151, 180
ritual/spiritual/religion, 102, 120, 121, 129, 131, 156, 160, 194
Rogers, Carl, 78
Rogers, Fred, 92, 157

Roper, Amanda, 93
Rosenberg, Brian, 63, 65, 178, 198
Rule, Nick, 59
Russell, Joyce E, 43

safety, 6, 12, 16, 17, 34, 78, 90, 91, 144, 145, 147, 167
sailboat metaphor, 15, 16, 37, 78, 188, 194
Samford University, 100
Sathy, Viji, 70
satisfaction, 38, 39, 51
Sbarra, David A., 37
Schiano, Bill, 13
Schmidt, Claire, 81
Schmidt, Isabell, 136
scholarship of teaching and learning (SoTL), 78, 82
Schwartz, Harriet L., 22, 31–32
Scott, Kim, 49
security, 16, 38, 167
Seeber, Barbara K., 55, 56, 65
self-acceptance, 23, 113, 121, 196
self-actualization/transcendence, 15, 16, 17, 24, 25, 38 112, 188, 195
self-esteem, 16, 17, 18, 195
sensations, 35, 137, 141
service learning, 26, 27, 68
service work (faculty), 61, 109
sexual orientation, 70, 71
shame, 23, 50, 59, 71, 110, 144
shared governance, 56, 198
shelters, 5, 54, 75, 76, 77–87, 91, 194
Shuman, Rebecca, 52
Sides, John, 84
silence, 118, 124, 125
Simmons University, 69
Sinek, Simon, 46–47, 52, 192
Slack, 41–43
sleep, 14, 110, 149, 178, 189
Smith, Clint, 88
Smith, Kate, 107–8
snacks, 33–34, 42, 46, 196
social dynamics, 1, 12, 46, 195
social media, 38, 55, 59, 76, 99, 104, 153, 197

social sciences, 37, 51, 196
social work, 17, 51, 109
Sorenson, Elian, 68
soul, 19, 65, 113, 119, 124, 125, 159
Sprokay, Susan, 31
Stanovich, Keith, 13
statistics, 43, 73, 102; errors, 43, 59
stereotypes, 103, 185
Stevenson, Bryan, 180–82, 201
Stommel, Jesse, 31, 196
stories/narratives, 90, 92–112, 105, 121, 125, 132, 133, 175–76, 180–82
strategies/practices, 32, 40, 112, 129, 137, 146, 155, 169
strength, 18, 52, 154, 159
stress, 2, 3, 4, 29, 39, 49, 72, 75, 113, 118, 157, 158, 160, 161, 167, 184, 189
structural/systems/systemic, 24, 44, 69, 103, 173, 183, 187, 198, 199
Supiano, Beckie, 48, 196
supports/supportive, 46, 67, 76, 180
SXSW, 23
syllabus, 40, 66, 69, 89, 185
Syman, Stefanie, 129
System 1 thinking, 13, 14
System 2 thinking, 13, 14

Tabur, Susanne, 87
Tagg, John, 14
technology, 78, 93
TED, 7, 12, 46, 50
tenure, 10, 20, 54, 61, 100, 107, 153, 198, 199
tests/exams, 40, 61–62
Texas A&M University, 102
text messages/Remind, 41–42, 193
The Professor Is Out, 38, 55, 76
therapy/therapist, 6, 29, 94, 96, 105, 139, 148
Thich Nhat Hanh, 9, 218
Times Higher Education, 57
Tinnell, Teresa L., 83
Title IX, 152–53
Tobin, Thomas, 80, 197
Tompkins, Jane, 68
transparent, 80, 99, 100
transportation, 43, 61, 178

trauma, 2, 3, 4, 38, 44, 69, 114, 118, 119, 139, 149, 187
Tree of Contemplative Practices, 118–21, 120, 139
trust, 18, 27, 31–33, 38, 40–43, 123–25, 147–48, 168, 176–77, 196
Tulshyan, Ruchika, 24–25
tutoring, 61, 102
Tversky, Amos, 13

University of Denver, 105
University of Houston, 51
University of Mull, 59
University of North Carolina Greensboro, 104
University of Notre Dame, 94
University of Oklahoma Press, 39
University of Texas at Dallas, 59

values, 1, 5, 40, 44, 60, 66, 97, 116, 153, 168, 189, 192, 194, 195
Vanderbilt University, 96
van der Kolk, Bessel, 2, 4
Verschelden, Cia, 73, 198
visualization, 148–50
vulnerability, 16, 23, 25, 27, 40, 50, 90, 94, 95, 97, 103, 146

Warby Parker, 48
Washington University, 100–102
West, Richard, 13
West Duffy, Mollie, 47–48
West Virginia University Press, 39, 200
Whiat, Matt, 54
wholeness/wholehearted, 18, 50
Wilkerson, Isabel, 62
Williams, Mark, 119
Williams, Tom, 57
Winerman, Lea, 135
Winter, Richard, 56
wonder, 124–225
woo, 123, 149, 196
Woods, Vanessa, 51–52
worth, 17–18, 22, 35, 59, 165
Wright, Mary, 78
writing, 26, 33, 59, 60, 92, 95, 97, 98, 106, 112, 134, 153, 155, 166

yoga, 72, 105, 121, 127–42, 200, 218; teacher training, 20, 134; teaching, 134, 136–38, 199
York University, 23

Zoom, 152, 197
Zorn, Diane, 23

Milton Keynes UK
Ingram Content Group UK Ltd.
UKHW030942261124
451566UK00017B/231/J